The American Presidents

in the Eyes of Voters

and Historians

ROBERT W. MERRY

WHERE THEY STAND

SIMON & SCHUSTER

NEW YORK   LONDON   TORONTO   SYDNEY   NEW DELHI

Simon & Schuster
1230 Avenue of the Americas
New York, NY 10020

First Simon & Schuster hardcover edition June 2012

SIMON & SCHUSTER and colophon are registered trademarks
of Simon & Schuster, Inc.

For information about special discounts for bulk purchases,
please contact Simon & Schuster Special Sales at
1-866-506-1949 or business@simonandschuster.com.

The Simon & Schuster Speakers Bureau can bring authors
to your live event. For more information or to book an event,
contact the Simon & Schuster Speakers Bureau at
1-866-248-3049 or visit our website at www.simonspeakers.com.

Designed by Ruth Lee-Mui

Manufactured in the United States of America

10 9 8 7 6 5 4 3 2 1

Library of Congress Cataloging-in-Publication Data
Merry, Robert W., date.
   Where they stand: The American presidents in the eyes of voters and historians /
   By Robert W. Merry.
        p. cm.
   Includes bibliographical references and index.
1. Presidents—Rating of—United States.   2. Presidents—United States—
Biography.   3. Presidents—United States—History.   4. Political leadership—United
States—History.   5. United States—Politics and government.   I. Title.
   E176.1.M468 2012
   973.009'9—dc23
   [B]   2011039883
ISBN 978-1-4516-2540-0
ISBN 978-1-4516-2543-1 (ebook)

All photos courtesy of the Library of Congress, except that of George W. Bush,
which is courtesy of the White House (photo by Eric Draper).

To Rob, Johanna, and Stephanie,
who sparkle in life like aspen leaves in an autumn breeze

Contents

Introduction: The Great White House Rating Game   xiii

PART I: THE HISTORIANS
1. The Judgment of History   3
2. The Vagaries of History   20

PART II: THE PEOPLE
3. The Making of the Presidency   43
4. The Presidential Referendum   51
5. The Judgment of the Electorate   67
6. The Stain of Failure   90

PART III: THE TEST OF GREATNESS
7. War and Peace   117
8. Split-Decision Presidents   144
9. Leaders of Destiny   164

PART IV: REPUTATIONS IN FLUX
10. Republican Resurgence   193
11. The Post–Cold War Presidents   212

Conclusion: Clear and Present Danger   235

Acknowledgments   241
Appendix A: Academic Polls   243
Appendix B: Presidents by Category Based on Voter Response   247
Notes   251
Bibliography   273
Index   283

WHERE THEY STAND

Introduction

THE GREAT WHITE HOUSE
RATING GAME

Mark Twain once wrote, "It is difference of opinion that makes horse-races." True enough. It's difference of opinion also that has fostered one of the most compelling political parlor games in the American democracy—assessing, rating, and ranking the presidents. We do the same with movies, of course, and sports teams and big-time athletes. But those assessments emerge in the realm of trivia, and few would argue that any lessons they convey could hold the keys to understanding the past—or perhaps even the future—of the American Republic. The presidency is different because the presidents—just 44 of them in nearly 225 years—have held in their hands the national destiny. " 'Ranking the Presidents' has always been a Favorite Indoor Sport of history-minded Americans," wrote Clinton Rossiter, a leading political scientist of the 1950s and 1960s, who himself enjoyed the game, even rendering an uncharitably harsh critique of Dwight D.

Eisenhower's presidency while the man still sat in the White House. (He said the game was "fun to play even on a muddy field and a murky day.")

As a longtime political journalist in Washington and a presidential biographer, I have succumbed to this indoor sport over the years. Now I propose to pull you into the Great White House Rating Game. It *is* fun to play, on a muddy or dry field, on a murky or clear day. That's partly because the game is ongoing and open to all. With horse races, the difference of opinion gets settled definitively at the finish line. In the White House Rating Game, there is no finish line—just endless difference of opinion. I believe that is one huge value derived from the periodic polls of academic experts on presidential success. They spark lively debate and generate in turn interest in the American past. I hope to do the same with this book.

But I'm less interested in who's up and who's down in this sweepstakes than I am in what the Rating Game teaches us about how the presidency works and how presidents succeed—or fail—or serve simply in a zone of ordinariness or mediocrity. I put forward just one insight I consider fresh and perhaps even of value—namely, that no rating game is worthy of the name if it ignores the contemporaneous judgment of the electorate. Like most of us, presidents have a boss—in their case, the American people. And if the boss was happy or unhappy with a particular employee of the past, then who are we—or even a collection of historians—to toss that aside? Presidential greatness, then, generally should be conferred upon presidents who governed successfully based on the popular sentiment of their times. As the British scholar Harold J. Laski put it, any president "must see what he sees with the eyes of the multitude upon whose shoulders he stands."

This idea had been percolating in my mind for some time when I received a phone call a couple years back from Mark Lotto, then an editor on the *New York Times* op-ed page. Would I be interested, he asked, in writing a piece for the *Times* on a recent intriguing re-mark by President Barack Obama during a television interview with Diane Sawyer of ABC News? Responding to her questions on the apparent unpopularity of some of his programs and proposals, the president turned a bit defensive. He said he would "rather be a re-ally good one-term president than a mediocre two-term president." Lotto wondered if I had some thoughts on that, given that my latest book was a biography of James K. Polk, the eleventh president, widely considered by historians to be the country's most successful one-term executive. Suggesting that I might consider some other one-termers, he mentioned William Howard Taft, a solid executive whose presi-dency was cut short at one term by the third-party intervention of his predecessor and one-time mentor, Theodore Roosevelt.

I proposed instead a focus on an interesting Rating Game phe-nomenon: that the judgment of history—in the form of presidential rankings by those periodic polls of historians—coincides to a signifi-cant degree with the contemporaneous judgment of the electorate. The *Times* piece, entitled "The Myth of the One-Term Wonder," ran just before Presidents Day in 2010. It raised the question whether Obama or any president can set himself above the voters with un-popular programs to such an extent that he gets tossed out at the next election—and yet rise to a high station in the eyes of historians. Not likely, based on the record. As I wrote, "A better approach for any chief executive is to assume that, in presidential politics, as in retailing, the customer is always right, and that the electorate's verdict will be consonant with history's consensus."

The point is that presidents who were successful with the voters have tended to be rated by historians as our greatest executives, while those who were rejected by the voters generally don't get smiles of approval from the scholars. There are exceptions, however, and some bounce into the Rating Game with some force. Does Ulysses S. Grant, for example, belong in the Failure category, where he languished for decades before beginning a slow journey up the register in recent years? What about Warren G. Harding? The mere mention of his name generates dismissive smiles as people conjure up the image of a colorless numbskull whose most prominent presidential qualification seemed to be that he looked like what people thought a president should look like. And yet, as I will seek to show, he gave the American people what they wanted (including one of the greatest years of Gross Domestic Product growth in the nation's history) before he died in office.

Then there are the presidents ranked highly by the historians who were, however, rejected by the voters. Grover Cleveland comes to mind. Ranked as high as eighth in the academic polls, he was the only president to preside over the defeat of his party in presidential elections not just once but twice (with himself on the ballot in one instance). John Adams similarly gets high rankings in most polls, and yet the voters showed him the door after a single term. I would add Woodrow Wilson, ranked consistently in the upper echelons by the historians. But his two presidential terms, based on voter assessments at the time, could be summed up as follows: first term, a gem of success; second term, a disaster.

Generally, though, the retrospective judgment of the historians coincides with the contemporaneous judgment of the electorate. Aficionados of American democracy can take heart in this. It says that the voting collective, sifting through the civic complexities of the day in a highly charged electoral environment, have as much sense about the direction of the country as academics looking back with the clarity of hindsight and the cool dispassion of time. This poses some interesting implications that bear upon the Rating Game and on the workings of American executive power.

With this book I seek to analyze the presidency through an intertwined exploration of both the academic polls and the ballot-box reactions to the various presidents. I will survey the body of literature spawned over the decades by those intermittent academic surveys, which clearly add value to any assessment of White House performance. And I will look at some of the more interesting presidential stories through the prism of the historians' judgments. But I also will look at what the voters were saying, or trying to say, while these men sat in the White House. Did the electorate cut them off at a single term or give them another four years? For two-termers, did the voters then reject the party in power at the next election or retain the incumbent party? What about midterm elections, those weather vanes that catch the winds of political sentiment? Public-opinion surveys also represent an ongoing assessment of the electoral mood, worth consideration in analyzing presidential performance.

All this will be brought into the mix as we explore American history through the prism of presidential performance. As you will see, I don't place much stock in the personal judgments of individual analysts or commentators (including myself), except insofar as they contribute to the ongoing Rating Game discussion. Instead, I place stock in collective assessments—the rankings of hundreds of historians through multiple surveys over several decades; and the collective judgment of the electorate as it hired and fired presidents through the course of American history. Those, I suggest, are the two fundamental indices for assessing the achievement levels of presidents. And they will guide me as I seek to craft this travelogue through presidential history.

This approach has another possible advantage. It militates against any tendency to insert partisan sentiments into the discussion. The voters have elected liberal and conservative presidents, and they have fired liberal and conservative presidents. Thus electoral outcomes are not a test of ideology but rather of promise and performance. By concentrating on voter sentiments we keep the focus on performance and away from anyone's political leanings. I believe, for example, that the two greatest presidents of the twentieth century were Franklin

Roosevelt and Ronald Reagan—one perhaps the century's most liberal president, the other perhaps its most conservative one. They also were the only twentieth-century presidents to be elected twice and then maintain party control of the White House after their second terms. In other words, they met the highest test of electoral success.

I break my study into four parts. Part I will explore the academic polls and the literature surrounding them. I believe these constitute the closest we can come to the judgment of history. It also will probe what I call the "vagaries of history"—the occasional fluctuations in presidential rankings brought about through changes in historical interpretation or vogues of thought. Part II will look at the role of the people through a series of chapters on the making of the presidency at the 1787 Constitutional Convention; the nature of presidential elections as referendums on the incumbent president or incumbent party; and the ways in which electoral judgments come into play in that referendum system. Part III explores the test of greatness. It looks at the war decision, fraught with political danger as well as opportunity for glory. It explores the phenomenon of what I call "split-decision presidents"—two-termers whose second-term performances led to a White House change of party at the next election. And it dissects those rare presidents—I call them Leaders of Destiny—who were revered by the electorate, have been extolled by history, and are notable for changing the country's political landscape and setting it upon a new course.

Finally, Part IV assesses the five most recent presidents, whose rankings remain fluid because history has yet to render a definitive judgment.

Some presidents inevitably don't fit neatly into the broad categories we tend to create in our efforts to bring order to presidential analyses. One is James Polk, who at first glance would seem to bolster Obama's dichotomy between two-term mediocrity and one-term success. Polk was a one-termer who still captured a high station in the pantheon of later historians (though he has remained highly controversial through history). In nearly all the serious academic polls on presidential success, he makes it into the historians "Near Great" category.* But in fact his story is singular, and he is the exception that tests the rule.

Polk did a remarkable thing when he got his party's nomination in 1844. He announced that, if elected, he would serve only one term. He not only kept his promise but also realized all of the big goals he set for himself in both domestic and foreign policy. Polk doesn't fit Obama's construction because he didn't lose his reelection bid by angering the voters while courting history. Instead, he consciously bet his presidential reputation on a single term, something that very few presidents have been willing to do. No other president has run on a one-term promise.

If Polk's exception proves the rule that one-term presidents do tend to get history's brush-off, who gets its accolades? The historian Arthur M. Schlesinger Jr. wrote in 1996—in conjunction with his own poll of presidential scholars—that surveys since 1948 have consistently identified nine Greats and Near Greats: Abraham Lincoln, George Washington, Franklin Roosevelt (usually in that order), followed in various rank order by Thomas Jefferson, Andrew Jackson, Polk, Theodore Roosevelt, Woodrow Wilson, and Harry S Truman. Leaving aside Polk, all these men either were two-term presidents or (as with TR and Truman) were elected after succeeding to the White

---

* The historian surveys explored in this volume are those by Arthur M. Schlesinger Sr. (*Life* magazine, 1948), Schlesinger Sr. (*New York Times Magazine,* 1962), David Porter (1981), Steve Neal (*Chicago Tribune Magazine,* 1982), Robert K. Murray and Tim H. Blessing (1982), published in the book *Greatness in the White House: Rating the Presidents from George Washington Through Ronald Reagan,* Murray-Blessing on Reagan (1988–1990) (published in the same book), Arthur M. Schlesinger Jr. (*New York Times Magazine,* 1996), and James Taranto and Leonard Leo (2005, sponsored by the *Wall Street Journal* and published in the 2005 book *Presidential Leadership*).

House upon the death of their predecessors. All persuaded the voters that they deserved to retain their jobs.

Consider the presidents judged by history to be presidential failures. The historians' polls generally focus on James Buchanan, Franklin Pierce, Andrew Johnson (who inherited Lincoln's second term), Millard Fillmore (who ascended to the presidency upon the death of Zachary Taylor), and Harding. Not a two-term president in the bunch. Grant is the single two-term outlier. He presided over nasty financial scandals involving White House and Cabinet officials. It is worth noting, however, that the worst of those scandals erupted in his second term, and his first term was characterized by a frothy economic boom that attended massive railroad construction. Hence, the voters had no particular reason to expel him based on his first-term record, and the historical ranking seems based mostly on his second administration. In any event, Grant's standing in history is on the rise for reasons we will discuss.

History generally consigns one-term presidents to the category of "Average," occasionally "Above Average." This tends to mean no unavoidable crises, no scandals of consequence, and no serious new directions for America. A 2005 *Wall Street Journal* poll of historians and other experts ranked one-termer John Adams, the second president, as Above Average and then populated the Average category mostly with other one-termers: Taft, John Quincy Adams, Martin Van Buren, Rutherford B. Hayes, Chester A. Arthur (who succeeded James Garfield at his death and never was elected in his own right), and George H. W. Bush.

The *Journal* poll included a couple of two-term presidents in the "Above Average" category—Calvin Coolidge and Bill Clinton. Coolidge, who inherited the presidency and then was elected, presided over the burst of economic expansion in the 1920s, and most Americans applauded him for it at the time. But some historians have argued that his policies contributed mightily to the Great Depression.

As for Clinton, it doesn't seem appropriate to credit a president's poll ranking rendered while he still inhabited the Oval Office, as the *Journal* poll did. In assessing a president's historical standing, it's best to allow the passage of some history, generally at least a generation. What can be said about the "Average" presidents in the *Journal* poll is that most were decent and forceful men who demonstrated serious political acumen in rising to the pinnacle of American politics. But they left little mark of historical dimension.

In embarking upon my exploration of the presidency, I confess to one prejudice. I consider the institution to be a work of genius—a unique governmental institution that contains within it centuries of civic experimentation, armed struggle, historical exploration, penetrating political analysis, and philosophical endeavor. It all came together, almost by accident, during that miraculous building session in Philadelphia during the hot summer of 1787. (Both George Washington and James Madison used the word "miracle" in letters to describe the outcome.) It isn't surprising that the American people take a proprietary view of their presidential office and demand from it an appropriate degree of dignity and solemnity—and success. It's difficult for us today, with 225 years of constitutional history at our backs, to conceive what a remarkably innovative and novel idea the presidency was. The great kings of the world are long gone now, but in the eighteenth century, at the time of our nation's birth, they were in their heyday, and it wasn't clear a mere president could rival the world's royalty in dignity and gravitas. But Americans, having been handed the gift of the presidency, never doubted it. That's because the president is a product of themselves in a way no king or potentate—or even prime minister—could ever be. That is one reason why the American presidency stirs so much interest, respect, and affection from the broad populace—and why, perhaps, so many Americans have always been captivated by the White House Rating Game.

Thus, the Rating Game is more than just a beguiling diversion. It actually can tell us something about how and why presidents succeed or fail, how they deflect or get crushed by history, and the dynamics that bring forth those rare Leaders of Destiny. I will seek in this volume to put forth my own thoughts and observations, whatever their merits, about how the country's presidential politics has unfolded over the centuries. I do so fully in the Rating Game spirit—and in the spirit of Twain's observation about difference of opinion.

Hence, if your views diverge significantly from those contained in this book, relax. As I say, the Great White House Rating Game is ongoing and endless—and open to everyone.

Wanna play?

Part I

THE

HISTORIANS

1

THE JUDGMENT OF HISTORY

In November 1948, *Life* magazine published an innovative article by Harvard historian Arthur M. Schlesinger Sr., a noted scholar of his time and father of the later historian Arthur M. Schlesinger Jr. Schlesinger's piece presented the first academic survey in the White House Rating Game and set in motion the ongoing discussion of presidential performance that has come down to our own time. Schlesinger polled fifty-five experts, mostly historians but also some journalists and political scientists, and asked them to place the presidents in one of five categories—Great, Near Great, Average, Below Average, and Failure. William Henry Harrison and James A. Garfield were left out because of the brevity of their presidential tenures. The professor instructed his respondents: "The test in each case is performance in office, omitting everything done before or after." Beyond that, Schlesinger left all criteria of judgment to the respondents.

The Schlesinger poll ranked the presidents based on the number of votes they received for each category. Lincoln, the only president to be rated unanimously as Great, emerged at the top of the presidential list. The other Greats, in descending order, were George Washington, Franklin Roosevelt, Woodrow Wilson, Thomas Jefferson, and Andrew Jackson. The Near Great category included (in rank order) Theodore Roosevelt, Grover Cleveland, John Adams, and James K. Polk. The Failure category consisted of Ulysses S. Grant and Warren G. Harding. The other presidents were scattered throughout the Average and Below Average categories.

The Schlesinger poll immediately demonstrated America's fascination with its presidents. It generated extensive discourse centered not just on the rankings themselves but on questions of the soundness of the Schlesinger methodology and even whether there was any particular value in such polling initiatives. Many Republicans questioned the high standing of Franklin Roosevelt, then still widely despised by his political opponents. Schlesinger Sr. never suggested his poll results represented any kind of definitive judgment on the presidents but rather were merely a "highly informed opinion" by a collection of worthy historical experts. Nevertheless, the 1948 *Life* article proved highly influential, and soon Schlesinger's poll was cited by many as a conclusive historical assessment.

More significantly, Schlesinger's innovative poll became the fountainhead of subsequent surveys that would flow over the decades to produce a large pool of academic presidential assessment. When we speak of history's judgment on the presidents and their rankings in relation to one another, these polls, taken collectively, form the single greatest body of evidence. They also have served over the decades as a constant source of discussion and debate on the presidents.

In 1962, fourteen years after Schlesinger Sr.'s first poll, he conducted a follow-up survey published in the *New York Times Magazine*, this time of seventy-five respondents—again mostly academic histo-

rians but with a smattering of journalists and political scientists. The
two polls yielded similar results, which was not surprising given that
many of the 1962 respondents also had participated in the 1948 survey. But it reinforced the Schlesinger rankings in the minds of many
as something approaching definitive. The top seven remained the
same, and in the same order—Lincoln, Washington, Franklin Roosevelt, Wilson, Jefferson, Jackson, Theodore Roosevelt. While Jackson
remained at number six, he dropped from Great to Near Great. Polk
rose from tenth to eighth, while Cleveland dropped from eighth to
eleventh. The two failures remained Grant and Harding. The Average and Below Average categories contained the same presidents in
both instances.

The most interesting aspect of the second Schlesinger poll was the
addition of Democrat Harry S Truman and Republican Dwight D.
Eisenhower to the rankings. Truman, who logged a Gallup approval
rating of just 22 percent during his final year in office, nevertheless
entered the lists at number nine, in the Near Great category, just
below Polk and just above John Adams. Eisenhower, by contrast,
was relegated to the low Average category, number twenty-two, just
below Chester A. Arthur, a caretaker president, and ahead of Andrew
Johnson, a notably ineffectual leader. Much of the controversy generated by Schlesinger's second poll centered on Truman's high standing
and the designation of Eisenhower as mediocre. Many Republicans
argued persuasively that these rankings reflected partisan sensibilities
among some respondents.

By this time the skeptics had become more pointed in their criticism of this form of presidential scholarship. The leading skeptic was
Thomas A. Bailey of Stanford University, who wrote a 1966 book
that questioned the soundness of the exercise. Called *Presidential
Greatness*, Bailey's treatise contended that the Schlesinger surveys
were inevitably slanted because the respondents personified certain
political biases—pro-Democratic, politically liberal, oriented toward

the Northeast and Midwest rather than the West or South. It was true that Democrats outnumbered Republicans by two to one. And perhaps the elder Schlesinger signaled his own political outlook when he identified the six Great presidents in his first poll as those who "took the side of progressivism and reform, as understood in their day."

Bailey conducted a study in the mid-1960s of the history departments of thirty leading universities and discovered that most were strongly pro-Democratic. In fact, only one department was evenly divided between Democrats and Republicans, while one other was pro-Republican. Some departments had no Republicans at all. He attributed this to a number of factors—historians tended to favor progress and experimentation, hence embraced activist government; they viewed Democratic leaders as being more "intellectual," like themselves; they tended to be internationalists and felt uncomfortable with Republican isolationism of the 1930s, '40s, and '50s; and many young professors, being not particularly well off, tended to identify with the party of the working man.

Certainly, during the time of Schlesinger Sr.'s two polls, the academic realm was highly influenced by the example of Franklin Roosevelt, who significantly expanded the size and scope of the federal government, both to fight the Great Depression and to wage World War II. It was voguish among intellectuals in those post-FDR days to glorify presidents who, like Roosevelt, sought to enlarge the office and to concentrate power in the federal government. That clearly accounts for the otherwise inexplicably low ranking for Eisenhower in the second Schlesinger Sr. poll. An example of this outlook would seem to be Clinton Rossiter's patronizing denigration of Eisenhower during his presidency: "He will be remembered, I fear, as the unadventurous president who held on one term too long in the new age of adventure."

Bailey also questioned whether it was historically appropriate to compare presidents who faced such different national challenges in such different historical times. He dismissed the Schlesinger polls as an effort "to measure the immeasurable."

This perception didn't stop Bailey from crafting his own rating system, which he deemed more accurate. He applied forty-three "yardsticks" to his evaluation, including such matters as administrative capacity, dealings with Congress, ethics, success in foreign affairs, even the kinds of enemies accumulated.

From these indices Bailey placed the presidents in categories corresponding with those of Schlesinger. But in the end he produced a ranking that wasn't far different from the two Schlesinger polls. The top three remained, in order, Lincoln, Washington, and Franklin Roosevelt. He drops Jefferson to Near Great, Jackson to Above Average "at best," Polk to Average, Cleveland to Average, and Truman to Average. He elevates Grant above his previous Failure designation, to Below Average, and also boosts Buchanan a few notches. Otherwise, Bailey's categorizations reflected the reality that, notwithstanding his critique of the Schlesinger polls, a consensus seemed to be building around the general Schlesinger framework.

That consensus, with small fluctuations, held up through subsequent polls. In 1977 the United States Historical Society surveyed the heads of a hundred history departments on the ten "greatest" presidents. The eighty-five respondents returned an unsurprising verdict: Lincoln, Washington, Franklin Roosevelt, Theodore Roosevelt, Jefferson, Wilson, Jackson, Truman, Polk, and John Adams. These were the same ten names on Schlesinger Sr.'s second poll, though the rankings varied a bit.

In 1981 a history professor at William Penn College in Iowa, David L. Porter, surveyed forty-one academics using much the same methodology as Schlesinger. Again, the results were similar, except for a couple of notable variations. Eisenhower, beginning an ascent that would continue in subsequent polls, rose to twelfth. Cleveland fell to fifteenth. Grant climbed out of the Failure category and made it into

Below Average, fifth from the bottom. Three new presidents were added—Lyndon Johnson, who entered at eleventh place, in the Near Great category; Richard M. Nixon, third from the bottom, a Failure; and Jimmy Carter, who placed twenty-third, in the Average category.

The next year Steve Neal, a *Chicago Tribune* political reporter and author of political biographies, queried forty-nine "leading historians and political scholars," all authors of published works on the presidency. He asked the respondents to classify the presidents on a scale of 0 to 5 in five specified areas—leadership, accomplishments, political skill, appointments, and character. He also asked them to rank the ten best and ten worst presidents. Again, similar results emerged, except that Eisenhower continued his climb, getting to ninth, just above Polk. John Adams dropped down to a tie for fifteenth (with James Monroe). Also, William McKinley, the stolid Republican elected twice but assassinated in 1901, came in at eleventh after languishing between fifteenth and eighteenth in the previous polls.

Then in 1982 two history professors brought to the Rating Game a more extensive and sophisticated methodology, with the idea of probing not just what their historical experts thought but what might be driving their responses. The academics were Robert K. Murray of Pennsylvania State University and Tim H. Blessing of Pennsylvania's Alvernia College. They mailed out nearly 2,000 questionnaires to Ph.D. historians who held academic positions as assistant professors or above. They adopted "[m]odern opinion research procedures," as they put it, and the results were categorized and analyzed by computer. The survey consisted of 180 questions, and the researchers bolstered their mail-questionnaire findings with face-to-face surveys and interviews with sixty of the respondents. They ended up with 846 completed questionnaires.

By questioning the respondents on their backgrounds, age, sex, academic specialties, political outlooks, and a host of other distinguishing traits, Murray and Blessing were able to determine correlations between some of these characteristics and the responses. Most are of interest largely to political scientists, but some are intriguing for our purposes. For example, subject-area specialties played a significant role in some outcomes. Specialists in southern history and African-American studies tended to give higher ratings to Carter, whereas military historians denigrated him. Military historians favored Eisenhower by a wide margin. African-American specialists particularly disliked Jackson and Polk (both slaveholders), while specialists in women's history were the harshest critics of Polk and Theodore Roosevelt (both viewed by many as enthusiasts of a martial spirit). To the extent that these specialties reflected political outlooks, it would seem that those outlooks also influenced the responses.

Particularly intriguing was the Murray-Blessing analysis of presidents who continue to generate controversy, as reflected in the wide distribution of their ratings. The most controversial, with a wide range of favorable and unfavorable responses, were Nixon, Lyndon Johnson, Hoover, and Jackson. Others with wide disparities included John Quincy Adams, Truman, Wilson, Polk, and Kennedy. The least controversial were Lincoln, Washington, and Franklin Roosevelt, whose high ratings were nearly universal.

Murray and Blessing speculate that the most recent controversial presidents are likely to have their rankings change in future polls, as the disparity in their ratings diminishes in one direction or the other with the perspective of time. For Jackson, however, they suggest, there isn't much likelihood his standing will change appreciably given how well entrenched his reputation seems to be after so much historical attention. (Jackson's historical standing will be explored in the next chapter.)

The Murray-Blessing rankings didn't change much from the earlier postings. The top three remained the same, while the top ten varied from some previous polls only in that Lyndon Johnson made it into that circle and John Adams returned to it. Eisenhower was eleventh, just ahead of Polk; McKinley dropped back once again to eighteenth; and Grant slipped back into the Failure category, along with Harding, Nixon, James Buchanan, and Andrew Johnson.

Our review of the academic polls now comes down to a final two, noteworthy in part for how they treated a single president, Ronald Reagan. In 1996, eight years after Reagan left office, Arthur Schlesinger Jr. conducted a new academic poll and published a piece in the *New York Times Magazine* designed to update the Rating Game discussion set in motion by his father. He called his article "The Ultimate Approval Rating," and in it he discussed at length the previous polls, digressed on the apparent elements of presidential success and failure, and offered a few words of admonition to then-President Bill Clinton. (He said Clinton should abandon the center and govern from the left if he wanted a high station in the esteem of history.)

One participant in the Schlesinger Jr. poll, Senate historian Donald A. Ritchie, noted what he considered a "peculiarity" in it—namely, that it ranked most of the late-nineteenth-century presidents higher than those in the late twentieth century, despite the latter having faced far greater issues and coped with more complexity than their predecessors. Perhaps, he speculated, historians feel more comfortable dealing with administrations whose papers are open and who present extensive historiographies.

In any event, Schlesinger's poll yielded some intriguing differences from past surveys. The top three remained the same, Lincoln, Washington, and Franklin Roosevelt (in that order). The Near Great category (from fourth to ninth) included, in order, Jefferson, Jackson, Theodore Roosevelt, Wilson, Truman, and Polk. Eisenhower, at tenth, was placed at the top of the High Average category, while John Adams managed to cling to eleventh. Lyndon Johnson slipped to fourteenth, behind Kennedy at twelfth and Cleveland at thirteenth. James Monroe inexplicably emerged from the shadows to make it into the High Average clique, at fifteenth, just ahead of McKinley, at sixteenth.

Then there was Reagan, a two-term president succeeded by a president of his own party, who transformed both the domestic and foreign policy debates in America. He came in at twenty-sixth, a clear signal that the respondents collectively considered him mediocre. He ranked below Chester Arthur, Benjamin Harrison, Gerald Ford, and even Carter, whose failed one-term presidency Reagan had succeeded.

No doubt the respondents' political leanings contributed to this outcome. Schlesinger's "jury" of thirty-two arbiters included two Democratic politicians (New York Governor Mario Cuomo and Illinois Senator Paul Simon) but no Republican politicians. The jury also included a number of academics whose liberal views were well known but only one who could be viewed as having conservative leanings (Forrest McDonald of the University of Alabama).

Schlesinger notes in his piece that Reagan's ratings were quite disparate, with seven Near Great votes but also nine Below Average designations and four Failures. This differs significantly from, for example, Carter's ratings, which were largely bunched in the middle, with just one Near Great vote and two Failures. Hence, following the Murray-Blessing formula for rankings that could change in subsequent surveys, it would appear that Reagan's standing in the Schlesinger poll may have been the result of a lack of the kind of historical perspective that comes with time.

That perception was reinforced by a 2005 survey conducted under the auspices of the *Wall Street Journal* editorial page and the Federalist Society, which polled eighty-two respondents, including nineteen historians, twenty-five political scientists, twenty-four law professors, and fourteen economists. The survey organizers, though conservative in outlook, adopted a method of choosing accomplished scholars designed to find a balance between those who leaned to the right and those to the left. "Our goal," wrote James Lindgren, a law professor at Northwestern University and a key architect of the study, "was to present the opinions of experts, controlling for political orientation."

Unlike the previous polls, the *Journal* survey ranked Washington at the top, followed by Lincoln and Franklin Roosevelt in the Great category. The Near Great compendium included the same names as before, with one big exception. Reagan came in sixth. Hence the Near Great representatives are, in order, Jefferson, Theodore Roosevelt, Reagan, Truman, Eisenhower, Polk, and Jackson. Wilson, at eleventh, dropped into the Above Average category. Adams dropped once again to thirteenth. And Grant resumed his upward trajectory, coming in at twenty-ninth, far from his old Failure habitat.

The *Journal* poll is not the only evidence that Reagan's historical standing may be improving. After Barack Obama's election, a political intelligence firm called Clarus Research Group conducted a national poll of U.S. voters asking them which past president they wanted Obama to emulate. The leader by a significant margin: Reagan. Clarus President Ron Faucheux said the results showed "the American people clearly want a President who leads boldly, embodies change, and who can effectively communicate that change." Results of a C-SPAN viewer poll in 1999 placed Reagan at the very top of the presidential list, while a 2000 ABC News poll of citizens placed him fifth. A 2007 Rasmussen Reports poll placed him at ninth. But Reagan still has a considerable distance to travel before he can fully surmount the lingering negative view of him among academics. This view was reflected in a special Murray-Blessing survey that showed widespread and deep hostility to Reagan's presidential leadership at the time of his retirement from office. We will discuss Reagan's presidential performance at length in a subsequent chapter.

Generally, though, the *Wall Street Journal* poll, published in a book with profiles of all the presidents, yielded results not far different from the previous polls discussed in this chapter, beginning with Schlesinger Sr.'s 1948 survey. Lindgren wrote that the correlation between the *Journal* poll and Schlesinger Jr.'s 1996 survey was 91 percent, and it would have been considerably closer except for the deviation in their respective Reagan rankings. He notes also that even the self-styled Democrats surveyed for the *Journal* poll had Reagan at fourteenth. Thus it would appear that the cooling winds of time had affected Reagan's standing positively with Democrats as well as Republicans (who ranked Reagan at second among all presidents—perhaps an indication that political passions of the moment can elevate a president as well as denigrate him).

This disparity reflects an intriguing aspect of the *Journal* study. Because it probed respondents on their political affiliations, it was possible to compare rankings of Democrats and Republicans who participated in the poll. Most often there were only small deviations based on political affiliation, but in a few instances beyond the Reagan example they were significant. Among Democrats, for instance, Lyndon Johnson and Kennedy are ranked ninth and tenth, respectively; among Republicans, thirty-first and twentieth. Wilson gets a seventh ranking from Democrats but is twenty-third among Republicans. Conversely, Republicans place George W. Bush in the Near Great category, at sixth, while Democrats drop him down to thirty-fifth, close to the Failure category.

Taken together, these postwar polls contain inevitable limitations and flaws, as Stanford's Thomas Bailey and others have pointed out. One particularly interesting recent critic is Alvin Stephen Felzenberg, author of a provocative book called *The Leaders We Deserved (And a Few We Didn't): Rethinking the Presidential Rating Game,* published in 2008. Felzenberg argues that the methodology used by most academic pollsters doesn't allow for consideration of the various categories of leadership—foreign affairs, economic policy, ethics, etc. Thus when the respondents rank Nixon in the Failure category—a reasonable assessment given that he is the only president to have resigned in disgrace—what happens to his successful foreign policy achievements, such as his diplomatic opening to China and his retreat from Vietnam under severe military and political circumstances? Similarly, Lyndon Johnson clearly was a failure in foreign policy, as reflected in his disastrous Vietnam adventure. But he transformed American domestic life with his civil rights legislation of the mid-1960s and the expansion of government under the aegis of his Great Society.

An interesting point. Perhaps triumph and failure add up to an average president. Or perhaps the failure—Watergate, for example—is so abject that it adds up to an overall failure, notwithstanding whatever good it came with. Nixon's managerial lapses, after all, sent the country into a crisis so severe that it poisoned American politics for years. One could argue that that is the fundamental wisdom inherent in the methodology of Schlesinger Sr., who let his respondents determine the criteria for judgment. Collectively, a judgment emerges that places all competing assessments into perspective.

Felzenberg, a conservative, criticizes the Rating Game on several grounds. He writes that his book was an angry response to Schlesinger Jr.'s 1996 poll in the *New York Times Magazine,* particularly the tag of mediocrity placed upon Reagan. He argues that the initial polls by the elder Schlesinger created an artificial consensus on presidential greatness, thus stamping upon the national consciousness a sense among Americans of who was great among presidents and who wasn't. This false consensus, he writes, became self-perpetuating in subsequent polls, as well as in the academic literature on the subject, in media accounts—and ultimately in the minds of Americans.

"The popularization of Schlesinger-style surveys . . . ," writes Felzenberg, "freed journalists, political commentators, museum curators, and students of all ages from having to offer *evidence* in support of their opinions. All they had to do was to cite the collective assessment of the 'experts.'"

Felzenberg cites the example of Truman and his 22 percent Gallup Poll approval rating during his final year in office. Yet a 2007 survey of American opinion by *USA Today*/Gallup indicated that Americans now rate Truman as seventh on the list of presidential success. Given that few of those who answered the poll had any recollection of Truman's presidency, writes Felzenberg, this assessment must be a product of "the periodic publicity that surveys of presidential greatness have received." He adds parenthetically that some recent favorable biographies of the man—not least David McCullough's magisterial work—probably played a part as well.

Felzenberg's complaint is less than compelling. After all, most Americans don't carry in their heads a memory of all the presidents, in rank order on their own scale of greatness. Hence, when asked their opinion by a pollster who calls on the telephone, they naturally consult their memories of the judgment of history, as reflected in those academic poll results and the consensus thinking they have spawned. There doesn't seem to be anything amiss here. Besides, Felzenberg himself, employing his own ranking system presumably free of the influences of the Schlesingers and their Rating Game colleagues, also places Truman at seventh place in the presidential pantheon (though tied with four other presidents).

Felzenberg is particularly exercised about what he considers to be the political bias driving many of the academic poll responses. In the instance of Reagan's standing in the 1996 Schlesinger Jr. poll, his vexation would seem well placed, just as Republicans in 1962 justifiably fumed over Eisenhower's low ranking in the second Schlesinger Sr. poll. But Reagan, as Eisenhower before him, seems to be rising to a higher station, and in any event it's difficult to see what a conservative effort to rate the presidents would yield that would be appreciably different from the current consensus view, arrived at through multiple polls over some six decades.

The problem here is that Felzenberg seeks to substitute the judgment of one man, however well reasoned, for the collective judgment of scores of scholars—and also for the contemporaneous judgment of the electorate. Another example of this historical genre is a 2009 book entitled *Recarving Rushmore: Ranking the Presidents on Peace, Prosperity, and Liberty,* by Ivan Eland. Eland is a libertarian and free-market advocate who views himself as a constitutionalist and opponent of executive power. He writes that "in U.S. history, presidential activism has proved pernicious for the republic." His book assesses each president based on criteria that emanate from his own political views, and he takes pride in noting that his rankings bear no resemblance to the polls of either the conservative *Wall Street Journal* in 2005 or the more liberal Siena Research Institute's 2002 survey of some two hundred history and political science professors. He notes correctly that these disparate organizations, with disparate political outlooks, actually rated the presidents quite similarly.

Eland abhors presidents who sought to use power in behalf of their goals and elevates those who didn't really want to do much. Hence, in his Excellent category he lists John Tyler, Cleveland, Martin Van Buren, and Rutherford B. Hayes. The Bad presidents include Jefferson, Jackson, Lincoln, Franklin Roosevelt, Reagan, Polk, Truman, and Wilson. Altogether, Eland identifies four Excellent and six Good presidents, with another four categorized as Average. Fully twenty-six presidents are relegated to the Poor and Bad categories, signifying that Eland doesn't hold much truck with the judgment of the historical poll respondents, not to mention the American voter. (Many of his top-ranked presidents were one-termers rejected by the electorate at reelection time.)

Eland's assessments manifest a curious inconsistency. He castigates Jackson for merely recognizing the Republic of Texas—"thus beginning the journey toward his dream of acquiring that large piece of land for the United States." Yet Eland's top-ranked president,

Tyler, actually initiated negotiations to bring Texas into the American Union, an action for which he doesn't get docked. (In truth, although Jackson did want Texas in the Union, he exercised great caution in his policy toward Texas lest he draw his country into serious hostilities with Mexico.) Eland praises Tyler for supporting a limited money supply and for opposing high tariffs, a national bank, and federal welfare to the states. But Jackson and Polk, both excoriated by Eland, pursued those same policies—and more effectively than Tyler. He scores Jackson's use of the veto but doesn't get exercised by the fact that Cleveland, who resides in his Excellent category, used the presidential veto more than twice as many times as all his predecessors combined.

Eland doesn't want any wars. Presidential ambition turns him off. When the economy stagnates and people are suffering, he doesn't want any appreciable governmental intervention. He ranks Lincoln twenty-ninth and confesses to "thoughts of tearing down the Lincoln Memorial." He says Lincoln should have let the South go in peace or perhaps, prior to the conflict, offered southerners compensated emancipation of their slaves. Economic developments and history would have led eventually to emancipation anyway, he writes.

This thinking lacks rigor. Nobody knew, at the beginning of the war, what kind of bloodbath would ensue, so the choice that Eland suggests in hindsight never really existed. And history makes clear that the South never would have embraced compensated emancipation. Besides, the president had uttered an oath—before the nation, with his hand on the Bible—to "preserve and protect" the Constitution. To sit by and let the South destroy that document would have been an act of ignominy for the ages. History isn't that tidy. It is filled with human passions, often driven (as in the Civil War) by clashes of cherished principle on all sides. Developments in this ongoing saga often unfold in uncontrolled chaos, sometimes with savage outcomes.

Any serious effort to assess the players in this civic drama must begin with this fundamental understanding, which Eland lacks.

Beyond that, Eland's work, and Felzenberg's, reflect a certain denigration of the American electorate. There's nothing wrong with any citizen arguing that the course of American history would have been far richer and more beneficial had the country only been directed by his particular viewpoint rather than the electorate's. But it's difficult to overlook the underlying political arrogance. Indeed, there's a whiff of antidemocratic sentiment in it. Had the Founders had that kind of faith in the judgment of one man, they probably would have opted for monarchy. But the Framers placed their faith in the value and validity of a collective judgment, as opposed to individual judgments.

The same holds true with the presidential Rating Game. The academic surveys used for this study encompass nearly 1,180 responses from experts over six decades, and this collective judgment is almost inevitably more valuable than the assessment of a single individual. Thus, taken together, these polls of historians represent more than just a worthy conversation piece. They pull together a substantial body of thought from largely distinguished scholars over a significant period of time. No doubt, given the realities of human nature, political leanings have clouded some responses in some instances, as evidenced by the initial Eisenhower and Reagan rankings. That is evident also in the deviations by partisan identity found in the *Wall Street Journal* survey. But overall there's little reason to conclude the fundamental outcomes have been consistently skewed through partisanship. Indeed, it's noteworthy that, notwithstanding the instances of partisan deviation among *Journal* respondents, the overall *Journal* rankings bear a remarkable correlation to the previous polls.

Thus if, as I have argued, there are only two serious ways of assessing presidential success—the judgment of history and the contemporaneous judgment of the electorate—then these polls, in aggregate, would seem to represent the closest we can come to the judgment of history. There's nothing definitive here, and certainly no finish line; these differences of opinion will continue as long as the Republic endures. The historical assessments also are subject to change. New thinking will emerge to nudge some of these men up or down the scale. But when we talk about history's verdict on presidents, this is it. There is no other way to derive it.

2

THE VAGARIES OF HISTORY

In the fall of 1945 a new book appeared that would shake the thinking of the country's historians. It was *The Age of Jackson*, by Arthur M. Schlesinger Jr., then just thirty-one and still waiting to be deployed back to America after overseas duty in the country's wartime intelligence service. The book was an instant success, going through eight printings before the end of 1945 and six more in 1946. It sold nearly 100,000 copies the first year and brought the young author a Pulitzer Prize. It brought to the nation an entirely fresh interpretation of the political essence and thrust of the Andrew Jackson presidency.

Before Schlesinger's book the standard interpretation of Jackson portrayed him as a frontier phenomenon, representing the rugged individualism of the backwoods West, where men thrilled to the opportunities of national expansion and harbored suspicions of eastern elites bent on taking control of the federal government for their own

ANDREW JACKSON

Tough-minded, bold, and quick to anger, Old Hickory also possessed a penetrating political wisdom. Revered and hated in his time, he remains controversial today. But he crafted a governing philosophy that retains considerable force in the country's political consciousness.

ends. Schlesinger sought to show that it was the eastern working classes and their intellectual champions who constituted the bedrock of Jacksonian politics as the industrial age dawned, and their ideological fuel was class consciousness and a hatred of business interests. In Jackson's time, he wrote, "the basic distinction was not, say, between farmers and city dwellers, but between the productive and unproductive classes, between those whose labor increased the national wealth and those whose labor did not."

Beyond the class interpretation, Schlesinger seemed seriously focused on the politics of his own time. As he explained years later in discussing the controversies generated by *The Age of Jackson*, "I was an ardent young New Dealer, and I sought precedents in American history for the problems that faced FDR." Schlesinger's aim was to portray Jackson as a progenitor of Franklin Roosevelt in order to portray Roosevelt as part of a grand tradition of American political liberalism stretching back to the early decades of the Republic. This thesis, however dubious, was embraced avidly and widely in the academic realm.

Just three years after publication of Schlesinger's book, his father's pioneering presidential poll appeared in *Life*. And it wasn't surprising that Jackson, freshly minted as a Franklin Roosevelt forerunner, should make it into the Great category, sixth on the list. The preponderance of academic thinking at that time embraced FDR's governmental activism as a kind of ideal in presidential politics. Since then, Jackson's standing in the academic polls has fluctuated between fifth and tenth.

But mention of his name today is just as likely to generate howls of opprobrium as expressions of respect. Many see his feisty demeanor and political rawness as evidence that he couldn't be trusted with power. He is scorned for owning slaves, for showing no discomfort over the fact that women couldn't vote in American elections, for his brutal policies to push American Indian tribes to the West to make room for Anglo-Saxon expansion—the tragic Trail of Tears episode. He is often viewed as an economic policy failure whose destruction of the Second Bank of the United States brought on the powerful depression known as the Panic of 1837.

A recent Broadway play called *Bloody Bloody Andrew Jackson* portrayed the seventh president as a kind of political rock star—"a childish, temper-prone teenager who wants what he wants when he wants it," as Jackson biographer Jon Meacham described the depiction in the *New York Times*. He added the play also suggested Jackson was "emotionally challenged and all too quick to fall into self-pity."

In 2006, a half century after his *Age of Jackson* appeared,

Schlesinger issued an apologia of sorts in the pages of the *New York Review of Books,* whose audience is largely urban liberals inclined to look upon Jackson with a certain revulsion. He wrote: "The predicament of slaves, of the red man and the 'trail of tears'—the forcible removal of the Cherokees and other Indians from Georgia to the far frontier—and the restricted opportunities for women of the period . . . were shamefully out of my mind." His excuse was that he had been "hopelessly absorbed in the dilemmas of democratic capitalism made vivid for my generation by FDR and the New Deal." Hence he "underplayed or ignored other aspects of the Age of Jackson."

Schlesinger's predicament suggests a fundamental element of the White House Rating Game—that history's judgment is always subject to new interpretations, new vogues of thought, new political impulses. We can't predict whether the gathering national discomfort with the old legend of Jackson will alter significantly his standing in future polls. But it's possible. Recall that the Murray-Blessing poll reflected a wide disparity in the respondents' rankings on Jackson, suggesting that he remained highly controversial even a century and a half after his presidency. (The other highly controversial presidents were much more recent: Nixon, Lyndon Johnson, and Hoover.)

In any event, the vagaries of history are real, and any serious exploration of the presidential Rating Game must take them into account. Sometimes developments that might seem artificial in the context of the country's full history can affect the historical judgment on particular presidents, at least for a time. Consider Grover Cleveland, ranked eighth in Arthur Schlesinger Sr.'s initial 1948 poll. There doesn't seem to be anything in Cleveland's presidential record or his standing with his constituency to justify such a high ranking. His historical standing has eroded through subsequent polls, and so it's possible the aberrational 1948 ranking stemmed from an admiring biography published some years before by the influential historian Allan

Nevins. Entitled *Grover Cleveland: A Study in Courage*, it garnered a Pulitzer Prize for its author and generated a flurry of attention for the Gilded Age president.

Another example is James Madison, generally considered a middling president in spite of his high standing with his fellow citizens at the time of his ascendancy. Some scholars have speculated that he never had a chance to rise substantially in history's regard because of Henry Adams's highly influential history of the Jefferson and Madison administrations. This magisterial, nine-volume work, entitled *History of the United States of America During the Administrations of Thomas Jefferson and James Madison*, manifested a certain prejudicial view of the author's two subjects, particularly Madison. As historian Drew R. McCoy wrote, "Henry Adams was a New Englander to the core, culturally undisposed to admire the so-called 'Virginia Dynasty' of American presidents; and his harshly critical portrait of Madison's ineptitude, unmistakably reflecting his personal and regional vantage point, set a pattern that succeeding generations of historians were prone to follow." It is worth noting, in addition, that Henry Adams's great-grandfather, John Adams, had seen his presidency cut short by Jefferson (with Madison at his side) in the 1800 election. Hence, in the view of some historians, Adams may have had a score to settle in rendering his portraits of the two presidents. As Henry Adams biographer Elizabeth Stevenson wrote of the *History*, "Every chapter quivers with Adams's own beliefs, doubts, struggles. It is—in spite of documentation—an intensely personal book."

Henry Adams also had a hand in diminishing the historical standing of Ulysses Grant, whom Adams portrayed as a backward, bumbling product of the country's corrupt Gilded Age. Indeed, Adams viewed Grant's failings as stemming from Jefferson's own belief in limited government and laissez-faire economics. As biographer Stevenson put it, in Adams's view, "Jefferson led to Grant." Grant's standing was influenced negatively also by the interpretation of the post–Civil War Reconstruction period that prevailed in academic circles until relatively recently. In the traditional view, put forth by such historians as W. A. Dunning and Claude Bowers, the harsh anti-South actions pushed by the so-called Radical Republicans—and often embraced by Grant during his presidency—delayed the sectional healing necessary to bring the country back together. According to that argument, it kept the prostrate South at the mercy of freed slaves and northern carpetbaggers. The more recent view, put forth most prominently by Columbia University's Eric Foner, suggests that the oppression of southern blacks that ensued when Reconstruction ended constituted a blot upon the country. "The change from the Dunning and Bowers school . . . to the work of Eric Foner," writes Schlesinger Jr., "was nothing less than a revolution in historians' handling of Reconstruction." As the latter view has gained currency, Grant's standing has improved.

Clearly, the changing winds and forces of history can, over time, affect various presidents' standing in the American consciousness. For the purposes of this chapter, we shall explore particularly the impact of history's changing attitudes on two presidents—Andrew Jackson and his devoted protégé, James Polk, the seventh and eleventh presidents. The reputations of both have been buffeted with particular force and variability through the decades, and hence each presents a worthy case study. But I bring Jackson forward for another reason as well—because I believe that a full understanding of American history requires an understanding of the Jackson era and of what this pivotal figure actually represented in the country's politics.

Probably no American president has been more widely and variously interpreted than Andrew Jackson, who held office from 1829 to 1837, then was succeeded by his protégé Martin Van Buren of New York. Probably this is because no other president presents the complexities of character and outlook that we see in Jackson. A Jackson biographer named Marvin Meyers, writing in the 1950s, said of him, "No man of his time was at once so widely loved and so deeply hated." Arthur Schlesinger Jr. added in a 1989 essay, "Every generation produces its own portrait of Jackson." The multiple portraits seem to flow endlessly from the multiple ambiguities of the man.

He grew up poor in the Carolinas, fought as an adolescent in the Revolutionary War, moved west to Tennessee as a young man, and gravitated to the law, politics, and military life. In personality he combined a defiant pugnacity in circumstances of contention with a charming courtliness in polite society. He was still in his thirties when his fellow Tennesseans selected him as major general of the state militia, a position conferred only after the most serious deliberation. In those days and in that locale, a white man, woman, or child was killed by Indian attack every ten days or so, and local citizens naturally demanded the highest qualities of leadership in their military protectors. During the War of 1812, he devastated a British army seeking to seize New Orleans and its strategic dominance over the Mississippi River Valley. The British reported 2,037 dead, wounded, and missing that day in 1815, while Jackson's troops suffered only 13 killed. Although this victory came after the signing of a peace treaty (word of which had not reached the Gulf city), Jackson quickly emerged as the nation's greatest military hero since George Washington—and an inevitable contender for the presidency.

His political emergence marked him as the country's leading "populist" of his time. This is a term that has assumed many meanings in the country's political history, but in its most distilled form populism denotes an essential optimism about people's ability to make decisions about their lives, which leads to an abiding suspicion toward entrenched power held by societal or governmental elites. Jackson's great rival and antagonist during his political career was Kentucky's Henry Clay, who wanted the power of federal Washington brought to bear boldly in behalf of domestic prosperity. Clay crafted a philosophy of governmental activism and devised a collection of federal programs and policies he considered essential to American prosperity—construction of roads, canals, and bridges; creation of a national university; high tariffs; sale of federal land at high prices to plenish government coffers and fund federal programs. Clay called it the American System, and it would become the bedrock of his Whig Party, which played a major role in American politics for more than two decades and galvanized the political sentiment of many leading politicians, including the young Abraham Lincoln.

Jackson, on the other hand, abhorred any degree of concentrated power in Washington, which he believed would lead inevitably to corruption and invidious governmental actions favoring the connected and powerful at the expense of ordinary citizens. He wanted political power to remain diffuse and as close to the people as possible. The catchphrases of his political ethos became limited government, strict construction of the Constitution, low tariffs, fiscal discipline, hard money, and westward expansion.

In May 1830, Jackson demonstrated his aversion to federal power, and his suspicion that it leads inevitably to corruption, by vetoing legislation to extend the so-called National Road from Maysville to Lexington, Kentucky. Opposing the idea of Congress appropriating federal money for local projects, he argued that the people had a right to expect a "prudent system of expenditure" that would allow the government to "pay the debts of the union and authorize the reduction of every tax to as low a point as . . . our national safety and independence will allow." If the government amassed the kind of power implied by the road project, he contended, it would lead inevitably to "a corrupting influence upon the elections" by giving people a sense that their votes could purchase beneficial governmental actions to "make navigable their neighboring creek or river, bring commerce to their doors, and increase the value of their property." This, he said, would prove "fatal to just legislation" and the "purity of public men."

That veto proved to be a forerunner to his even more famous veto of legislation extending the charter of the Second Bank of the United States, the controversial private institution fostered by the federal government to serve as repository of federal monies and to maintain currency stability. Jackson viewed the bank as a "hydra headed monster" of federal power in league with elitist financial interests. He later killed the bank by withdrawing all federal funds from it.

In his veto message Jackson made clear he harbored no impulse toward economic equality or societal leveling, but wished merely to ensure that the levers of government were not used to bestow special favors upon a well-positioned few. "Distinctions in society will always exist under every just government," he wrote. "Equality of talents, of education, or of wealth can not be produced by human institutions." And government should protect all citizens in "the full enjoyment of the gifts of Heaven and the fruits of superior industry, economy, and virtue." But he added that "when the laws undertake to add to these natural and just advantages artificial distinctions, to grant titles, gratuities, and exclusive privileges, to make the rich richer and the potent more powerful, the humble members of society . . . have a right to complain of the injustice of the Government."

This veto message served as a manifesto for Jackson's bold brand of politics that brought into the political fold a new mass electorate with populist sensibilities and a yen for westward expansion. Thus did Jackson transform America's political landscape.

Jackson also protected the federal union from a growing movement in some states, notably South Carolina, toward declaring the right to "nullify" federal laws they disliked. Jackson saw this correctly as leading to secession and a mortal threat to the constitutional system crafted by the Founders. It wasn't clear in those early days of the Republic whether the federal government would resist such a movement, but Jackson left no doubt. "Please give my compliments to my friends in your state," he told a South Carolina congressman.

"And say to them, that if a single drop of blood shall be shed there in opposition to the laws of the United States, I will hang the first man I can lay my hand on engaged in such treasonable conduct, upon the first tree I can reach." The nullification movement faded (though Jackson also helped craft a compromise solution on tariff rates, the issue then stirring nullification sentiment).

Then there is the issue of Jackson's policy of Indian removal—forcing the Cherokees and other southeastern tribes to relocate to new and supposedly protected homelands west of the Mississippi, so their lands east of that great divide could be settled by whites. Jackson did not believe that Indians and whites could coexist peaceably in the same location, and he professed to be motivated by a protective regard for the Indians. No doubt there was some truth in that. But of course he was accommodating the voracious land appetites of the country's whites, and in any event his policy led to a dark episode in which thousands of Indians died on the Trail of Tears as they were forced to march west.

History's first phase in the evolving Jackson legend emerged between 1859 and 1861, with publication of James Parton's three-volume *Life of Andrew Jackson*. Parton brought to his sprawling work extensive documentary research as well as numerous interviews with surviving figures from the Jackson era. He views Old Hickory as the quintessential figure of his time, characterized as the "combative-rebellious period of American history," when the country was full of sap and a bit rough around the edges. No other figure of that era, he suggests, personified this combative-rebellious ethos with the larger-than-life dimension of Jackson—soldier, frontiersman, Indian fighter, duelist, pugilistic politician, self-styled protector of the country's ordinary folk.

But Parton was critical of many aspects of the Jackson presidency, most emphatically his introduction of the "spoils system"—filling government jobs with loyal adherents (a practice that later biographers, including Schlesinger, defended as consistent with Jackson's populist outlook since it ensured the federal government would remain under the popular will). Parton condemned this as "an evil so great . . . , that if all his other public acts had been perfectly wise and right, this single feature of his administration would suffice to render it deplorable."

The next phase began some forty years later with the emergence of Frederick Jackson Turner's famous thesis on the impact of the American frontier on the country's development. Turner viewed the American West as a magnet for easterners willing to brave hardship and danger in search of the abundant opportunities to be found there; hence it served as a kind of political safety valve, relieving social and economic pressures that might otherwise have built up to a high intensity in the East. And, once those westward adventurers encountered the "primitive conditions along the continually advancing frontier line," says Turner, the experience shaped the outlook not only of these pioneers but also that of the nation at large. The result was a host of peculiarly American traits—"that coarseness and strength combined with acuteness and acquisitiveness; that practical inventive turn of mind, quick to find expedients; that masterful grasp of material things . . . that restless, nervous energy; that dominant individualism."

It was inevitable that subsequent biographers would view Jackson as a product of this national phenomenon and the greatest spokesman for those sentiments welling up along the frontier. In his famous *Main Currents in American Thought* (Vol. II), published in 1927, Vernon L. Parrington profiles Jackson as representing "the best which the new West could breed in the way of capable and self-reliant individualism, and the backwoodsmen loved him for the enemies he made, and backed him loudly in his fight against the aristocratic East."

The Turner-Parrington view became the thrust of the next great Jackson biography, Marquis James's two-volume *Life of Andrew Jackson* (distilled into a single volume in 1938). James won a Pulitzer Prize for his work, and his prose captures the Jackson story with more lilt and verve than perhaps any other biography. He applauds Jackson's assault on the Bank of the United States and his fight against state nullification. Indeed, he sympathizes unabashedly with nearly all of Jackson's presidential initiatives and thrusts, even including his Indian removal policies. In discussing the president's conviction that the Cherokees and other tribes must abandon the Southeast and move beyond the Mississippi lest they face destruction at the hands of growing numbers of land-hungry whites, James writes without irony: "Jackson expressed the more enlightened frontier point of view in that his remarks included some concern for the fate of the Indians."

Still, James exposes without flinching some of the contradictions and defects in Jackson's national leadership—for example, his pugnacious resolve to confront South Carolina's nullification drive while allowing Georgia nearly free rein to influence the federal government's Indian policies.

The James biography might have fostered a widespread national view of Jackson for a considerable time, except for the emergence of Schlesinger's provocative *Age of Jackson* at the end of World War II. Its widespread embrace in academia was accompanied, however, by some pungent intellectual attacks, most notably from the prominent historian Richard Hofstadter, who scored Schlesinger for ignoring the entrepreneurial spirit that animated American thought and activity at that time.

It is not the purpose of this book to sort out academic arguments for or against particular presidents, but rather to trace their historical standing over time. Jackson requires special treatment for purposes of this discussion, however, because he represents a pivotal period in our history. Getting him wrong carries a substantial risk of misinterpreting the course of American history. And Schlesinger gets him wrong.

There is no doubt that the Industrial Revolution was spawning a growing sense of class consciousness among northeastern working classes during Jackson's time, and they certainly gravitated to his banner. Schlesinger establishes this clearly by profiling and quoting a long queue of class-conscious, antibusiness intellectuals from the time and detailing the social ferment among growing numbers of factory workers in places such as Lowell, Massachusetts. But he doesn't demonstrate that this was the dominant political force, and he fails to show that these were the primary sentiments driving Jackson's political decisions.

The problem is that Schlesinger began with a mission—to show a connection between Jackson's politics and those of Schlesinger's great hero, FDR. In order to do that, he had to choose carefully. Historian Daniel Walker Howe, whose survey history of America from 1815 to 1848 demonstrated he was no admirer of Jackson, writes, "Schlesinger preferred to avoid any topic that might cast doubt on his characterization of Jackson as an appropriate hero for New Deal liberals." Hence he gives scant attention to Indian removal and Jackson's views of slavery. Schlesinger also takes great pains to demonstrate that Jackson, far from an advocate of limited government, actually wanted to aggrandize federal governmental power in pursuit of his aims—such as the curtailment of business—much as Roosevelt did more than a century later.

Hofstadter rebuts this interpretation by pointing out fundamental differences between Jackson and Roosevelt. True, Jackson attacked the Bank in much the same way FDR attacked Wall Street. But Jackson wanted to break up the centralized power represented by the Bank-government alliance; hence his aim was decentralization. Roosevelt, by contrast, centralized federal power in order to take on Wall Street and pursue his domestic aims. Further, Jackson never wavered in his opposition to federal projects such as roads, bridges, and canals, whereas Roosevelt fully embraced the Henry Clay advocacy of federal public works—and took that policy prescription far beyond anything ever before contemplated by any president.

In a 1989 piece in the *New York Review of Books* (one of two in that publication that he wrote on the subject), Schlesinger acknowledged that he had crafted his thesis perhaps a bit too starkly in his Jackson biography (though he still held fast to his fundamental thesis). "In doctrine the Jacksonians were indisputably antistatist," he writes. "On this level, my critics have a point when they claim the Whigs, and not the Jacksonians, as the real forerunners of the New Deal." He adds that the tradition of affirmative government was the tradition of Hamilton and Clay, not of Jefferson, and that Clay's American System could be characterized as "a great dream of economic development under the leadership of the national state."

This is correct and immensely significant. Jackson's populism, by contrast, was fundamentally a faith in ordinary citizens to conduct their own lives, unimpeded by government or elites aligned with government, and a faith in the citizens at large to manage the national economy. His rhetoric—particularly the Maysville Road veto message (which Schlesinger doesn't quote in his Jackson biography) and the Bank veto message—makes clear his target was invidious governmental actions favoring the well connected. It was not antibusiness per se. Jackson's brand of populism often emerges in American politics during times of economic growth and entrepreneurial fervor. The 1830s, as Hofstadter notes, were such a time. Robert Remini, author of an exhaustive three-volume Jackson biography, writes: "The continuing development of the industrial revolution, the rapid economic growth, the revolution in transportation most recently advanced by the advent of railroads . . . the preoccupation with work, money and 'getting ahead'—all these shaped a new and modern American society to which politicians quite naturally responded."

The progenitor of Franklin Roosevelt is not Jackson; it is Henry Clay. Jackson represents a separate political tradition, best exemplified in the twentieth century by Ronald Reagan. The Jackson-Clay rivalry represents an inevitable and ongoing tension in American politics—

the tension between those who wish to consolidate more power in the federal government in order to strengthen the American democracy; and those who believe such power consolidations weaken the ties of democracy. This tension has ebbed and flowed in the country's civic life since the beginning and seems to be at a particular state of intensity in today's political environment. It should be viewed as a healthy political agitation that helps define the American experience and also sometimes determines the national direction.

Schlesinger's thesis continued to exert a strong influence well into the following decades. Then in 1975 came a potent treatise called *Fathers and Children: Andrew Jackson and the Subjugation of the American Indian,* by Michael Paul Rogin. Rogin helped set in motion a new wave of scholarship focused on the injustices suffered by North America's native Indians at the hands of the ascendant white race. The book came out a few years after publication of the seminal *Bury My Heart at Wounded Knee: An Indian History of the American West,* by Dee Brown. This book catalogued what *Time* magazine described as the "broken promises and treaties, the provocations, massacres, discriminatory policies and condescending diplomacy" toward the Indians of the American West from 1860 to 1890. Brown's book lingered on bestseller lists for a year and was translated into seventeen languages. Rogin brought the story back to the 1830s and implicated Jackson as a leading figure in the tale of abuse.

But he went further, portraying Jackson as not just a misguided national leader with insufficient regard for American Indians but as a man whose policies flowed from his character flaws, exposed through a kind of biographical psychoanalysis. Rogin and subsequent debunking biographers characterized Jackson as vindictive, hypersensitive to slights, oblivious of reality, wildly pugnacious—generally, a man out of control. These portrayals have sustained a minority but strongly held view of Jackson as a nearly villainous president.

The traditional heartland view of Jackson, however, continues to exercise a strong pull on the American consciousness. The most recent general biographies have put forth laudatory portrayals while dealing head-on with his faults and lapses—and generally ignoring Schlesinger's class-struggle interpretation. Remini calls Jackson at his death "a fallen hero" and applauds Melville's tribute: "Bear me out in it, thou great democratic God! ... Thou who didst pick up Andrew Jackson from the pebbles; who didst hurl him upon a warhorse; who didst thunder him higher than a throne!" H. W. Brands's 2005 *Andrew Jackson: His Life and Times* echoes the Marquis James portrayal of Jackson as a truly national figure, although he treats the tragedies of Indian removal more forthrightly. The debacle, he writes, "made a mockery of Jackson's claim that his policy was founded in humanity." A. J. Langguth elaborates on this in his book *Driven West*, which portrays Jackson's implacable resolve to remove Indian tribes from eastern states even as he expressed sympathy for their fate.

More recently, Jon Meacham's 2008 entry, *American Lion: Andrew Jackson in the White House*, depicts Jackson as a flawed giant but a giant nonetheless. Noting that the old general's slave quarters still stand at his Tennessee plantation, the Hermitage, he calls them "a rebuke to the generations of white Americans who limited crusades for life and liberty to their own kind." He adds, "The tragedy of Jackson's life is that a man dedicated to freedom failed to see liberty as a universal, not a particular, gift. The triumph of his life is that he held together a country whose experiment in liberty ultimately extended its protections and promises to all." Meacham quotes Stephen A. Douglas as saying, at the dedication of the Jackson statue in Washington's Lafayette Park, "He still lives in the bright pages of history." To which the author adds, *"He still lives*—and we live in the country he made, children of a distant and commanding father, a father long dead yet ever with us."

Thus, Jackson continues to enjoy a hallowed place in the pantheon of American history, even as agitated critics gnaw away at his stand-

JAMES K. POLK

"Young Hickory," as this Jackson protégé was known, is the country's greatest one-term president. He expanded U.S. territory by a third through negotiations with Britain and war with Mexico. Then he voluntarily relinquished presidential power and died four months later at age fifty-three.

ing. No other president of his historical stature continues to generate the kind of emotional debate that surrounds Jackson. Whether he can retain his favorable standing indefinitely is a question cast to future historians.

When Jackson's protégé, Polk, got his party's presidential nomination in 1844 and announced he would serve only one term, his motivation was twofold—one public and principled, the other private and calculated. Publicly, he professed that, as a small-government man, he held a philosophical aversion to entrenched power and hence would back up this civic principle by renouncing any national ambition beyond a single term. But privately he was motivated more by the volcanic ambitions rumbling within the breasts of the big figures in his Democratic Party, notably Martin Van Buren (who had been president and hungered for a White House return), Thomas Hart Benton, Lewis Cass, and John C. Calhoun. Polk calculated that, if these men thought he would be in the White House for eight years, they would never extend themselves in his behalf, and he would face a likely defeat at the hands of the Democrats' most despised nemesis—that Whig, Henry Clay. Better, he thought, to forswear any second-term aims and get those men behind him in the general election.

It worked. He beat Clay by only 39,490 votes out of 2,703,659 cast. Had he not made his promise, he most likely would have lost the election.

But Polk's one-term promise contained within it big presidential dreams. He was in many ways a smaller-than-life figure—sanctimonious, suspicious, uncomfortable in social settings. But he harbored larger-than-life ambitions. Upon getting elected, he set for himself four outsized goals: he would reduce tariff rates to foster foreign trade; create an independent treasury to serve as a repository for federal monies and maintain currency stability; bring into the Union the bulk of Oregon Territory, which had been jointly occupied by Britain and America for some twenty-seven years; and acquire California from Mexico.

None of this would be easy. Tariff rates in those days generated political passions akin to those generated by the tax issue today. And the independent treasury stirred the ire of Americans who remembered how Polk's great mentor, Andrew Jackson, had killed the Second Bank of the United States during the Jackson presidency. Had he not done that, many felt, the independent treasury wouldn't be needed at all.

But it was Polk's foreign policy goals that would agitate the nation most of all. The president pushed right to the brink of war with Great Britain before finally settling for most of Oregon in what ended up as a deft negotiation but came close to disaster. And he knew from the beginning that the acquisition of California would almost inevitably entail a war with Mexico. He got his war and, with it, California, along with a huge swath of land in what is now the American Southwest. He thought the war would be short and relatively painless, but it turned out to be long and costly. Congress and the country turned on him with a vengeance for his miscalculation.

In the end, though, he fulfilled all four goals, and also pulled off the annexation of Texas (which had been set in motion by his predecessor, John Tyler). His tenacity and political adroitness extended the country's territorial expanse by a third and established America as a transcontinental power positioned to dominate two oceans and vie for global preeminence. Not a bad record for a four-year presidency. That record seems reflected in Polk's historical standing. As noted, he ranked tenth, within the Near Great category, in Schlesinger Sr.'s first poll in 1948 and rose to eighth in his second poll. An aggregate ranking of some twelve academic and citizen polls conducted since 1948 would place Polk at eleventh among all presidents, with a high of eighth and a low of fourteenth.

And yet probably no other president presents such a chasm in our own time between actual accomplishment and popular recognition. Among American intellectuals Polk has generated abundant controversy through history in much the same way he did during his own presidency. Whereas the contemporary critics of John Adams, Jefferson, Lincoln, and the two Roosevelts exercise almost no lingering influence on those presidents' historical reputations, Polk's historical standing seems trapped in the arguments and controversies that swirled around him during his momentous White House years. Some historians have suggested that these arguments and controversies took on added intensity after the country had become inflamed by the Vietnam war in the 1960s and 1970s.

Thus, Polk often is viewed as an imperialist manipulator who bent the truth and the nation's will to his questionable objectives. He is accused of assuming illegitimate power to manufacture his war; of lying about the actual events that generated hostilities with Mexican troops; of stealing territory from a weaker nation that lacked the resources to fight back; of casting his nation into the role of international aggressor. And it has been suggested through history, as it was during Polk's time, that he embarked upon his territorial ambitions largely to enhance the nation's southern slave power.

These views have been widespread in America the past forty years. Former vice president Al Gore stated flatly in 2008 that Polk's war had been "condemned by history." Historian John H. Schroeder has argued the conflict emerged from "dubious beginnings and questionable motives." When a documentary producer named Sylvia Komatsu sought to produce a public television film on the "U.S.-Mexican War" in 1998, the subject generated so much controversy that normally generous corporate sponsors declined to back the project for fear of getting caught in an ideological crossfire. One adviser to the effort, Ron Tyler, director of the Texas State Historical Association, extolled the documentary for presenting the notion "that this is the War of Yankee aggression and to call it anything else is wrong."

I suggested in my book on the Polk presidency, *A Country of Vast Designs*, that such lingering sentiments are not surprising in a nation with a powerful strain of foreign policy liberalism—which deprecates wars fought for national interest and glorifies those fought for humanitarian ideals. Certainly, when the United States fought the Mexican War, it decisively chose national interest over humanitarianism, and that breeds still a sense of discomfort among some Americans. And I noted that the humanitarian critique of Polk's war is not without traces of truth. All American wars, including those of Wilson and Franklin Roosevelt as well as those of Lyndon Johnson and George W. Bush, have generated their own special hypocrisy and presidential deceit. Polk certainly contributed his share to that historical record.

But some of the lingering criticisms of Polk do not hold up when placed against the complexities of his time and the facts in the case—that there was no provocation in Mexico's actions toward the United States, for example, or that his war was unconstitutional. And the allegation that Polk was a tool of the slave power is, as Princeton's liberal historian Sean Wilentz has put it, "simply false." Beyond that, it is perhaps important to note that Polk ultimately was the instrument of the popular political sentiment of his time, which embraced with a powerful passion the notion of American expansionism—or Manifest Destiny, as it became known—with the aim of establishing a nation that extended from sea to sea. As I summed up my exploration of the Polk presidency, "But in the end he succeeded and fulfilled the vision and dream of his constituency. In a democratic system that is the ultimate measure of political success."

Part II

THE
PEOPLE

3

THE MAKING OF
THE PRESIDENCY

On June 18, 1787, during the arduous deliberations of the Constitutional Convention, Alexander Hamilton rose to outline the kind of government he wished to see emerge at the Philadelphia assembly. The brilliant New Yorker, just thirty at the time, held the floor for five hours, offering a comprehensive vision of the American polity. He talked extensively about the country's chief executive, which he thought should be as close to the English king in power and prerogative as the citizens of the new nation would accept. "I believe," declared Hamilton, "the British government forms the best model the world ever produced."

Hamilton was willing to bow to democratic sentiments of the New World sufficiently to accept that the American president—or "governor," as he called the officeholder—should be selected by electors who in turn would be selected by popular means in the various states. And the national governor, he added, should be subject to impeachment for serious wrongdoing. But—and here was the kicker—absent impeachment this governor should serve for life. Further, he should have an absolute veto power, meaning he could negate any bills passed by the legislature. For good measure, Hamilton added that senators in the new Congress also should serve for life—as an agency of the aristocracy he wished to see in the new nation.

This was preposterous stuff—far too close to monarchy to be taken seriously by any delegates save perhaps a couple. But no one rose to dispute Hamilton. There wasn't much point, as his outlook was so far removed from consensus thinking as to be almost shocking. Still, Hamilton's radical traditionalism reflected a reality of that convention that enlightens our efforts today to understand the American presidency—namely, that the Founders, when they began their work, had no clear sense of how to fashion a national executive or even what it should be.

Another view of the presidency came from Connecticut's Roger Sherman, then sixty-six and a man of considerable stature. John Adams considered him "as honest as an angel," and Thomas Jefferson once observed that he had "never said a foolish thing in his life." Sherman projected a concept that was the polar opposite of Hamilton's. The American magistracy, he argued, should be "nothing more than an institution for carrying the will of the legislature into effect . . . the person or persons ought to be appointed by and accountable to the legislature only, which [is] the depository of the supreme will of the society." In other words, the executive would have no independent power.

Most delegates assumed the final result would lie somewhere between the polar positions of Hamilton and Sherman. But, when they got down to details, they seemed incapable of fashioning a consensus. Should the national executive be more like a king or like a prime minister? Should his enumerated powers be slight or robust?

Should he be a handmaiden of the legislature or operate from an independent power base? How should he be selected? How long should he serve? Should he be eligible for reelection or limited to a single term? There was even talk of investing executive power in two persons or perhaps three.

Ultimately, the institution was born of two interlocking and competing imperatives that troubled the Founders—the need to curtail the whims and abuses of executive power; and the need to employ executive power to limit the whims and abuses of legislative power. The delegates spent considerable time in search of a compromise that encompassed both of these imperatives. It wasn't easy. The Founders thought deeply about such concepts as divided government, checks and balances, consent of the governed, and a carefully calibrated distribution of powers. But it wasn't clear how all this could be pulled together into a functioning governmental system. Although their Revolutionary War experiences had instilled a profound distrust of executive power, later experiences had taught them that unchecked legislative power could be equally dangerous. After the Revolution, most of the new states, following the lessons of King George III, had crafted governmental systems with feeble executives and potent legislatures. The result over the years had been a growing catalogue of legislative abuse.

In early deliberations, fear of executive power won out. The Founders settled upon what seemed like a default position: The president would be selected by a vote of Congress and would serve for seven years, after which he would be ineligible for reelection. His duties would be minimal—to execute the laws enacted by the legislature and make appointments not vested in the legislature (which, it was assumed, would not be many; even judges, according to the prevailing thinking, would be appointed exclusively through legislative prerogative). Thus, the convention seemed headed for something more like the Roger Sherman approach.

This emerging concept reflected the fact, as historian Allan Nevins has noted, that the experience of the Revolution had rendered it difficult to draw a distinction between a royal governor and a popularly elected one. The Founders did not yet see that the latter could be held accountable to the people in ways a king never could be. On the other hand, without an independent executive, the delegates were unable to craft a system with an appropriate degree of equilibrium, with all the various parts of the governmental machinery working in harmony and with appropriate checks and balances.

For example, if the legislature chose the executive, what was the point in giving him broad powers of personnel appointment or command over the executive departments? Ultimately, those powers would be snatched away by the powerful legislature. Also, it was widely agreed that, if the president were to be selected by Congress, he must be ineligible for reelection; otherwise, any president wishing to retain his office would crumble under the sway of the legislative electors, and executive independence would be lost. But this curtailment on executive longevity, a necessity of the prevailing selection mode, struck some troubled delegates as a curtailment of democracy and executive efficiency.

Some of the convention's most influential participants began to weigh in with serious objections to the prevailing concept. Virginia's James Madison suggested the legislative selection process would generate "intrigues and contentions that ought not to be unnecessarily admitted." He favored "the people at large" as the best repository of presidential selection.

The most powerful arguments came from Pennsylvania's Gouverneur Morris, an eloquent and blunt aristocrat whose loss of a leg in a carriage accident had never seemed to diminish his famous success as a ladies' man. Morris harbored a vision of America as a broad, expanding power guided by a free citizenry. He was a populist in the sense that he possessed a firm faith in the collective judgment of the electorate. And he felt an independent executive was necessary to curb the inevitable abuses of an unconstrained legislature.

"One great object of the Executive," he declared, "is to control the Legislature." He pictured the independent presidency as "the guardian of the people, even of the lower classes, [against] Legislative tyranny." Inevitably, he argued, the "Great and the wealthy . . . in the course of things will necessarily compose the Legislative body," and without a check on it the people would be endangered. "Of all possible modes of appointment, that by the Legislature is the worst."

At this point a change of outlook by Morris on one aspect of the presidency transformed the debate for numerous delegates. Morris had opposed any impeachment prerogative for Congress as a threat to executive independence. But now, he said, he could see that impeachment would be necessary to protect the system from executive malfeasance that could undermine the people's consent.

"The Magistrate is not the King," said Morris, "but the prime-minister; the people are the King."

That expression constituted a pivotal moment in the convention debate—and in the course of American history. For centuries in the West, kings had embodied national sovereignty. In America, where kings were not wanted, many had come to view the legislative assembly as embodying sovereignty. That was Roger Sherman's concept. But now Morris seemed to be articulating a new idea—the people as sovereign. This distilled the essential concept that Morris, Madison, and others had been developing in a kind of halting way. The people would judge the success and failure—and determine the rise and fall—of the public servants who toiled in the executive branch of government. Just as a prime minister was the king's servant in governments of old, now the president would be the people's servant—and would be accountable to them.

This was huge. Now it could be seen by holdouts that an independent presidency was not only possible in theory but perhaps necessary in practice. It took some time and further debate before this notion captured the imagination of the convention majority. But, when it did, it gave birth to a new way of looking at executive power. Under the new concept the president would be selected by an Electoral College whose members would be chosen by any means deemed appropriate by each state. Electors would equal the sum of each state's senators and representatives in Congress. The president would serve for four years, with no restriction on his right to seek reelection. If no candidate got a majority of electoral votes, the decision would devolve to the Senate (a grant of power that the Founders transferred in later deliberations to the House because they considered that chamber closer to the people).

This approach addressed most of the lingering concerns and imperatives of various delegates. Alexander Hamilton got his presidency for life, so long as the occupant could retain the people's consent every four years. (This was upended—unfortunately, in my view—in 1951 by the Twenty-Second Amendment, which limited presidential tenure to two terms.) He also got a president with a powerful standing within the vortex of national government. Roger Sherman got congressional selection in instances when the Electoral College could not produce a majority winner (which many, including Sherman, thought would be the norm). He also got, through subsequent compromise, a president whose powers were curtailed through a series of checks and balances. Gouverneur Morris got his independent executive answerable to the people and capable of speaking for the nation at large.

But the convention had one last big job—crafting the relationship between the executive and legislative branches. Here's where Roger Sherman's concern over executive power merged with the delegates' capacity for innovation. Now it wasn't so much which branch would control which governmental functions but how the branches would share those functions. The Framers crafted a system of separate and competing branches of government in terms of personnel, but a system whose powers were shared intricately by those independent branches.

Hence, the president was empowered to select his top governmental ministers but only with the "advice and consent" of the Senate. Judges would be nominated by the president but confirmed by the Senate. While the president would dominate selection of judges, Congress would control the process of their impeachment. The president would negotiate treaties with foreign powers, but they would not take effect without the Senate's two-thirds ratification. The president would command the country's armed forces, but only Congress could declare war. Congress could pass legislation, but it could be vetoed by the president—and then overturned by a two-thirds vote of Congress.

All this intermingling of function was new, not only in practice but also in most of the literature of political philosophy. What emerged was a matrix of shared powers binding the two branches and forcing them to work together in the course of governing. The so-called strong-executive delegates won out, but the ultimate office was embedded into the American system in ways that were highly complex, intricately balanced, and ultimately as safe as the Framers could conceivably make them.

And thus was born the modern presidency with all of its majesty—a majesty that emerges from a central reality: The people own the office; the office belongs to the people. The president is the only American leader who holds his position exclusively through the sufferance of the broad electorate. (Technically, the vice president also is, but he is merely a sidecar on the presidential motorcycle.) Hence the president is the single national leader who can claim to speak for the people. No parliamentary system has such a leader, and no legislature can produce one. Limited in his prerogatives though he may be; beset though he is with the weight of legislative authority; frustrated though he inevitably feels with checks on his free hand— the president nevertheless possesses one commanding attribute: his direct connection with the people, wherein the Founders placed the national sovereignty.

Woodrow Wilson expressed it well when he said: "Let him once win the admiration and confidence of the country, and no other single force can withstand him, no combination of forces will easily overpower him. . . . If he rightly interpret the national thought and boldly insist upon it, he is irresistible."

But it is immensely difficult for any president to capture precisely that national moment and thus become the irresistible force that Wilson envisioned. Therein lies the challenge of the presidency. Therein can we find the true nature of the political crucible that has beckoned and diminished and elevated so many ambitious and forceful Americans absorbed by the call of destiny and the lure of greatness. The presidency is the fulcrum of American politics and hence of American history.

4

THE
PRESIDENTIAL REFERENDUM

In the spring of 1990, Madison Books published a work entitled *The 13 Keys to the Presidency*, by Allan J. Lichtman and Ken DeCell. This work of history and political science immediately stirred my interest because I had never before encountered a view of presidential elections quite like the one fashioned by these authors. Their formulation brought into focus some of my own observations and perceptions about what drives the voters every four years as they choose their national leaders.

Even during my years as a political reporter, tethered to presidential campaign planes and fixated on every political development, however fleeting or minor, I never quite bought the notion that those fleeting and minor developments actually made much difference in the outcome of campaigns. Most of them, I felt, get filtered out by the electorate, which somehow manages to bring a collective judgment—perhaps even a collective wisdom—to the job of selecting U.S. presidents. While many of my colleagues on the political beat believed the electorate often was manipulated into faulty decisions by negative ads or clever slogans or fund-raising disparities, I believed that the electorate operates generally on a higher plane, sorting out the unimportant debris of campaigns and rendering decisions based mostly on more fundamental questions of national direction and the performance of the incumbent (or incumbent party).

So I naturally perked up when *The 13 Keys* of Lichtman and DeCell put forth the argument that presidential campaigns turn on questions of governance, not on the fine points of campaigning. "Effective government, not packaging or image-making, keeps executive parties in control of the White House," they wrote. In short, they viewed presidential elections as referendums on the incumbent or incumbent party. If the incumbent's record was adjudged to be exemplary, they suggested, it didn't matter much who the challenger was or what he said or did. The incumbent would win. If that record was judged to be faulty, then again it didn't matter much who the challenger was or what he said or did. The incumbent would lose.

This concept of presidential elections as largely referendums struck me as powerful and an appropriate prism through which to view America's presidential succession. I wrote a column on *The 13 Keys* for the *Congressional Quarterly Weekly Report* in which I suggested that its thesis was essentially optimistic. "It posits," I wrote, "that the voters, exercising their collective franchise, bring sound judgment to the task of choosing their leaders, that their decisions are based on big-picture considerations and not trivia, that the country's presidential guidance system is working as well today as it did during any halcyon days of yore." The thesis of *The 13 Keys* is worth pondering, for it isn't quite possible to understand the presidency without understanding the dynamics of presidential selection.

The Lichtman-DeCell thesis was embedded in a broader effort to demonstrate a means of predicting presidential elections based largely on the performance of the incumbent president (or the incumbent party if it puts forth a new candidate). The authors identified thirteen "keys," or fundamental questions, that illuminate the political standing of the party in power. Assessing each presidential election since Lincoln's 1860 victory, they note that when five or fewer of these questions turn against the incumbent party, the voters keep the incumbent or incumbent party in the White House. When six or more turn against the incumbent party, it gets tossed out.

The keys include such questions as these: Has the incumbent party increased its share of House seats in the past two elections? Is there a serious contest for the incumbent-party nomination? Is the incumbent-party candidate the sitting president (thus projecting a small advantage of incumbency when the sitting president is seeking reelection)? Is there a significant independent campaign in the general election? Has the economy fared well over the previous four years, and is it turning upward in the campaign year? Have there been major changes in national policy? Has there been a major failure or success in foreign affairs? Has there been sustained social unrest in the country? Has there been a major scandal in the incumbent administration? Is the incumbent-party nominee a man of "charisma" or a national hero? Is the challenger a man of charisma or a national hero? This analytical matrix applies to politics a mathematical technique called "pattern recognition," which seeks to illuminate the politics of today by discerning patterns of circumstance that have guided the country's political path through history.

Since the book in your hands is written not for political scientists but for political aficionados, we needn't explore the Lichtman-DeCell methodology in detail. Suffice it to say that the academic in the partnership—Lichtman, a history professor at American University in Washington, D.C. (DeCell is a longtime editor at the *Washingtonian* magazine)—devised his keys through a complex pattern of algorithms. There may be flaws in the concept. Historical patterns, however finely analyzed, could be broken at some point in the future. And some of the key questions call for subjective judgments that may skew the political analysis. For example, one of the keys seeks to assess whether the incumbent president had been beset by a major scandal. In their discussion of Ronald Reagan's second term, the authors conclude that the Iran-Contra scandal was not of sufficient magnitude to turn that particular key against the Republicans at the next election. This is difficult to credit, given the long agony of congressional hearings, the career destruction of so many people near the president, and the persistent talk of impeachment or resignation. (In this particular instance, even if that key had turned against the Republicans, the outcome would not have changed.)

Or consider the key based on whether the incumbent president had brought about a major domestic achievement. Certainly, Barack Obama's massive health-care bill would qualify as such an achievement. And yet rarely in American history has the majority party pushed through Congress legislation of such magnitude that also stirs such powerful opposition on the part of voters. The simple equation represented by that particular key may not be sufficiently nuanced to account for such a rare political development.

Still, the book's thirteen keys, based on voting patterns through thirty-three elections at the time of its publication (and five since), do offer a useful window on the nature of presidential politics. What one sees through that window differs markedly from the view of presidential politics generally put forth in most of the campaign coverage and analysis. The conventional view is the "horse race" view, which focuses primarily on campaign dynamics—the candidates' electoral strategy and tactics, political gaffes, positioning on issues. These are seen as the fundamental factors propelling one horse ahead in the race or retarding the progress of another. The index for assessing all this during the campaign is the polls, which determine who's up and who's down at any given moment.

This approach has a powerful etymology. It can be traced to the famous and hugely popular work of Theodore H. White, who chronicled presidential elections with his *Making of the President* book series, beginning with John F. Kennedy's stirring 1960 triumph. White concentrated his considerable narrative skills on human endeavor and drama—high-risk decision-making in the thick of a primary; backroom deals yielding eddies of cigar smoke and blocs of convention delegates; fatigued candidates in hotel rooms watching the returns. This approach ignored the candidate's message and how it was going over with the voters. In reporting the Democrats' 1960 Los Angeles convention, White devoted not a line to Kennedy's acceptance speech.

Then following the 1968 election between Richard M. Nixon and Hubert H. Humphrey, there appeared an influential book by Joe McGinniss—*The Selling of the President*—about Nixon's efforts at media manipulation. The success of that study heightened political journalists' concentration on the techniques and tactics of campaign politics. Pushed even further from their range of interest were the larger themes of any campaign year, the ideas that emerge when politician and polity come together to work out the future of the country. By the 1980s, this approach had taken on a disturbing new cast—a view that elections are essentially stolen every four years from an unsuspecting and crass electorate.

This outlook emerged most starkly in the campaign books of two venerable political reporters, Jack W. Germond and Jules Witcover, whose book on the 1984 presidential campaign between incumbent Ronald Reagan and Democratic challenger Walter Mondale was entitled *Wake Us When It's Over*. The authors wrote, "And surely there was no evidence in 1984 of growing sophistication on the part of the electorate. On the contrary, too many voters seemed smugly willing to make their judgments based on those flickering images on their tele-vision screens." They added that American society had developed "an attention span roughly comparable to that of a twelve-year-old ..." Their political analysis, it seemed, boiled down to blaming the voters for an election outcome they obviously didn't like.

Four years later the two journalists titled their study of the 1988 campaign between Republican George H. W. Bush and Democrat Michael Dukakis, *Whose Broad Stripes and Bright Stars?* The subtitle: *The Trivial Pursuit of the Presidency.*

At the time of the book's publication both authors had been professional friends of mine for years, Germond an occasional dinner companion on the campaign trail. Producing a column on the essence of their campaign chronicle, I described them as fine reporters who viewed the multitudinous political maneuverings of any campaign year as a vast excavation site that always yielded up, from their digging, a compelling tale of political ambition, technique, and strategy. But I added there was always something missing from their narratives—any true sense of the voters. "The electorate," I wrote, "emerges in these pages as a vast collective of malleable minds to be massaged and manipulated by Republican victor George Bush, himself massaged and manipulated by the political pros around him." As Germond and Witcover put it, in summing up their view of Bush's campaign against Dukakis, "In the hands of Bush's hired guns, the concept of campaign as educational exercise crumbled before the concept of campaign as warfare and Dukakis was gunned down in the process."

There was some irony in these replicas of the famous Teddy White approach because White himself had repudiated his own style of reporting by the time of his death in 1986. It began when he un-dertook to report his fifth campaign, the 1976 presidential election, and found himself stymied by his traditional reliance on the dramatic moment and telling anecdote. Recognizing he was missing something important, he sought to address it by retreating from the fray, pausing for thought, and reassessing his previous reporting techniques. The result was a pair of books aimed at summing up the lessons of his journalistic life—a 1978 memoir and a later survey volume entitled *America in Search of Itself.* In contrast to the Germond-Witcover approach, both books took an expansive view of American politics— politicians searching for a stirring message and a means of getting it out; voters carefully listening for political prose that captured their vision of their country's future.

As White wrote in his memoir, *In Search of History: A Personal Adventure,* for years he had believed history to be the product of ambitious men striving to define themselves, an epic clash of heroes driven to leave some shard of remembrance in the sands of time. But now, he said, he was coming to the conclusion that the primal force in society wasn't personality but ideas. He added, referring to himself in the third person: "The men he had ... reported in politics were all of them the vessels of ideas. Their cruelties and nobilities, their creations and tragedies, flowed far more certainly from what was in their minds than from what was in their glands."

I quoted that in my review of the Germond-Witcover book as an example of a better analytical sensibility. By then I already had rejected the horse-race approach to reporting or following a presidential campaign. And I certainly had rejected the idea that the voters operate collectively on the basis of widespread stupidity (however stupid any individual voter may be). I was convinced that the better approach would account for the role of the voters, the role of ideas, and a sense of the collective judgment of the electorate. Then a few months later came the Lichtman-DeCell book, and I added to my range of perceptions the concept of presidential elections as referendums. I concluded then, and I think today, that these elements constitute the best analytical framework for understanding that mystical national conversation through which American presidents are chosen.

Of course, like any analytical framework (including Lichtman's and DeCell's), it shouldn't be too rigidly applied, particularly given the complexity of the presidential selection process. But, when the Founders created the presidency and gave it to the American people, they set in motion a democratic process that included, as we have seen, a major role for the voters, a powerful invitation to an intermittent national conversation, and an accountability system designed to keep the governmental executive in check—and allow for his firing by the voters at regular intervals.

And it is to those regular intervals—the four-year term—that we now turn in our analysis of the presidency and its relationship to the people. It can be argued that the four-year term constitutes a significant part of the genius of the system, ensuring its equilibrium and hence its stability. To understand this concept, it helps to travel back to the Founding Fathers as they grappled with the concept of the presidency—and then sought to sell it to the American people during the ratification process.

The Framers became increasingly frustrated during that Philadelphia summer as they struggled with the question of the president's duration in office. If selected by Congress, it was concluded, the president must have a longer term and be barred from reelection. Otherwise, he would lose his independence and become a mere tool of the legislature. But that approach never seemed entirely workable. In the view of many, the seven-year duration that had emerged as the consensus time frame seemed too long, particularly given that it wasn't clear that the executive's independence would be protected in any event. Only after the idea of popular selection emerged did the Framers fix on a shorter term, and four years seemed about right.

How this compromise emerged, and how the precise four-year duration was arrived at, has never been fully understood because the committee that crafted it didn't keep notes on its deliberations. But subsequent developments, particularly during the ratification process, provide a glimpse into the Founders' thinking about how all this would work. During the deliberations of the Constitutional Convention, Gouverneur Morris argued that the prospect for reelection was necessary to give the executive an incentive to work hard and perform at peak capacity. Everyone wants recognition for his accomplishments, he argued, and the prospect of reelection offers the greatest recognition a president could seek.

Besides, added Morris, a prohibition against reelection "may give a dangerous turn to one of the strongest passions in the human breast." He explained, "The love of fame is the great spring to noble and illustrious actions." But, if the road to glory is thwarted by the Constitution, a president "might be compelled to seek it by the sword." The answer, said Morris, was to give him a free rein to glory but keep him under check through intermittent elections. "Let him be of short duration, that he may with propriety be re-eligible."

The man who emerged as the greatest exponent of the proposed constitution's presidential institution turned out to be Alexander Hamilton, who abandoned his earlier advocacy of presidential life tenure. In eleven of the Federalist Papers distributed by Hamilton, Madison, and John Jay during the ratification process, Hamilton probed this proposed new institution in minute detail, figuratively holding it up to the light, turning it slowly and carefully, and considering it from every angle.

In discussing the president's duration in office, Hamilton emphasized that "a general principle of human nature" suggested that the longer the tenure, the greater the tendency for the officeholder to cling to the office with a growing sense of entitlement. He added that a long tenure without any prospect of recognition through reelection could also, given human nature, sap a president's zest for his duties. Thus an extended, nonrenewable duration could serve to "corrupt his integrity, or debase his fortitude."

On the other hand, argued Hamilton, the tenure must be of sufficient duration to ensure presidential independence not just from

Congress but also from the whims of the electorate. The "deliberate sense of the community" should direct presidential decision-making in a general way, he said, but "it does not require an unqualified complaisance to every sudden breeze of passion, or to every transient impulse which the people may receive from the arts of men, who flatter their prejudices to betray their interests." To some extent the president should be above such shifting currents of political sentiment in order to operate in the interest of the nation as a whole.

The key, Hamilton argued, was to provide enough time in office to ensure presidential resolve and potential for accomplishment while curtailing abuse that could emerge with entrenched power. "As, on the one hand, a duration of four years will contribute to the firmness of the Executive in a sufficient degree to render it a very valuable ingredient in the composition; so, on the other, it is not enough to justify any alarm for the public liberty." Hamilton noted that the New York governor served for three years, and he didn't seem positioned to "establish a dangerous influence" in that time. Thus, he added, if it couldn't be done at the state level in three years, then by extension it probably couldn't be done nationally in four.

Consider the four-year term in the context of the Lichtman-DeCell thesis that presidential elections are largely referendums, popular judgments at election time on the performance of the man or party in power. The four-year duration, in that context, seems right. As voters pass judgment on the incumbent (ignoring, in the Lichtman-DeCell formulation, the challenger), four years is more than adequate to justify whatever judgment emerges. At the same time, the electorate has no particular reason to fear the challenger or what he will do once elected. After all, he has only four years before a subsequent judgment will be rendered. And, as Hamilton argued, that isn't enough time to "establish a dangerous influence."

After decades of watching presidents up close and following their elections, I have concluded that this may be the fountainhead of

American political stability. I like to view it as akin to the element of baseball that holds the game together and ensures its equilibrium—ninety feet between the bases. That's precisely the right distance for ensuring a balance among all the things that come into play on the field—running, throwing, pitching, bat speed, hand-eye coordination, reaction time. If the ninety feet were reduced to eighty-five or increased to ninety-four, the game's equilibrium would be lost, and some talents would consistently win out over others.

My grandfather, an avid fan of the old Seattle Rainiers in the Pacific Coast League, used to call baseball, with great admiration, "a game of inches," which is a related observation. It is the game's equilibrium, ensured by the ninety feet, that renders it a game of inches—and provides so much of its drama.

Likewise, America's four-year presidential term provides stability by holding the political system together. Suppose the presidential term were a mere two years. Presidents would almost inevitably become irresponsible in their effort to make a mark before having to face the voters once again, while voters would judge the man without feeling comfortable that he had had a sufficient time to prove himself. If the presidential term were six years and it emerged in the electorate's collective consciousness after a year that the man in office was taking the country in troublesome or even dangerous directions, a heightened sense of civic anxiety could threaten the country's political stability.

But under the four-year approach, if the electorate concludes it has installed in the White House an incompetent, there is no need for any sense of urgency in getting rid of him. The next election will roll around soon enough. Meanwhile, the voters can clip his wings by reducing his party's congressional standing at the next midterm elections. For truly egregious behavior, there is always the impeachment option.

Over the years, many political scientists and politicians have advocated replacing the four-year term with a six-year, nonrenewable

tenure. Some two hundred constitutional amendments to that effect have been introduced in Congress over the decades. It has been
advocated by a number of presidents, including Andrew Johnson,
William Henry Harrison, Hayes, Taft, Lyndon Johnson, and Carter.
(The indisputably great presidents have not seemed interested in the
idea.) The rationales are numerous: The president would have more
time to accomplish his objectives before exiting the stage; he would
feel less pressure from voters and hence could operate with greater
independence; he wouldn't be distracted by the necessities and time
commitments of reelection campaigns.

This is not an idea that would be good for America. The advocates seem to want "an antiseptic, apolitical presidency that is neither
possible nor wise," as University of Virginia political scientist Larry
J. Sabato puts it. He's right. The Founders had it correct when they
crafted a presidency that is forever and always under the influence of
the people. The four-year term guarantees that.

It also cements that special relationship between the people and
the presidency. In the Introduction, I discussed the notable conver-
gence between the presidential rankings rendered by history, in the
form of the polls of historians, and the contemporaneous judgment of
the electorate. But here we must note that these two assessments of
presidential performance operate in very different ways. For the historians the question is how the president performed throughout his full
tenure, whatever that might be. But the electorate judges presidents
quite differently—in rigid four-year increments; or, put another way,
through the prism of presidential referendum politics.

This will become important in subsequent chapters as we explore
further these two sources of assessment. For now I should like to il-
lustrate the matter by invoking the example of Harry Truman. Here
was a man who never enjoyed much respect from the electorate during his presidency, was barely elected in his own right in 1948, and
was so unpopular by the end of his full term that any thought of a

HARRY S TRUMAN

A modest Midwesterner who loved history, Truman took power at FDR's death and shaped the postwar world with a series of brilliant, audacious moves. This inherited term shines as one of the greatest in U.S. history, but his second term proved less than stellar.

reelection bid seemed ridiculous. And yet the historians have placed him near the top of their ratings—either eighth or ninth in most polls since his presidency. How does one square that?

Easily explained. Historians assess Truman's overall record and find it remarkably successful. These successes include the difficult but bold decision to drop the atomic bomb on Japan, thus ending World War II and saving perhaps a million American lives; America's instrumental role in creating the United Nations and embracing the Bretton Woods structures designed to ensure a stable international system and global economy; the policy of "containment" that saved Western Europe from the threat of Soviet communism; the Marshall Plan; the National Security Act of 1947, which revamped the military and intelligence apparatus of the country, creating the Department of

Defense, the National Security Council, and the Central Intelligence Agency; the difficult but ultimately successful transition from a wartime economy to a peacetime economy; the heroic decision to save West Berlin with an airlift.

The Berlin Airlift decision is revealing of a president willing to make tough decisions in highly pressurized circumstances. On June 28, 1948, Truman summoned to his office Defense Secretary James Forrestal, Army Secretary Kenneth Royall, and Undersecretary of State Robert Lovett (representing Secretary of State George Marshall, who was ill). The question was what to do about the Soviets' Berlin Blockade, designed to starve out the city, bring it under the Soviet yoke, and deliver a stunning defeat to the West. All three argued strenuously that there was no hope for the city; it had to be abandoned. When Lovett began discussing options for how to execute the withdrawal, Truman cut him off.

"We stay in Berlin. Period," he said, and left the room.

That decision helps explain why Truman is ranked so highly by the historians.

And yet all of the powerful successes listed above came in his first term, which Truman inherited at Roosevelt's death in April 1945. In addition, the economy was growing during the 1948 campaign year. By the calculation of Lichtman and DeCell in their *13 Keys,* five keys turned against Truman, which was the maximum he could sustain and still win the 1948 referendum.

The second Truman term, by contrast, was a failure by most standards of assessment, and certainly by the electorate's standard. There were some bright spots—notably, creation of the North Atlantic Treaty Organization and General Douglas MacArthur's brilliant Inchon landing to turn the tide in the Korean War. But all that was outweighed by a wave of unfortunate developments: the communist takeover of China; ultimate stalemate in the Korean War after China intervened and pushed the allied forces back to the 38th parallel; a series of scandals involving the president's closest administration cronies; sluggish economic growth throughout the second term. Hence the voters, in their unsentimental way, tossed out Truman's Democratic Party at the next election.

It can be argued that both historians and voters were correct in their separate assessments of Truman's presidency, with the historians concentrating on his overall record and the voters sticking to their four-year evaluations. Indeed, the disparity in how these two evaluation sources operate should be borne in mind as we explore the performance of presidents.

The essence of presidential referendum politics has at times been captured by men seeking the Oval Office. One was Jimmy Carter, whose 1976 campaign inserted into the national consciousness something he called the "misery index"—the sum of the unemployment rate and the inflation rate. He used this number—nearly 14—as a scimitar to cut up the candidacy of incumbent President Gerald Ford, the only president who reached the White House after having been appointed to the vice presidency. There is no doubt that that index captured a significant part of the faulty record upon which Ford was running, although the incumbent was a haphazard campaigner and carried a heavy burden from his decision to pardon the disgraced Richard Nixon for his Watergate crimes. When it came time for Carter to defend his own record four years later, the misery index had soared to 21, and the scimitar sliced up his own career.

Reagan captured the referendum nature of presidential politics probably more concisely and effectively than any other presidential candidate. During the single debate between himself and Carter, the Californian gazed into the camera and said, "Ask yourself, are you better off today than you were four years ago?" He was urging voters to treat the election as a referendum on Carter. They did, and Reagan won.

But, if presidential elections are simply referendums in which

the electorate focuses largely on the record of incumbency, what difference does it make what the challenger says? I've concluded that
it doesn't make much difference in terms of the electoral outcome.
But it carries abundant weight as a blueprint of how he will govern.
Should he find himself the victor based on the incumbent's unaccept-
able performance, the challenger will have four years to demonstrate
that he's worthy of a second term. And how he governs—based on
the blueprint he brings to the office—will determine his success or
failure. The American voters, in their collective judgment (and with a
largely nonideological temperament), will give him a blank slate, will
accept just about whatever governmental experimentation he wishes
to pursue. But it has to work. If it does, retention; if not, good-by.

Thus does the continuous succession of American executive power
unfold, term after term, election to election, as the country sets its
path through history.

5

THE JUDGMENT OF
THE ELECTORATE

Stephen Grover Cleveland was not a man whose youthful presence stirred people to view him as a future U.S. president. Although somewhat imposing, he was a plodder, a man of limited imagination and modest energy. Yet he was a hail-fellow who managed to acquire well-connected benefactors, and he moved through the ranks of New York politics—Erie County sheriff, mayor of Buffalo, New York governor—so smoothly that he soon was viewed as presidential timber. He received the Democratic Party nomination in 1884, at age forty-seven, and went on to defeat Republican James G. Blaine and end the GOP's twenty-four-year White House reign.

From there Cleveland went on to gain the distinction of being the only president to win two nonconsecutive terms. Furthermore, his party lost the White House after each term, and so he is also the only

GROVER CLEVELAND

The only president to serve two nonconsecutive terms, Cleveland also presided over two presidential defeats, including one when he was on the ballot for reelection. Thus the electorate in his own time rendered him a two-time failure. History has been kinder to him.

president to preside over two separate party defeats in the country's presidential referendum politics.

The first defeat, in 1888, with Cleveland himself on the Democratic ballot for reelection, was a near thing. He won the popular vote but lost to Republican Benjamin Harrison in the Electoral College (a disparity that has occurred four times in American history, reflecting the Founders' intent that states should retain their identity over the mass electorate in presidential elections). According to the Lichtman-DeCell 13 Keys formula, only five of the thirteen keys turned against him, which should have assured his reelection. But the keys, say the authors, only predict the popular vote. During Cleveland's first administration, the economy expanded nicely. He signed the Interstate Commerce Act, designed to rein in abusive railroad trusts, although he had done little to promote the law and didn't identify himself with it. He curtailed abuses in the expansive Civil War pension and disability program. But his administration lacked energy. The president brought forth no major domestic initiatives and no foreign policy actions of note. His efforts to reduce tariff rates, a hallmark Democratic position, faltered in Congress.

Worst of all, Cleveland's tenure was beset by extensive labor protests that led to a significant loss of life and property damage. America's first national labor organization, the Knights of Labor, organized mass protests and strikes that went beyond calls for higher pay and better working conditions. The protesters wanted political initiatives such as an eight-hour workday, employee-dominated cooperatives, and curbs on child labor. In 1886 some 600,000 workers participated in more than a thousand strikes and lockouts, double the number from the previous year. In May 1886, during a series of nationwide strikes and rallies, Chicago police fired on protesting workers, killing several. The next day a retaliatory bomb killed 8 police officers and injured 67. A police counteroffensive led to several deaths among protesters. As labor unrest continued through Cleveland's tenure, with intermittent deaths, many Americans felt the country was coming unhinged, and some feared a dark radical conspiracy.

That anxiety undermined Cleveland's political standing. His performance was widely viewed as undistinguished and ultimately unworthy of reelection in the decisive Electoral College. The key was New York, which Cleveland lost in 1888 after capturing it in 1884. That turned out to be his margin of defeat, just as it had been his margin of victory four years earlier. Had he retained his home state in 1888, he would have retained the White House.

Cleveland ran again in 1892 and won, largely as a result of Harrison's deficiencies. But his second term could reasonably be called a clear failure, characterized by a persistent economic downturn that unleashed extensive bank failures, corporate bankruptcies, and devastation in the farm sector. Cleveland seemed inert in the face of the crisis and proved incapable of acting effectively when domestic tranquility was shattered with further massive labor strikes and governmental efforts to quell street protests. Cleveland enraged his own party further when he deflected calls to expand the money supply through the coinage of silver. Hence the Democratic convention of 1896 rejected him in favor of the fiery free-silver advocate William Jennings Bryan, and the party went on to a decisive November defeat.

Given that Cleveland is the only president who twice failed to retain party control, it's difficult to view him as a presidential success based on his contemporaries' judgment. If it is presumed that the voters know what they are doing, then Cleveland would have to be viewed as a middling president at best. Yet in the first Schlesinger Sr. poll of 1948, he was ranked eighth among presidents, and even in Schlesinger's 1962 poll he was cast in the Near Great category, at eleventh. In Schlesinger Jr.'s 1996 poll, he came in at twelfth, the same station he enjoyed in the *Wall Street Journal*'s 2005 poll.

The Cleveland case suggests that the dichotomy between history's judgment and the electorate's can sometimes be traced to artificial vogues of thought. As noted earlier, this dichotomy could be attributable in part to the popularity of Allan Nevins's reverential 1932 biography, *Grover Cleveland: A Study in Courage,* which won a Pulitzer Prize and greatly enhanced Cleveland's reputation among academics. That's the view of Thomas Bailey in his book *Presidential Greatness.* Cleveland's decline in subsequent polls, says Bailey, indicates that perhaps "the bloom had worn off" Nevins's admiring biography.

Thus, while history's judgment is significant in the White House Rating Game, it should not be considered definitive—and should be weighed against the electorate's contemporaneous assessments. As we have seen, there is a significant correlation between history's calculations and the electorate's. But some big exceptions cry out for attention. Cleveland's presidency provides a case in point. If his presidential leadership was as effective as the historians suggest, why did the voters toss his party out of the White House after each of his two terms? Clearly, history's judgment must be assessed against the backdrop of voter assessments in real time.

This imperative takes on added significance if one accepts the view, put forth in the last chapter, that presidential elections operate generally as referendums. Sometimes, no doubt, elections can be affected by seemingly small factors, such as whether the challenger is a colorless man and weak opponent as opposed to a charismatic figure. But generally presidential elections, as noted earlier, turn largely on fundamental questions of presidential performance and not on minor campaign aspects such as points scored in debates, verbal gaffes, or endorsements. If the referendum concept is valid, then elections represent a powerful index of presidential assessment.

In exploring these voter assessments, several clear categories emerge. First, there are the two-term presidents who are succeeded by their own party. In terms strictly of the voters' contemporaneous judgment, these would seem by definition to be successful presidents. Then there are the two-termers whose party lost control of the White House at the eight-year mark. These are relatively successful but not in the first rank. One-term presidents populate the middle and lower registers on the scale of presidential success.

These categories pose some difficulties, however, which stir discussion and debate. How much credit should be allocated, for example, to a president who inherits the office at the death of his predecessor? And how much to the dead president? This approach also has limitations when it comes to assessing the presidency of James Polk, who promised not to seek voter approval for a second term. Clearly, this categorization formula should not be applied so rigidly that we lose sight of exceptional circumstances.

We begin with two-term presidents succeeded by their own party, a level of political success not easily attained. First, the candidate must get elected. Then he must pass the test of having the voters wish to retain him in office. Then he must pass the added test of having the voters retain his party for another term. (I'm speaking here, of course, in terms of the Twenty-Second Amendment; prior to its 1951 ratification, the party nominee after a president's two terms could have been the sitting president himself, but it happened only in the case of Franklin Roosevelt.) It's the longevity of success—eight full years judged worthy by the electorate—that renders this test daunting. That's a long time to avoid being beset by some fatal combination of economic travail, foreign difficulties, domestic disturbance, scandal, and a general loss of governmental control. The severity of this test is reflected in the fact that only two twentieth-century presidents managed to pass it—Franklin Roosevelt and Ronald Reagan. (The number would be four if we include Theodore Roosevelt and Calvin Coolidge, who inherited the presidency, were elected, then maintained party retention.)

Eight of the country's forty-four presidents served two full terms and maintained party succession—Washington, Jefferson, Madison, Monroe, Jackson, Grant, Franklin Roosevelt, and Reagan. Now let's add those who died during their second terms, with those terms being succeeded by the same party—Lincoln and McKinley. Finally, Theodore Roosevelt and Calvin Coolidge. Altogether, twelve.

What can we say about these twelve? First, that inclusion within this group does not automatically confer inclusion into history's tiers of Great or Near Great. But there is a significant overlap. Six reside in the upper reaches of the historians' rankings—Lincoln, Washington, Franklin Roosevelt, Theodore Roosevelt, Jefferson, and Jackson.

Second, the low historical ratings for some contrast starkly with their success with the voters. This is most notably the case with Madison, Monroe, Grant, McKinley, and Coolidge. Then there are the presidents who were treated roughly by the voters but still get high ratings from history—most notably, Cleveland and John Adams.

JAMES MADISON

Small of stature and lacking in flair, Madison has been docked by history for the national humiliation of the War of 1812. But Americans of his day loved him, and a survey of his record shows why. Madison's war actually produced solid benefits for America.

A look at the records of these presidents suggests that perhaps the judgment of the historians may be subject to debate and that voter assessments can enlighten that debate. Let's take, as an example, James Madison, generally considered Average in the academic polls but clearly appreciated by his constituents in his own time.

History has been hard on Madison's presidency, in part because of the way he is portrayed in Henry Adams's multivolume history of the Jefferson-Madison era. Adams's profile accentuated with some glee Madison's personal weaknesses and executive mistakes and glossed over other perspectives that seemingly impressed the electorate he served. Adams's portrayal would prove influential when later historians undertook to probe the same subject.

The traditional interpretation goes something like this: Though clearly a civic genius as manifest in his performance during the Revolution and at the nation's founding, Madison was small of stature, with a weak constitution and a natural timidity. One biographer suggested with a touch of malice that he was the kind of fellow who jumped at the sound of a gun. Hence he seemed entirely ill suited to the role of national leader, even in tranquil times. But he didn't preside during tranquil times. He led his country into the War of 1812 with Great Britain, for which it was ill prepared. The result of this folly was the greatest humiliation his country had ever suffered—or would suffer. This indignity is most markedly reflected in the White House being torched by the British, along with just about all of Washington's other civic buildings. Madison barely eluded capture and returned to a smoldering capital only after his safety could be assured.

The War of 1812 unleashed fearsome domestic forces resulting largely from maritime New England's intense opposition to the conflict. Partisan opposition from that region rained copiously upon the president; threats of secession were commonplace; regional banks, in a display of opposition, took to hoarding the country's meager reserves of hard currency, setting off a menacing wave of inflation as banks in other regions were forced to rely largely on printed money. That Madison managed to maintain a high level of popularity in the face of these failures (so the conventional interpretation goes) was a testament largely to Andrew Jackson's military victory at New Orleans, which occurred after a peace settlement had been officially negotiated in Belgium. The settlement gained little that justified the war in the first place.

Now let's look at the perspective of the voters in Madison's day. Americans at that time, leaving aside New England, had a far different view of the man. They saw a president reluctantly pushed to war by British seizure of American citizens, or "impressment," on the high seas and British harassment of American shipping designed to thwart the president's neutrality policy in the persistent British-French wars of that Napoleonic period. They saw a man committed to the Jeffersonian ideal of an agrarian society producing agricultural surpluses for world consumption under free-trade principles, and they also saw those ideals trampled by British and French global ambitions. Jefferson had sought to maintain America's neutrality rights through the "peaceable coercion" of an embargo on goods to the belligerents, but Congress had repealed that law at the time of Madison's presidential ascension. Thus the country stood weak and helpless in the face of the British abuse. Passivity in such circumstances, in Madison's view and that of many Americans, would have stamped the United States as an easy mark in a hostile world.

When war came, Madison personally led American troops, though he had had no military experience. He rode with his troops, spending up to fifteen hours a day in the saddle, issued orders to military and civilian officials attempting to avoid the superior British forces, and came under fire at the battle of Bladensburg. He never managed to lead a successful assault on the enemy, but he displayed uncommon courage in putting himself in harm's way and fulfilling the role he perceived for himself as the country's commander in chief. Although actions of the New England opposition seriously undermined his war effort, Madison never hinted at responses that would curtail freedom of speech, press, or protest. An ardent opponent of the harsh Alien and Sedition Acts of John Adams's Federalist presidency, which came close to equating peacetime political opposition to treason, Madison adhered to his traditional principles in the face of actions that could have been construed as wartime treason. Many of Madison's contemporaries marveled at his forbearance, which some perceived as contributing to his later success in soothing the bitter recriminations of war and reuniting the nation at the dawn of peace.

The Treaty of Ghent that ended the war didn't yield much for the Americans, as the pact didn't settle the impressment or neutrality issues. (With Britain's victory over Napoleon those issues soon faded.)

But it did thwart for all time Britain's aim of extending its dominance south of the Great Lakes, into the Ohio and Mississippi river valleys, which would have shattered America's dream of a transcontinental nation. Hence the war helped consolidate the U.S. position upon the North American landmass. Indeed, the perception of American success in the war was so widespread among Madison's countrymen that a wave of nationalist sentiment swept the land, and the country soon moved into what was called "the era of good feelings." The opposition Federalist Party soon faded from the scene.

Turning his attention to domestic matters at war's end, Madison demonstrated sufficient flexibility of mind to accept reestablishment of the Second Bank of the United States, which he had previously opposed but which now seemed necessary to curb New England banking abuses and to ensure currency stability. He also accepted, contrary to his general principles, a modest tariff to protect American manufacturers beset by years of embargo and war. Prosperity reigned, and Madison left the presidency in 1817 surrounded by popular adulation. The "era of good feelings" fostered by Madison buoyed the nation and the subsequent eight-year presidency of Madison's chosen successor, James Monroe.

It isn't difficult to see why Madison's contemporaries appreciated the man, notwithstanding the travails of war, and why they kept the White House in the hands of his Democratic-Republican Party in the 1816 election. Thus, by the standards of voter judgment, his was a successful presidency. But it's also fair to note that the two-party system in that time had not developed into the sturdy political force that it later would become, and hence the referendum nature of presidential elections had yet to take hold fully. With the Federalist Party fading from the scene, Monroe was able to govern at a time when hardly any opposition forces could muster a serious political threat to his tenure. The "era of good feelings" spawned in part by Madison was so strong that Monroe gained 183 electoral votes in 1816 to only 34 for his opponent, Rufus King. In 1820, Monroe ran essentially unopposed, with only a single electoral vote cast against him—by an elector bent on preventing Monroe from joining the hallowed Washington as a unanimous winner in the Electoral College.

Based on this, does Madison deserve a higher ranking in history's judgment? Though I remain skeptical of individual assessments in rating presidents, including my own, I offer a few thoughts in the spirit of the Twain analogy and in keeping with the thesis of this book that the electorate's contemporaneous judgment deserves consideration in presidential assessments. Among the presidents who have placed higher than Madison, it would seem reasonable to question the rankings of four relative to his own—John Adams, Monroe, Cleveland, and John F. Kennedy (who never had a chance to leave a substantial stamp upon the nation).

Adams's White House story is particularly instructive. Like Madison, he clearly was a man of greatness, manifested in his long and illustrious career as lawyer, Continental Congress delegate, political theorist, and diplomat to France and Great Britain. Whether that success extended to his single term as president is another question.

Adams's presidency was marked first and foremost by an undeclared naval war with France, which drove a wedge through the country and seriously complicated his ability to govern. The Democratic-Republican Party, under Jefferson, maintained a rather self-indulgent reverence for France and vehemently opposed any declared hostilities with that country. Adams's Federalist Party favored Great Britain in its epic struggle with France for European dominance and naval superiority. Adams sought to maintain a stance of neutrality, but France wouldn't accept any U.S. commerce with Britain. The French navy seized more than three hundred U.S. trading vessels, wounding many Americans in the process, and in one particularly gruesome incident tortured an American captain with thumbscrews in an unsuccessful effort to make him confess to carrying British cargo.

Partisan strife in the country became so intense that the two factions would hardly acknowledge one another. "Men who have been intimate all their lives," wrote Jefferson at one point, "cross the streets to avoid meeting and turn their heads another way, lest they should be obliged to touch their hats."

Adams's approach to this crisis seems sound in historical perspective. He desperately sought to avoid an open war with France for which the United States was ill-prepared while at the same time investing heavily in naval armaments to fortify the country should an all-out war prove unavoidable. The problem was that this approach left him looking weak to Federalists while the Jeffersonians, bent on destroying his presidency at the next election, gave him no credit for his forbearance. Hence, he found himself in a troublesome political vise. Worse, to pay for his military buildup, Adams increased taxes substantially; the government was soon spending twice as much as it had spent during the Washington years. And he signed the notorious series of laws called the Alien and Sedition Acts, which criminalized public criticism of the government. At least fourteen citizens were indicted under the Sedition Act, which was clearly unconstitutional, and ten were convicted and jailed.

It would seem that Adams, in signing these questionable measures, allowed his critics to get the better of him. One admiring biographer, David McCullough, notes that, while Adams remained silent on the legislation, "it is hard to imagine him not taking a measure of satisfaction from the prospect of the tables turned on those who had tormented him for so long." He seemed to feel the same way about using the Sedition Act to root out French émigrés considered potentially hostile to Federalist sensibilities. One refugee from the French Reign of Terror, a quiet bookstore owner in Philadelphia, inquired why he had been singled out for deportation. The reply came back from officials who quoted the president as saying, "Nothing in particular, but he's too French."

At one point, frustrated by the pressures and intrigues of the capital city (Philadelphia), Adams fled to his home near Boston for nearly eight months, insisting he could perform his presidential duties from afar and resisting entreaties that he return to Philadelphia in order to demonstrate his leadership. Only a series of intrigues within the Cabinet he had retained from Washington's presidency (a serious political blunder) and warnings that his Federalist rival Alexander Hamilton and Hamilton's allies were undermining Adams's policy decisions induced Adams to return to his official desk. At the next opportunity, in 1800, the voters ousted him in favor of Thomas Jefferson.

Whatever we may say today about Adams's presidency, it is not difficult to see why the voters held him to a single term—or why his elevated station in the historians' polls may be a little too favorable. As for Monroe, he had the great fortune to preside during a time when partisan politics was essentially suspended. Thus, it would seem reasonable to suggest, based on contemporaneous voter assessments, that the two-term Madison deserves to rise a number of notches while some others should perhaps be dropped a few.

Ulysses Grant is another case in point. He took office at a time when the Senate was dominated by the post–Civil War Radical Republicans, who pushed for harsh Reconstruction initiatives against the South and insisted that postwar policies should be established by Congress and not the president. Grant largely accepted this formulation. He sought to steer a middle course on Reconstruction between congressional hardliners and the more compassionate approaches advocated by Lincoln and later Andrew Johnson. But on many issues he bowed to the Radical Republicans. One historian, David C. Whitney, wrote, "The Radical Republicans in Congress . . . treated him as a puppet." This can be attributed in part to his lack of political force and effectiveness in the civilian world—and in part to his sympathy for the fate of freed blacks in the South. But he allowed Congress

ULYSSES S. GRANT

A brilliant general by all measures, Grant was considered a failure in the White House by historians over many decades. But new thinking about Reconstruction has boosted his standing in the polls of historians, and some believe his stock will continue to rise.

to sap the power of his office. This was considered a lapse on Grant's part, it seems, by those polled in the early Schlesinger Sr. surveys, who favored strong presidents.

Grant reacted decisively when southern resistance movements sprang up to subvert the rights of the region's blacks. He fostered enactment of the Ku Klux Klan Act, designed to bring federal prosecution to those who sought to terrorize blacks through violence. He also pushed for various Force Acts authorizing the redeployment of U.S. troops into the South to maintain order. He fought for the Fifteenth Amendment, which banned disfranchisement based on race or previous condition of servitude. He supported creation of the modern Justice Department, with its network of federal prosecuting attorneys around the country. He even suspended the right of habeas corpus in going after southern whites accused of terrorizing blacks and their white sympathizers. The result was some six hundred convictions, and the Klan and other forces of violent intimidation were effectively curtailed.

Grant also scored a major foreign policy success with the Treaty of Washington, designed to settle U.S. claims arising from British shipbuilders providing warships to the Confederacy during the war. The claims were referred to an arbitration board, which called for a British apology and payment of $15.5 million to the U.S. Treasury. The settlement established a precedent for resolution of international disputes through arbitration and created a climate for a new level of friendship between the United States and Britain.

Grant's first term brought forth a powerful wave of economic growth born of massive railroad development, fostered in part by federal land grants and subsidies. This burgeoning industry spawned numerous corollary industries such as iron, steel, timber, and glass. In his first term there was a strong national sense of prosperity.

Thus it is difficult to see how this record could be considered a presidential failure, as later historians would characterize it. Grant's first-term success is reflected in the magnitude of his 1872 reelection victory, in which he collected 55.6 percent of the popular vote and about four-fifths of the electoral ballots. In that same election, Republicans expanded their House majority to 65 percent from 55 percent, signifying that Democrats now could capture few districts outside the former Confederacy. According to the Lichtman-DeCell 13 Keys formula, only three keys turned against the incumbent, thus ensuring his reelection.

Still, certain weaknesses in Grant's leadership style, discernible during his first term, would destroy prospects for second-term success. Reflecting his military temperament, he delegated extensively to subordinates whose actions he didn't monitor with any particular attentiveness. He didn't consult widely with advisers before making decisions, relying on his instincts rather than an accumulated base of knowledge. Also, he seemed naïve about human nature, often surrounding himself with persons of questionable competence and character. The result was a series of scandals that erupted in his second term, although in many instances the seeds of abuse were sown during the first term. The most damaging involved the so-called Whiskey Ring, in which the collector of internal revenue in St. Louis, General John A. McDonald, conspired with Grant's own private secretary, General Orville E. Babcock, to evade taxes on distilleries. The pair, along with a number of collaborators, defrauded the government of millions of dollars.

Particularly disturbing to Grant's constituency was his attempt to protect Babcock during his legal travail. The president provided a court deposition on his assistant's behalf and, after his acquittal (partly on the strength of the deposition), Grant gave Babcock a federal job as inspector of lighthouses. Worse, Grant harassed Treasury Secretary Benjamin H. Bristow, who had pursued the Whiskey Ring suspects aggressively, until Bristow finally resigned—thus raising questions about Grant's seriousness in bringing wrongdoers to justice, particularly if they happened to be his friends.

But Grant's largest second-term problem was the national economy, which collapsed with the 1873 bankruptcy of the country's top banking firm, Jay Cooke & Company. This triggered further bank failures, a severe credit contraction, and an oppressive deflationary spiral. Unemployment increased; wages, prices, and farm income plummeted; and businesses went under throughout the land. Grant, true to his hard-currency principles, declined to foster efforts to expand liquidity, and the recession continued to ravage the nation until 1878. Altogether, according to the 13 Keys formulation, nine keys had turned against the incumbent party by the end of Grant's second term.

The voters responded in 1876 by giving Democrat Samuel J. Tilden 51 percent of the popular vote to 48 percent for the Republican candidate, Rutherford B. Hayes. Tilden also outpolled Hayes in the Electoral College, 203 to 184. But Republican Party leaders, determined to hold on to power, protested that blacks had been barred from voting in South Carolina, Florida, and Louisiana. They challenged the Democratic victories in those states (as well as in Oregon for other reasons), and, if upheld, their challenge would give Tilden a one-vote electoral victory. The country's political leaders didn't know what to do as the country languished in uncertainty for nearly three months. Finally, congressional leaders of both parties met in secret and devised a plan to resolve the deadlock: They would appoint a fifteen-member commission to decide the validity of the disputed ballots—five from the Republican Senate, five from the Democratic House, and five from the Supreme Court.

It was assumed that the senators on the commission would be Republicans, while the House members would be Democrats, and the five Supreme Court members would be impartial. But it didn't turn out that way. The Supreme Court participants split along partisan lines—3 to 2 in favor of the Republicans—and the commission split 8 to 7, along partisan lines, in favor of Hayes. Congress validated that outcome on the basis of a deal in which Hayes offered to withdraw remaining federal troops from the South and effectively end Reconstruction in exchange for the votes of southern Democrats. The Republicans retained the presidency in what was clearly a stolen election.

Thus, if we look at the Grant presidency as his contemporaries did—as two separate four-year terms, each assessed on its own basis—we see that one was a clear success, rewarded by the voters with retention in office, while the other was a clear failure that stirred a resolve in the electorate to switch parties (thwarted in the end by questionable maneuverings). Notwithstanding the second-term problems, it is difficult to see how this record squares with the early historians' polls that relegated Grant to the Failure category, second from the bottom of all presidents. Even in Schlesinger Jr.'s 1996 poll, he languishes at fourth from the bottom. Only with the *Wall Street Journal*'s 2005 survey does he manage to rise to twenty-ninth, which seems a more fitting locus for the man, based on the electorate's mixed view of him at the time of his presidency.

Grant has been the subject of a kind of miniboomlet of late. A number of biographies in recent years have enhanced his reputation, and Princeton's Sean Wilentz rose to his defense a couple years ago when a movement emerged to replace Grant's visage on the $50 bill with a likeness of Ronald Reagan. "Though much of the public and even some historians haven't yet heard the news," wrote Wilentz in the *New York Times*, "the vindication of Ulysses S. Grant is well under way. I expect that before too long Grant will be returned to the standing he deserves—not only as the military savior of the Union but as one of the great presidents of his era, and possibly one of the greatest in all American history." While that latter prediction may be a bit of a stretch, Wilentz's potent defense reflects a clear evolution in Grant's historical standing.

Thus do we see the value in adding the voters' contemporaneous judgments to the historians' assessments in probing presidential performance. But there are limitations. Consider the two presidents who died in office during their second terms, with their party retaining the White House at the next election—Lincoln and McKinley. In terms of voter assessment, they reside in the same category. But of course they are not in the same category at all. McKinley was a solid if colorless national leader who presided over national prosperity and took his nation into the world with two decisive naval victories in the Spanish-American War. As a result of that war, which claimed only 385 U.S. combat casualties, the United States acquired Puerto Rico, the Philippines, and Guam. Hawaii also came under American dominion on his watch. In the historians' polls he has been ranked as low as eighteenth, which is probably too low, and as high as eleventh, perhaps a touch too high. The Schlesinger Jr. poll had him at sixteenth, while the *Wall Street Journal* survey placed him at fourteenth. That probably constitutes an appropriate range.

Lincoln of course is in an altogether different category, heralded nearly universally as the country's greatest president—"Restorer and Liberator," as U.S. Chief Justice Salmon P. Chase put it at the time of Lincoln's assassination, adding that those are two of the most powerful words that could be placed next to the name of a great leader. But it is noteworthy that Lincoln appeared headed to defeat in his 1864 reelection bid, with a stalemated war that had claimed hundreds of thousands of American lives without any resolution in sight. Even Lincoln himself, some ten weeks before the election, anticipated a humiliation. On August 23 he wrote a note to himself and sealed it in an envelope, to be opened only after his electoral fate was known. "This morning," he wrote, "as for some days past, it seems exceedingly probable that this Administration will not be reelected. Then it will be my duty to cooperate with the president-elect so as to save the Union between the election and the inauguration; as he will have secured his selection on such ground that he cannot possibly save it afterwards." Even contemplating a political indignity, the president was calculating how he might fulfill his constitutional commitment as president in the four months between his defeat and the inauguration of his successor.

Lichtman and DeCell write in their book that even into the fall of that campaign year it appeared that their keys would turn against Lincoln in sufficient numbers to ensure his defeat. "Then," they write, "for the first and, to date, only time in American history, events occurring after the major parties had nominated their candidates influenced enough keys to affect the outcome of the election." On September 3, word reached Washington that General William Sherman had captured Atlanta. Six weeks later General Philip Sheridan gained dominance over the Shenandoah Valley, a crucial Confederate supply source. Then the last Confederate ramming vessel, the *Albe-*

marle, was sunk in the Roanoke River, ending rebel resistance to the Union's naval blockade of the South. These military victories in the field altered favorably the political landscape at home, write Lichtman and DeCell, adding, "Where defeat had loomed just a few weeks earlier, victory was now assured."

This reflects one powerful element of Lincoln's greatness: He bet his entire store of political capital on one desperate gamble involving huge ideas and national imperatives, and he brought uncommon determination and steadfastness to the crisis he faced. He pulled it off— but just barely. Had those crucial military battles in the final weeks before the election gone the other way, Lincoln would reside further down on the register of presidents. And the history of America would have been far different.

Now let's consider the two presidents who assumed office at the death of their predecessors, then went on to get elected in their own right, and subsequently were succeeded by their own party—Theodore Roosevelt and Calvin Coolidge. Again, we see two presidents who reside in the same category in terms of voter assessments but whose presidencies were not comparable in the eyes of the historians. Coolidge may represent the largest disparity between voter and historical assessments. He simply gets no respect from history. Ranked variously between twenty-third and thirty-second, he presided over five-and-a-half years of peace, prosperity, and domestic tranquility. When he ran for president in his own right in 1924 (after assuming office at the death of the generally underrated Warren Harding), the voters gave him more than 54 percent of the popular vote. Four years later, after his full term, his Republican colleague, Herbert Hoover, received more than 58 percent of the popular vote, a highly unusual vote allocation for a nonincumbent, higher even than Franklin Roosevelt would receive four years later when he ran in the midst of the Great Depression. Ronald Reagan appreciated Coolidge to such a degree that he had a painting of the man placed in the White House Cabinet Room.

There seem to be two reasons for Coolidge's low standing in history. First, he rejected the philosophy, a hallmark of both Presidents Wilson and Theodore Roosevelt, of governmental reform and political progressivism. He curbed immigration, reduced income-tax rates, nudged tariffs upward just a bit, eased up on regulation, and generally fostered a free-market climate. Economic growth soared during much of his tenure (though not in his final two years). But he did not believe in major presidential initiatives, and thus historians view him as a caretaker president. Secondly, some have argued that his economic policies, by fostering massive corporate investment that ultimately outstripped consumers' spending power and fueling an unsustainable stock market boom, created an imbalance in the national economy that led inevitably to the Great Depression. Still, the argument that Coolidge bears responsibility for the Great Depression is more theoretical than provable, and he seems underrated by the historians.

By contrast to the largely passive Coolidge, Theodore Roosevelt was a man of force and civic enthusiasms, a visionary with an expansive view of American greatness, a progressive who wanted to unleash governmental power upon national problems and opportunities. Inheriting McKinley's second term about a year into it, Roosevelt fashioned an entirely new model of the activist president. He successfully went after the expanding business entities known as the "trusts." He pushed through a reluctant Congress the breakthrough Hepburn Act authorizing the Interstate Commerce Commission to set the rates charged by railroads to their shipping customers. He personally—and adroitly—handled a coal-strike crisis that threatened the national economy. Responding to his friends in the "muckraking" press, he fostered passage of the Meat Inspection Act and the Pure

Food and Drug Act. He preserved some 230 million acres in public trust through creation of a multitude of national parks, forests, and monuments.

In foreign affairs, he brought a brutal Philippine insurrection to a successful conclusion (though he accepted a great deal of brutality to do it). He set in motion the building of the Panama Canal, in part by fomenting a successful Panamanian revolt against Colombia and then negotiating with the new Panamanian nation for rights to the swath of isthmus needed for the canal. "We stole it fair and square," California's Republican Senator S. I. Hayakawa said of the canal decades later. Roosevelt built a two-ocean navy and sent his "Great White Fleet" around the world as a demonstration of America's arrival upon the global scene. He put himself forward as mediator to foster a negotiated end to the Russo-Japanese War, a bit of diplomacy that earned him a Nobel Peace Prize.

The man was irrepressible, ego-driven, full of bustle and stirring proclamations of enthusiasm and outrage. His relations with Congress were abysmal, largely because he didn't deign to work with or even consult legislative leaders on major initiatives hatched at the White House. He once suggested to a friend that he wished he had "sixteen lions to turn loose in Congress." When the friend asked if they might maul the wrong people, TR replied: "Not if they stayed long enough."

Roosevelt had his implacable detractors. Mark Twain called him "far and away the worst President we have ever had." Yet somehow he managed to lead the nation into a new era of moderate progressivism with a minimum of civic friction and with broad national support. His countrymen generally loved him; in his 1904 presidential race he scored the most lopsided popular vote total up to that point—56.4 percent to only 37.6 percent for his opponent, Democrat Alton B. Parker. And the historians, as we have seen, consistently place him in the top tier of U.S. presidents. Thus do we see, with the first Roosevelt, a tidy correlation between the judgment of the electorate in real time and the later judgment of history.

And that, in most instances, is the crossroads of presidential greatness—not just those adjudged Great or Near Great by history but those who also brought forth great accomplishments appreciated at the time by the electorate (hence, two-term presidents succeeded by their own party). Into that singular circle, then, we see Washington, Lincoln, Franklin Roosevelt, Jefferson, Jackson, and Theodore Roosevelt. Add to the list those who often bubble up into the historians' inner circle but who weren't consistently applauded by the electorate—Truman, Wilson, and Eisenhower. These three had highly successful first terms but faltered in subsequent efforts. Then add Polk, consistently heralded by history for his manifold one-term accomplishments but without a record establishing his political standing as a result of those accomplishments. Finally, add Reagan, one of the rare presidents who served two full terms and maintained party succession afterward. He left office with plenty of national adulation, but history's judgment thus far is indeterminate as to where he belongs in the rankings.

If these are the presidents of greatness or nearly so, what is the essence of greatness? What are the common traits of vision, temperament, character, commitment, resolve, and cunning that fostered their uncommon success and placed them in the highest circle of American national leadership? And what are the civic forces, pressures, crises, and developments that bring forth such rare presidents? These are questions for attention as we proceed with our intertwined exploration of the two most important modes of presidential assessment, that of history and that of the electorate. But first we must look at what constitutes presidential failure.

6

THE STAIN OF FAILURE

No president has managed to sink in history's estimation to a level below that of Warren Gamaliel Harding, the small-town Ohio newspaperman who seemed to stumble into the office in 1920, then died some twenty-nine months into his tenure. In the seven academic polls used as a collective baseline for this volume, he ranks dead last in six of them (nosed out by James Buchanan in the *Wall Street Journal*'s 2005 survey). Historian Paula S. Fass of Berkeley writes, "The Presidency of Warren G. Harding began in mediocrity and ended in corruption."

He is remembered mostly for that corruption—the famous "Teapot Dome" bribery scandal that ensnared his grasping secretary of the interior and attorney general. But he is widely viewed also as a vacuous suit of clothes whose career was fueled mostly by the fact that he looked like a president. People shake their heads over his fifteen-year

WARREN G. HARDING

With this plodding figure we see a stark dichotomy between the assessment of history (the worst failure of all) and the contemporaneous judgment of the electorate (a fine leader). His reputation was marred by scandal, but the country wanted a man to lead it away from Wilsonian politics, and Harding complied.

affair with Carrie Phillips, his best friend's wife. They snicker at the spectacle of the president's sexual trysts—in a coat closet adjacent to the president's White House office—with a starry-eyed young woman named Nan Britton, thirty-one years his junior.

Harding generally is dismissed as a weak and inert chief executive of petite ambitions who let Congress set a national agenda that shunned the progressivism and internationalism of Woodrow Wilson and tethered the government to business interests. No doubt that framework militated against him in the historical surveys, but the driving factor seems to be Teapot Dome.

Still, as Arthur Schlesinger Jr. has written, Harding was careless more than villainous—overly protective of cronies he should have jettisoned decisively. As Theodore Roosevelt's daughter, Alice Long-worth, put it, "Harding was not a bad man. He was just a slob."

But Harding was never implicated in any venality of his own. Nothing bad happened to the country during his stewardship. He didn't get the nation into any intractable war. Once he managed to reverse the steep recession he inherited from Wilson, he generated a robust economy—including real Gross Domestic Product growth in 1922 of nearly 14 percent, one of the best years of economic expansion in the country's history. Labor and racial unrest declined significantly. Aside from the scandals, it seems the worst that we can say is that the American people elected Harding to nullify Wilsonism, and he dutifully complied with that mandate.

Harding's historical standing, viewed against his times' political tempo, doesn't make much sense. Indeed, the most curious aspect of the historians' string of polls is the Failure category. It isn't clear what considerations drove the academics when they populated this classification of the lowliest. Harding probably represents the most puzzling example, but there are others. We have explored the ranking of Grant, twice elected by the American people, with a relatively strong first term followed by a middling second term (and succeeded by his own party only through the manipulations of Republican miscreants). Nixon, who went straight to the Failure rank upon being included in the surveys, raises questions about whether Watergate should nullify all the rest of his presidency. And one poll places Coolidge in the bottom five, a highly dubious designation.

Then there are those who have escaped the Failure designation despite questionable White House performances. The colorless and unimaginative Benjamin Harrison fostered currency and tariff policies that generated one of the worst recessions in the nation's history. Martin Van Buren also presided over a devastating economic collapse and shunned the policy flexibility needed to end it. Herbert Hoover is placed in the bottom five in only one of the seven academic surveys, but he presided over a total collapse of the American economy and seemed helpless in the face of it. There is John Quincy Adams, whose stewardship was marked by a mix of huge national ambitions far beyond the public's appetite (hardly any of it passed Congress) and an almost comical lack of political finesse. Historian Richard Norton Smith wrote that his presidency "degenerated into a train wreck of embarrassments." One could add Jimmy Carter, whose presidency was decisively repudiated by the voters after a single undistinguished term.

By looking at voter reactions to presidents who have faltered, we see the electorate's unsentimental and businesslike approach to the presidential selection process. Occasionally, the people turn almost cruel in their dismissal of a president. But generally they exercise their ownership of the office with cool dispassion. Consider Gerald R. Ford, a veteran congressman who never sought the presidency or even the vice presidency. After his elevation to vice president (nominated by Nixon and confirmed by Congress after the resignation of Vice President Spiro T. Agnew), Ford succeeded Nixon when that disgraced leader resigned in 1974. He was a man of simple tastes, unaffected speech, and unadorned directness. His probity and sound judgment were just what the country needed, and his civic contribution, by any objective measure, was immense. He inherited a nation shocked by scandal, rent by a faltering economy, stung by an Arab oil embargo, anguished over the Vietnam legacy, and suffering from a loss of national confidence. He brought improvements in all those areas but particularly in restoring honesty and integrity to government.

Yet he never had a chance in the country's referendum system when the 1976 elections came around. The presidential performance of the previous four years simply didn't justify Republican retention. According to the Lichtman-DeCell 13 Keys formula, fully eight keys turned against the administration in 1976, many of them legacies from Nixon. And so the country turned to the challenger, Carter. Academics at the time credited Ford with winning the hearts of the

American people even if they felt it necessary to let him go. Robert K. Murray, the Pennsylvania State University professor who helped spearhead the most comprehensive academic poll on presidential performance, said at the time of Ford's departure: "I believe he can ... sleep easily with the assurance that history will handle him kindly. His was a caretaker presidency, of course, but it was a caretakership that will have more positive than negative aspects."

In the seven academic polls we have been citing, ten presidents are placed in the bottom five at least once. They are Harding (in the bottom five all seven times); Buchanan (seven times); Grant (five); Pierce (five); Nixon (four of the five times in which his presidency was considered); Andrew Johnson (three); Fillmore (once); Taylor (once); Coolidge (once); and Hoover (once). These presidents provide fodder for analyzing what constitutes failure and what presidential traits lead to White House fiascos.

It's important to reiterate that presidents get the credit or blame for what happens under their stewardship. This is healthy, as it ensures accountability. Some historians have suggested that Hoover, for example, was victimized by the policies of his predecessor, Coolidge. As Will Rogers once complained, "Nobody ever asked Coolidge to fix a thing" when things were fine. "But now everyone wanted Hoover to fix everything." Similarly, some conservatives have argued that Clinton's economic successes were attributable to the lingering impact of Ronald Reagan's policy initiatives.

There is probably some merit in both arguments, but it is all beside the point. Even stipulating that Coolidge presided over an asset bubble that burst on Hoover's watch, the incumbent's job was to shepherd the country effectively out of the crisis. Hoover attacked the problem with vigor; he was a far more activist president than history has acknowledged. But his efforts didn't work, and he was tossed aside. Further, even granting that Reagan's fiscal policies unleashed a long-term wave of digital entrepreneurialism that in turn fueled high productivity and economic growth in the Clinton years, Clinton's job was to exploit all opportunities available to ensure a strong economy. He did that and appropriately got credit for it.

To explore the nature of presidential failure, we shall inspect the presidencies of those ten chief executives placed in the bottom five in at least one academic poll (taking them in order of service).

Zachary Taylor (in bottom five once): An angular-faced man with a rugged countenance and confident air, Taylor came from a family that had amassed large landholdings in Virginia and Kentucky. A figure of little spark or imagination, he showed almost no curiosity about subjects beyond his immediate involvement. But in war he manifested an instinct for action that had served him well, particularly in the Mexican War, where he led his troops to some brilliant victories. As president, his dour nature and phlegmatic temperament militated against any serious ambition or action. His sixteen months in office are marked by no memorable successes. His one notable failure was his inability to address the country's most pressing need in the wake of the Mexican War—getting through Congress legislation establishing governments in the new territories. In 1850 he sought to thwart the efforts of Kentucky's Henry Clay to calm the nation's political waters through a series of compromise measures on slavery. His death helped pave the way for passage of that legislation.

Millard Fillmore (once): The New Yorker and fervent Whig succeeded Taylor when the slavery issue was destroying the Whig Party. But Fillmore stepped up to the challenge of establishing governmental authority in the areas of the Mexican Cession. First, he abandoned Taylor's rigid approach and embraced Clay's compromise framework. Then he replaced Taylor's Cabinet members en masse and replaced them with men who also favored Clay's approach. He followed up by helping to shepherd through Congress five legislative acts that constituted the Compromise of 1850: California would enter the Union as a free state; a territorial dispute between Texas and New Mexico was settled; New Mexico and Utah would become U.S. territories with the right to determine their slave or free status at a later time; slave auctions would be banned in the District of Columbia; and Fugitive Slave Act procedures and requirements were established that placed a burden on northern officials to assist in capturing fugitive slaves and returning them to their southern owners.

Legislation settling these crucial issues had eluded Congress and government officials for four years, but now there was at least a chance for a lasting accommodation. Perhaps it would have worked, too, had not the Kansas-Nebraska Act upset the delicate equilibrium of the compromise measure. In any event, it represents a significant accomplishment for a president who assumed office in what many would have considered a caretaker situation. It seems unfortunate that Fillmore's presidency is lost to the country's historical memory. True, he served merely a partial term (thirty-one months) at a time that doesn't resonate much in the consciousness of Americans. But he probably deserves better than the historians' rankings—between fifth and eighth from the bottom. He saw what needed to be done and directed the power of his office toward that end.

Franklin Pierce (five times): Known as "Young Hickory of the Granite Hills," Pierce of New Hampshire was a conventional Democratic politician in the tradition of Andrew Jackson—an advocate of limited government, states' rights, and strict construction of the Constitution. He also appreciated the American expansionism that exploded upon the scene during the presidencies of Tyler and Polk. But Pierce succeeded Fillmore in the early 1850s, when the intensifying slavery controversy was overwhelming all the old issues of the Jackson era. Pierce couldn't see this powerful development, and that undermined his presidency.

He emerged in American politics at an early age despite a colorless demeanor and a robust taste for alcohol—New Hampshire legislature at age twenty-five, U.S. House at twenty-nine, U.S. Senate at thirty-two. But before his fortieth birthday he retired from the Senate and returned home to practice law and serve as a leading official of his state's Democratic Party. He fought in the Mexican War, rising to the rank of general in a New Hampshire military unit he helped recruit. Two developments conspired to elevate him to the White House at age forty-eight. First, the Democratic split over slavery generated a nomination stalemate at the 1852 Democratic convention. The party broke the logjam by nominating Pierce, a northerner with southern sympathies, on the forty-ninth ballot. Then, in the general election, the collapse of the Whig Party in the South opened the way for an Electoral College romp for the Democrat. Pierce collected 254 electoral votes to just 42 for his opponent, Winfield Scott.

Pierce entered the White House resolved to battle the declining Whigs on the traditional issues, but the assault on his presidency came from within his own party. His political fate was sealed when he allowed himself to be lured by Illinois Senator Stephen A. Douglas into supporting Douglas's troublesome Kansas-Nebraska Act, designed to forge a particular parcel of land west of the Mississippi into the full-fledged states of Kansas and Nebraska. Douglas, for whom slavery was not a particularly pressing issue, was motivated by desires to open up those lands to greater settlement and enhance prospects for a central railroad route to the Pacific. But, to get southern votes for his bill, the Illinois senator accepted language repealing the Missouri Compromise prohibition of slavery above latitude 36°30'. That prohibition, embraced by northerners for decades, had been part of a major 1820 sectional accommodation that also brought Missouri into the Union as a slave state while Maine, which had been part of Massachusetts, came in as a free state. That preserved the numerical parity between slave and free states, thus soothing sectional fevers for years.

But the proposed Kansas-Nebraska legislation stated that the 1850 Compromise language had superseded the Missouri Compro-

mise, though there was no explicit language in the 1850 bill repealing the previous Missouri legislation. Douglas knew he would need
Pierce's endorsement to get his bill passed, and on a fateful Sunday
in 1854 he went to see the president at the White House. Pierce's
secretary of state, William Marcy, and Michigan Senator Lewis Cass,
a close adviser, both had warned the president against endorsing the
Douglas bill. It would unleash a political firestorm in the North, they
predicted, if territory long protected from slavery would now become
open to bondage. Neither Marcy nor Cass was invited to the meeting
with Douglas. War Secretary Jefferson Davis, from Mississippi, was
there, however, and he strongly urged Pierce to endorse the bill. The
compliant president succumbed to pressure and signed on.

Douglas, aware that the wispy-willed Pierce was known for wrig-
gling out of stated positions when counterpressures emerged, asked
the president to write out a statement of support. Pierce dutifully
wrote that the Missouri Compromise "was superseded by the principles of the legislation of 1850, commonly called the compromise
measures and is hereby declared inoperative and void." Pierce's house-
organ newspaper, the *Daily Union*, promptly declared support for the
Kansas-Nebraska legislation to be "a test of Democratic orthodoxy."

The men who spawned the Kansas-Nebraska bill, writes historian
Allan Nevins, "had thrown the nation into turmoil, and unleashed
forces which no man knew how to control." Many northerners were
shocked to learn that the 1850 Compromise had positioned the South
to spread slavery throughout the Southwest—added to the region's already stated resolve to acquire Cuba as another slave state. With a pli-
able executive in the White House, writes Nevins, "Douglas suddenly
brought out . . . a measure resting on assumptions never approved by
the voters and erecting a principle they had never endorsed."

The resulting anger destroyed the Democratic Party in the North.
At the next election the party managed to retain all but four of its
sixty-seven slave-state House seats, but it lost all but twenty-five of

its ninety-one free-state seats. Northern voters expelled all but seven of the forty-four Democrats from that region who had voted for the legislation. A coalition of anti-Democratic House members took control of the chamber from Pierce's party, and the president, who never understood the implications of his action, lost his ability to govern effectively.

Then when bloody violence erupted in Kansas, he proved incapable of taking hold of the situation. He sent four successive territorial governors to Kansas, and all failed. He refused to consider military action to restore order to this American territory, but no other approach held out any hope of success. The result was that he looked weak and vacillating.

On other domestic matters, Pierce seemed content that everything that mattered had been taken care of during the Jackson and Polk administrations. He assumed a defensive posture, protecting Democratic programs from Whig attack. In foreign policy, he roiled the nation by declaring his intent to seize Cuba from Spain, and he harbored designs on territory in Mexico and Central America. Mercifully for the nation, none of that was realistic, and hence nothing came of it. But he did manage to acquire a strip of southwestern land from Mexico—the so-called Gadsden Purchase—that eased the way for a southern railroad route to the Pacific. And under his leadership U.S. Naval Commodore Matthew Perry negotiated treaties with Japan that opened ports there to U.S. trade.

Pierce manifested interest in getting his party's nomination for a second term, but his standing in the country was so tattered, and his party so demoralized, that his prospect was nil. "By the time he left office . . . ," said a twenty-first-century admirer, Jayme Simões, "Pierce couldn't have been elected dogcatcher." The party and the nation got James Buchanan, who was to govern much as Pierce had—only worse.

James Buchanan (seven times): Long before he became president,

JAMES BUCHANAN

Self-centered, devious, dishonest, and cowardly, Old Buck presided over a gathering national crisis that he failed to understand and refused to address. His politics of drift helped render the Civil War unavoidable, and history consistently has him at or near the bottom of the presidential lists.

Buchanan demonstrated that he lacked the character required for strong presidential leadership. His weakness wasn't grubby venality; he had made a tidy fortune as an effective Pennsylvania lawyer before going into politics, and he felt no need to seek financial gain through public office. Rather, Buchanan was a man of no fixed principles and no consistent political or personal loyalties. With ease he could flit from one position to an opposing one without so much as an explanation to those left behind. Any contorted rationalization could justify in his mind whatever actions he considered in his interest at any time. And, while he took pride in his personal incorruptibility, he was not above corrupting others in pursuit of his policy aims.

As secretary of state to James Polk in the 1840s, Buchanan showed no loyalty to his president. He promiscuously embraced

various contradictory positions as dictated by his presidential ambition. As Polk lamented to his diary: "I cannot rely upon his honest
and disinterested advice."

When he assumed the presidency in March 1857, Buchanan's
credentials for the office were far more impressive than those of
most presidents—congressman, senator, secretary of state, leader of
the Democratic Party, minister to Russia, ambassador to the Court
of St. James's. But such credentials, alas, are not a predictor of presidential success. Similarly impressive backgrounds were accumulated
by Hoover and Nixon.

In Buchanan's case, his crimped and ego-driven behavior emerged
before he even entered the White House. In selecting his Cabinet, he
chose second-raters who easily could be brought under his sway. Buchanan was a "doughface"—a northerner with southern sentiments—
and he surrounded himself with southerners and other doughfaces.
Hence, from the beginning he announced implicitly that he had no
intention of seeking any kind of compromise solution to the yawning
political and cultural differences that threatened the country.

Early on, he demonstrated a lack of any clear-headed understanding of the competing political forces then swirling through the body
politic. Although publicly he nominally opposed slavery, in truth he
didn't care much about it one way or the other. But he hated the
abolitionists of the Northeast, whose fulminations he denounced
as generating "great evils to the master, the slave, and to the whole
country." Polk had held similar views a decade earlier, but in Polk's
time the abolitionists operated on the fringes of politics. Now, with
the nation in turmoil over the incendiary issue of slavery in the new
territories, abolitionist sentiment was entering the political main-
stream—and growing. It had to be taken into account because it was
a major force in the country. The president couldn't see—or refused
to see—this fundamental political reality.

He dissembled to the American people in the very act of be-

coming president—during his inaugural speech—when he solemnly
declared he would accept whatever decision the Supreme Court
handed down in the looming Dred Scott case. In fact, at that moment Buchanan already knew the Court was about to issue a highly
controversial decision favoring the South (which it did three days
later). He had violated propriety—and the separation of powers—by
lobbying key justices on the issue in the weeks before his inauguration.

Buchanan never understood the ominous implication of the
Kansas-Nebraska Act's repeal of the sturdy Missouri Compromise of
1820 and its slavery prohibition above latitude 36°30'. The antislavery
agitations generated throughout the North intensified when Kansas
became a roiling cauldron of venomous conflict over its slavery policy.
A kind of demographic battle ensued, with northern settlers moving
in to ensure its free-state future while large numbers of proslavery
Missourians flowed in to tilt the referendum voting. Violent eruptions
became commonplace, and the territory became known as "Bleeding
Kansas."

Buchanan's job was to ensure an honest process of balloting on
the slavery matter, but he didn't. When he appointed as territorial
governor a high-profile politician named Robert Walker (a Missis-
sippian, but born and reared in Pennsylvania), the president issued
a ringing promise. "A constitution shall be submitted to the people
of the Territory," he declared, "[and] they must be protected in their
right of voting for or against that instrument and the fair expression
of the popular will must not be interrupted by fraud and violence."

When border-crossing Missourians overran the balloting, established an ersatz capital at Lecompton, and introduced fraud into
subsequent voting, Walker rebelled. He threw out the returns from
several counties in balloting designed to establish the territorial legislature and elect a delegate to the U.S. Congress. Buchanan promptly
withdrew his support from Walker. Later, when a compromise effort
gave Kansas residents a chance to vote on the slavery question but not

on a constitution, Buchanan endorsed it, despite his previous promise to ensure a vote on the state constitution.

When the Lecompton document reached Congress, Buchanan pushed it through by buying votes in the House through various inducements, including contracts for shipbuilding and mail routes, commissions, and patronage jobs ("either removal or extensions," as one Buchanan biographer put it). In some instances cash changed hands, according to a later congressional investigation, which hinted also that prostitutes were offered to some holdout congressmen. Biographer Jean H. Baker writes that "by the spring of 1858 most of official Washington agreed that the power of the executive had bought congressmen 'like hogs.'"

Buchanan's one-sided approach to the burgeoning national crisis infuriated the North, drove a wedge through the Democratic Party, finished off the Whigs, and fueled the ascendancy of the new Republican Party. When Abraham Lincoln, then a rising Illinois politician, was declaring that a house divided against itself could not stand, President Buchanan was struggling manfully to prop up that divided house.

Could he have averted the war with a more balanced governing approach? We'll never know. We do know that his presidency deepened the crisis and severely attenuated any effort to deflect the rush to war. When Lincoln was elected and the most fiery southern states moved to secession, Buchanan responded in typical fashion. He said no state had a right to secede, but the federal government had no power to prevent it. New York's William Seward suggested wryly that Buchanan's position boiled down to a conviction that no state could secede unless it wanted to and the government must save the Union unless somebody objected.

Buchanan's place in history, like Harding's, seems well established. The historians' various surveys have him vying for second from the bottom. That would seem to be a notch too high.

ANDREW JOHNSON

Lincoln's successor ran afoul of Congress's Radical Republicans over Reconstruction policy. Impeached by the House, he came within a vote of being convicted by the Senate. Some consider him courageous, others a fool. But he lost control of the government and thus couldn't govern effectively.

Andrew Johnson (three times): This post–Civil War president, a Democrat placed on Lincoln's 1864 "Union Party" ticket, ranks in the bottom five in three of the seven surveys employed in this analysis. What's interesting is that this low ranking emerges in the three most recent surveys. Before that, he was more highly regarded by history, even getting a ranking of nineteenth in Schlesinger Sr.'s pioneering 1948 poll. Then it was down to twenty-third in 1962, thirty-first in 1981, and thirtieth in 1982 (*Chicago Tribune*). From there he fell consistently to the bottom five.

What accounts for this descent? Probably, it is the flip side of what we have seen with Grant—whose stock, as noted earlier, has ascended with new academic thinking about Reconstruction. The Radical Republicans are now more highly regarded, viewed as representing a wider span of thinking than previously noticed, and perceived as forerunners of the twentieth century's civil rights activists. Grant's approach to Reconstruction paralleled their thinking to a significant degree, whereas Johnson fought the Radical elements—even, as some historians view it, when he might have been able to compromise with more moderate members of his party.

Though a Tennessean and a slaveholder at the time of the Civil War (he possessed a slave couple and their three children), Johnson despised the planter class. He fancied himself a champion of the South's rural yeomanry, poor folks like those from his own heritage. Thus, when he found himself thrust by fate into the presidency in the spring of 1865, he sought to shape a Reconstruction policy aimed at bringing that yeoman class to the fore while keeping the planters at bay. But ultimately he sought to cement the planters' loyalty by fashioning a plan for them to apply for individual pardons. He figured he had to deal with the former slaveholders politically in order to keep the Radicals at bay. Throughout his tenure he seemed determined to ensure that freed slaves did not get a foothold into the democratic process. And his terms for readmitting former Confederate states into the Union turned out to be remarkably mild.

That leniency generated a backlash from agitated Radical Republicans in Congress. In early 1866, Congress passed two measures designed to protect freed southern blacks from local measures aimed at excluding them from politics and locking them into a subservient social status. Of course, these measures also would have radically altered the relative shares of power and prerogative between the federal government and the states. Johnson vetoed both bills, largely on the ground of states' rights, but his veto messages also were laced with elements of racialist sentiments. He then opposed ratification of the Fourteenth Amendment to the Constitution, which established birth citizenship and guaranteed all U.S. citizens equal protection of the law, including state law.

These actions, reflecting Johnson's insensitivity to political opinion in the victorious North, destroyed his standing with the voters, who at the next congressional elections gave the Republican opposition veto-proof dominance over both houses of Congress. That began Congress's Radical Reconstruction, which pushed Johnson onto the political defensive. Congress essentially ran the government, often in league with Johnson's own Cabinet members, particularly War Secretary Edwin Stanton. Fearing Johnson would fire Stanton, Congress passed, over Johnson's veto, the Tenure of Office Act, which placed restrictions on the president's ability to discharge his subordinates.

Defying that act, Johnson sought to fire Stanton. That contributed to his House impeachment and a Senate trial in which he escaped conviction, and removal from office, by a single vote. It was this episode particularly that led some sympathetic historians of an earlier era to cast Johnson as having "fought the bravest battle for constitutional liberty and for the preservation of our institutions ever waged by an Executive," as historian Claude G. Bowers put it. Bowers is now challenged by historians who view Johnson as a stubborn impediment to racial progress in America.

But there were serious issues involved, not least whether it was a healthy precedent to have Congress take over the government's executive branch, even in a time of crisis. Indeed, the Tenure of Office Act was patently unconstitutional, as later affirmed by the U.S. Supreme Court in a 1926 case involving similar issues. The Court cited the Tenure Act as an unconstitutional congressional infringement upon presidential prerogative. Thus we have the spectacle of Congress seeking to destroy a president for resisting its own illicit law.*

---

* The 1926 case, *Myers v. United States*, affirmed the president's exclusive power to remove staff whose duties were an extension of presidential authority. Writing for the majority, Chief Justice William Howard Taft struck down the statute at issue in the case and also expressly found the Tenure of Office Act, which had been repealed before the *Myers* ruling, to have been unconstitutional.

But the first rule of presidential leadership is that it must be effective. That means the president must pull together a popular consensus that in turn buoys the administration effort. And of course it has to work. Johnson failed to do that. Some recent historians of the period suggest he should have identified the more moderate members of the Republican majority and worked with them in behalf of a measured approach designed to bring the South back into the Union on reasonable terms while opening the way for inclusion of blacks in society—and, in the process, assuaging the more moderate elements of public opinion in the North.

It's impossible to know if that could have kept the truly Radical Republicans at bay and spared the country the many agonies of Reconstruction. In any event, Johnson's approach resulted in his getting crushed by the opposition. And a crushed president can never be a successful president.

Ulysses Grant (five times): To reiterate previous observations, Grant's standing in the early academic polls doesn't seem consistent with the voters' assessment in his own time and a careful scrutiny of his presidential record. But, as noted, his standing seems on the rise, and he escaped the bottom five in the last two surveys in our study— Schlesinger Jr.'s 1996 poll and the *Wall Street Journal*'s 2005 survey. That rise likely will continue as the new academic interpretation of Reconstruction takes root. I view Grant's standing in the 2005 *Journal* poll—twenty-ninth—as about right.

Warren Harding (seven times): He is faulted for putting in place men of questionable character, particularly Attorney General Harry Daugherty, Interior Secretary Albert Fall, and Postmaster General Will Hays. They in turn brought to Washington a coterie of freebooters and scoundrels bent on joining those Cabinet officials in grabbing whatever booty they could. The result was disaster, and hence this is a valid and serious criticism. But Harding also brought to government men of high stature and clear probity, including Commerce

Secretary Hoover, famous worldwide as administrator of European relief after World War I; Secretary of State Charles Evans Hughes, renowned lawyer and future U.S. chief justice; and Treasury Secretary Andrew W. Mellon, mastermind of the economic boom of the 1920s. These men, along with the innovative agriculture secretary Henry C. Wallace, brought sound conservative principles to Harding's steward-ship. Harding also nominated former president William Howard Taft as chief justice of the United States, a choice that has stood up well in history.

It is certainly true that Harding demonstrated only marginal interest as these men did their jobs—and as their crooked colleagues pursued their devious endeavors. But some important initiatives emerged during his brief stewardship.

On the economic front, Harding signed the Fordney-McCumber Tariff of 1922, which imposed import duties on a host of agricultural and manufactured goods. The legislation was not particularly onerous, bringing rates to levels that were still below the levels in effect before Democrats had reduced them under Woodrow Wilson. Any negative economic impact was offset by big reductions in personal income tax rates—down to a top rate of 57 percent in 1921 and then to 46 percent the next year. Also, the threshold at which the top bracket kicked in went up substantially. Gross Domestic Product shot up to $85 billion in 1923 from $69.1 billion in 1921.

The Harding years also saw a sharp curtailment in immigration. Congress passed legislation establishing quotas to match incoming residents to the same proportion of ethnic groups that had prevailed in the 1910 census. The Harding presidency reflected a growing cultural divide, as more and more Americans, including immigrants, filled the increasingly cosmopolitan cities. This stirred rural and small-town citizens, clinging to the simpler ways of the past, to push back against what they saw as an assault on their cultural values. Manifesta-tions of this unrest included Prohibition and a resurgence of Ku Klux

Klan activity, not just in the South but also in many midwestern and Rocky Mountain states.

It's impossible to know what kind of presidential record Harding would have accumulated had he survived his first term. He died in August 1923 of an apparent stroke in San Francisco during an extended western sojourn—a trip that reflected his desultory engagement as president. Then the revelations of Teapot Dome, which riveted the nation for years as various prosecutions slowly unfolded, brought him low in the eyes of his countrymen. "After his death," writes Harding biographer Francis Russell, "his reputation plummeted so quickly that only with the greatest reluctance could a Republican successor be persuaded to dedicate his tomb."

Russell sees something of a double standard here. Harding never leveraged his governmental position to enhance his Ohio newspaper enterprise—unlike Lyndon Johnson, who got rich using political benefactors to get into the television business (under his wife's name). Russell catalogues the scandals of the Truman White House, perpetrated by presidential cronies who had gravitated to Truman during his days as a shill for Kansas City's Pendergast political machine. He also notes the scandal involving Eisenhower's chief of staff, Sherman Adams. Such episodes, he says, are mere historical footnotes, while the Harding episodes have been judged as defining. But the scandals of the Grant administration, not mentioned by Russell, greatly influenced Grant's historical standing in much the same way Teapot Dome influenced Harding's, and certainly Teapot Dome represented a greater blight on the government than most other scandals touching White House occupants. (Russell wrote before Watergate and the Bill Clinton impeachment.)

In any event, Harding's position in history probably won't change anytime soon, notwithstanding his high regard with his constituency during his presidency.

Calvin Coolidge (once): Any dispassionate sketch of his presidency would suggest that he simply doesn't belong in this lowly bracket. By the standard of voter assessment, he merits respect for retaining the presidency after his nineteen-month incumbency and then retaining it for his party four years later. He presided over peace, prosperity, and domestic tranquility for nearly six years, and he effectively cleaned up the scandal bequeathed to him by Harding. Thus, Ronald Reagan seems justified in placing Silent Cal's portrait in the White House Cabinet Room, and Coolidge detractors might inquire whether their ratings stem from the fact that he was among the twentieth century's most concise exponents of limited government.

Herbert Hoover (once): The Hoover story is a political tragedy. Brilliant, industrious, compassionate, flexible of mind, pleasant of demeanor, he possessed all the makings of a successful president. Yet he was a failure. Certainly, the vilification he received from the American people during his tenure was unfair. But American presidential politics wasn't designed to be fair; it was designed to address the two ancient and fundamental problems of governance—the problem of legitimacy and the problem of succession. In the American system, both reside with the people, and in times of turmoil the people can become harsh and unfeeling in their sentiments. That was Hoover's fate.

It isn't enough to say he failed to subdue an economic crisis that descended upon him. Hoover helped bring on the crisis by signing the Smoot-Hawley Tariff bill on June 16, 1930. A month earlier 1,028 American economists had petitioned Hoover to veto the bill as economic poison. "Countries cannot permanently buy from us unless they are permitted to sell to us," the economists warned, "and the more we restrict the importation of goods from them by means of even higher tariffs, the more we reduce the possibility of our exporting to them." The economists added that America, as a creditor nation, would suffer if its foreign debtors couldn't pay interest to Americans who had invested in foreign enterprises. The tariffs would drive a wedge through those international transactions.

It was classical economics, and Hoover ignored it in the face of rising political pressures, largely from the farm sector. When the economy tumbled, as the economists had predicted, Hoover executed the second element of his double-whammy on economic policy. He raised personal income-tax rates—to a top rate of 63 percent on $1 million from 25 percent at $100,000; and a bottom rate of 4 percent at $4,000 instead of 1 percent at that income. Numerous new business taxes were added. Hoover signed that bill on June 6, 1932, but it was retroactive to the first of the year. Jude Wanniski, the supply-side advocate of the 1970s and 1980s, wrote that this retroactivity was "Hoover's last gift to Roosevelt." Wanniski argued that the widespread bank failures of early 1933 emerged in part because many Americans had to withdraw money from their savings accounts to pay unexpectedly high tax bills.

The historians have gifted Hoover with remarkably high ratings given the economic wreckage of his administration. He ranked twentieth in Schlesinger Sr.'s initial 1948 poll, nineteenth in his subsequent 1962 survey, twenty-second in Porter, and twenty-first in both the *Chicago Tribune* survey and in Murray-Blessing. Finally, in Schlesinger Jr.'s 1996 survey, he drops to thirty-fifth (slipping into the bottom five) and comes in at thirty-first in the *WSJ* poll of 2005.

But the electorate manifested a different view during the man's presidency. In the 1930 midterm elections, opposition Democrats took control of the House of Representatives with a gain of fifty-three seats. They came within a single seat of capturing the Senate. Two years later, with Roosevelt on the ballot, the Democrats gained another ninety-seven House seats and twelve in the Senate. Hoover himself, on the ballot for reelection, didn't crack 40 percent of the popular vote.

Perhaps the academics went easy on Hoover in those early polls because he presented a strong image of brilliance and goodwill, as compared to, say, the wan personalities and sluggish intellects of Zachary Taylor and Millard Fillmore. But those presidencies never brought to the country the kind of woe that ensued during Hoover's tenure. And thus perhaps in his case the contemporaneous judgment of the electorate, as brutal and insensitive as it was, captures the man's performance more accurately than those academic surveys.

Richard Nixon (four times out of five): Nixon is exempted from the circle of ignominy only by the *Wall Street Journal* poll of 2005, which places him at thirty-second. In the 1982 *Chicago Tribune* survey he is second from the bottom; in two other polls, third from the bottom. But Nixon, as I will seek to demonstrate, was an effective president in many realms—and in some a brilliant one. The question remains whether his manifest achievements should be swept from consideration as history focuses on Watergate and the character flaws exposed in the man through the agonizing revelations of that scandal. The man's mixed legacy will be explored in subsequent chapters.

It seems more difficult to make a comfortable determination on who should be at the bottom of the presidential heap than to determine who were the greatest of the great. Perhaps this accounts for the wider disparity, at the bottom, between the judgment of history and the contemporaneous assessment of the voters. Buchanan and Pierce are easy enough. Andrew Johnson probably belongs there—in part, it can be argued, because he was on the wrong side of the issues but also because he lost control of the country he was supposed to lead. Hoover would seem to be an easier case than history has acknowledged. But Harding and Grant seem tougher cases, and Nixon poses ongoing puzzlement.

Taylor and Fillmore, while clearly not up to the job, escaped the office without any serious damage to the country. The same can't be said, for example, about Woodrow Wilson, whose flaws of personality contributed mightily to a second-term stewardship that was repudiated by the voters about as soundly as any repudiation in presidential history. Perhaps the historians have him wrong, and he should be down there among the lowly. We will discuss this complex president in subsequent chapters. And perhaps history has been too kind to one-term wonders Quincy Adams, Benjamin Harrison, Van Buren, and Carter.

As for the voters, they don't rank presidents when rendering their judgments every four years. They simply turn thumbs up or thumbs down on the incumbent or incumbent party based on what they feel the country needed and what it got. Then they move on, looking to the future, comfortable in the knowledge that they will have ongoing opportunities to weed out the failures along the way.

Part III

THE TEST OF GREATNESS

7

WAR AND PEACE

At seven o'clock on the evening of February 20, 1848, President
Polk convened a Cabinet meeting to discuss whether he should
send to the Senate, for ratification, a treaty negotiated in Mexico for
the termination of the Mexican War. Polk saw two problems with the
treaty: First, while it conformed to his previous demands for a substantial land transfer to the United States, Mexican intransigence in
the meantime had stirred Polk to want even more land as recompense
for the intervening loss of American money and blood; and, second,
the treaty had been negotiated by Nicholas Trist, who had been sent
to Mexico to negotiate it but had been fired by Polk later because of
his seemingly soft bargaining style. Since Trist had no authority to
negotiate the treaty, Polk questioned its validity.

A majority of the Cabinet recommended accepting the treaty, but
two argued for continuing the war and holding out for better terms.

Polk dismissed the Cabinet, pondered the matter overnight, then reconvened his advisers the next day. He said he would seek Senate ratification.

He could justify demanding more territory, he explained. But that would mean resumed hostilities in a war that was becoming ominously unpopular at home, and the political consequences could be dire. Opposition Whigs in Congress likely would cut off men and money for the war. Polk's occupation army would be "constantly wasting and diminishing in numbers." He might be forced to withdraw U.S. troops simply for their own protection, and both New Mexico and California—two big parcels of land coveted by Polk—could be lost.

In short, concluded Polk, if he rejected his own terms, he didn't see any possibility "for my administration to be sustained."

Polk's stark analysis reflected the predicament that threatens every president who takes his country to war: When hostilities linger, extracting a higher price than the perceived benefits justify, the voters turn against the war—and turn on the president. No presidential decision is more politically dangerous than the war decision.

These dangers aren't readily discernible at the war's outset. Then the country nearly always rallies behind the president. But when the country's young men and women return home in body bags without an end in sight; when budget deficits swell ominously; when the social fabric begins to fray; and particularly when the cause seems lost—then the voters assess the war's costs anew. And, if the equation doesn't hold up, a wave of dissent ensues. If an election comes during such a time, the party in power inevitably suffers.

We begin our assessment of presidential greatness with the executive war-making power because it can breed presidential ignominy just as easily as presidential glory. History gives us numerous examples of both. Remember how close Lincoln's war came to undoing him before it helped transport him to his hallowed place in history. Truman and

Johnson *were* undone by wars, at least in part, while Franklin Roosevelt's expeditionary triumph cemented his elevated station in history. No doubt a major factor in the Republicans' loss of the White House in 2008 was the lingering and ill-defined military effort in Iraq.

Of the country's forty-four presidents, thirteen were serious war presidents—Madison, Polk, Lincoln, McKinley, Wilson, Franklin Roosevelt, Truman, Eisenhower, Lyndon Johnson, Nixon, George H. W. Bush, George W. Bush, and Obama. Of these, Truman, Eisenhower, Nixon, and Obama inherited wars, while the rest (plus Truman again) initiated them. In all instances (leaving aside Obama, whose tenure is too recent for a fair assessment), their handling of the conflicts played a key role in the voters' contemporaneous assessments as well as in history's judgments. For purposes of analysis, I shall place these presidents into three categories:

Clearly Successful: Into this category we can place Madison, Polk, Lincoln, McKinley, Franklin Roosevelt, and George H. W. Bush. All accomplished their stated war aims and avoided serious political difficulties at the next election (H. W. Bush lost his reelection bid, but there's no reason to believe his war policy contributed to his defeat).

Clear Wartime Failures: Wilson, Truman, Johnson, and George W. Bush—presidents whose stated war aims proved elusive, with a resulting significant loss in political standing.

War Presidents Through Inheritance: Truman (fits two categories), Eisenhower, Nixon, and Obama. These men took power during wars established by their predecessors.

Just as all war issues inevitably take on a high degree of intensity, my categorizations here are likely to stir debate. That's good. Matters of war and peace should be hotly contested—both politically and philosophically—because they are fundamental to the definition of the nation. A look at the military performance of the war presidents follows (leaving George W. Bush and Obama for consideration in the final chapter):

James Madison (success): By categorizing Madison's war as successful, I anticipate a lively debate among historians, many of whom have derided his wartime performance. Indeed, we have explored previously the disparity between history's judgment of Madison and the voter assessment in his time. The electorate was pleased with his performance. And, looking at the 1812 War in the context of all other U.S. wars, it can be argued that "Mr. Madison's War," as it was derisively labeled by Federalists, yielded some important strategic benefits for America. It helped pave the way for the country's westward expansion.

The war emanated from the confluence of three issues that generated a war fever: first, the incendiary "impressment" issue—Britain's practice of abducting American seamen from their ships upon the high seas; second, Britain's refusal to accept American neutrality in the ongoing European wars; and, third, a desire among many Americans to thwart British-inspired Indian agitations south of the Great Lakes. These issues generated powerful anger among large segments of the populace.

Responding to this war fever, fanned by a coterie of forceful young politicians led by Kentucky's Henry Clay, Madison asked for a declaration of war on June 1, 1812, and Congress complied. What's impressive is that Madison conducted his war with a clear-headed understanding of his country's military weakness. At the very beginning of hostilities, when Russia offered to mediate a settlement, Madison jumped at it. When Britain instead insisted on direct negotiations without interlocutors, Madison accepted that approach as a way of preventing his war from slipping out of control. Hence, efforts for a negotiated solution began almost immediately at the war's commencement. The American negotiators, including Quincy Adams and Henry Clay, had to deal with Britain's superior military power and its effort to draw out negotiations in hopes that military victories would enhance British leverage.

In the end, the Americans gave way on the minor issues (impressment, neutrality rights) while getting major concessions that thwarted Britain's strategic aim of curbing America's movement toward the West, a powerful national imperative in the country's consciousness at the time. He also met the first imperative of presidential war-making: Never go to the next election with a war that has been going on too long and seems out of control. Hence, I place Madison's war in the "successful" category, recognizing that it may be a close call.

James Polk (success): Although the eleventh president ultimately won his war, some of his actions pose war policy lessons. One relates to Polk's lack of forthrightness in maneuvering his country into war. True, Mexico had adopted a belligerent stance toward the United States after the annexation of Texas. And there was a lingering issue of reparations owed by Mexico to Americans who had been abused and looted by Mexicans over the years. France invaded Mexico to get reparations for its citizens, and Britain threatened the same to win appropriate payments. Mexico remained intransigent on American claims.

In the face of these tensions, Polk sent an army under General Zachary Taylor into disputed territory along the Rio Grande River (or Rio del Norte, as it was often called). Then, when elements of that army clashed with Mexican troops, resulting in eleven dead Americans, Polk sent an urgent message to Congress. "Mexico," he declared, "has . . . shed American blood upon the American soil. She has proclaimed that hostilities have commenced, and that the two nations are now at war." He asked Congress to confirm that state of war and authorize money and troops for the effort.

A large contingent of senators expressed a willingness to authorize troops to fortify Taylor, who remained highly vulnerable to a larger Mexican force. But many disputed Polk's rendition of events leading to hostilities. South Carolina's John C. Calhoun, leading the opposition, said the facts did not support Polk's narrative and there was "no conflict but that between the two armies on the Rio del Norte; and yet you affirm . . . that mere local conflict, not authorized by either government, is a state of war! That every American is an enemy of every Mexican!" He called the doctrine "monstrous."

Hence Polk's war was born in controversy, and that haunted his war effort when it proved far more long and costly than anticipated. His adversaries delighted in dredging up old arguments about the war's origins in order to force Polk on the defensive.

Another Polk lesson is that no war unfolds as expected. Polk had not anticipated a protracted war, but he got one. He hadn't foreseen a need to conquer Mexican territory he didn't want, but Mexico's refusal to negotiate a settlement forced him to do so. He couldn't foresee that the command structure under General Winfield Scott would break down, with various officers brought under courts-martial and Scott himself charged with dereliction of duty. But all that happened. And he certainly didn't anticipate that a political movement would emerge advocating that the United States annex all of Mexico or perhaps dominate it in conquest as ancient Rome did its provinces. But such a movement surfaced.

In the end, Polk managed to bring his war to a successful conclusion and get a settlement sufficiently beneficial to the United States to justify the effort and its costs, at least in the eyes of the American people at the time. The conflict claimed 13,780 American lives and cost some hundred million in U.S. dollars. But it brought into the United States some 600,000 square miles of continental expanse and gave the new transcontinental nation a vast Pacific coastline with some of the best harbors in the world. Few presidents would enhance their country's geopolitical standing on such a scale.

Abraham Lincoln (success): Lincoln's great curse as commander in chief was his lack of aggressive military leaders needed for the struggle. He rushed headlong into an intense personal course of study designed to acquire the military expertise needed for his role as commander in chief. He pored over the writings of Napoleon's strategist Henri Jomini and West Point's Dennis Hart Mahan. He wrote incessantly to his generals, asking for information and suggesting particular maneuvers. He appeared at the front on eleven occasions. He promoted and then fired various generals in seeking the leaders he needed. He finally found them in Ulysses Grant and William T. Sherman—the two men who engineered, barely in time, the field victories needed by the president to prevail in the 1864 election.

Lincoln paid scant attention to domestic matters. He happily accepted the Republican domestic agenda, as outlined in the 1860 convention platform, and left it to Congress to enact it—including homestead legislation, the Pacific Railway Act, land-grant college legislation, an income tax, and a National Banking System. Neither did he involve his Cabinet much in war planning or decision-making. He let his Cabinet officers run their various departments without much interference, but generally his Cabinet sessions were infrequent and light on serious discussion about the war. That was his domain.

By the time the voters had an opportunity to pass judgment on his presidency, the war had been brought under control, and victory was at hand. Lincoln won reelection with 55 percent of the popular vote.

William McKinley (success): The last president of the nineteenth century doesn't enjoy the respect from history that he probably deserves. Schlesinger Sr.'s first poll of historians in 1948 ranks him eighteenth, and he has never risen much above that, with one exception—eleventh in Steve Neal's 1982 *Chicago Tribune* poll. He was fifteenth in Schlesinger Sr.'s 1962 poll, sixteenth in Porter, eighteenth in Murray-Blessing, sixteenth in Schlesinger Jr.'s 1996 poll, and fourteenth in the *WSJ* 2005 survey. Commentator Fred Barnes, profiling McKinley in a book on the presidency, writes, "He was America's most underrated president."

Lacking in flamboyance or intellectual flair, he nevertheless created the modern presidency after three decades of congressional dom-

WILLIAM McKINLEY

Unimaginative, stolid, and virtuous, McKinley was not one to produce a powerful vision of his country's future. But, reacting to events that converged upon him, he led America into a new age of imperialism through his "splendid little war" with Spain. Neither the country nor the world would ever be the same.

inance. A large factor, as we have seen, was the Spanish-American War. As a Civil War veteran who had seen his share of death, McKinley abhorred war. But ultimately he concluded the country's growing tensions with Spain were untenable.

There is a popular myth that the United States, spurred by the "yellow press" of William Randolph Hearst and others, swooped down on a pretext and grabbed Spanish possessions. This is untrue. McKinley, outraged by the yellow journalism of his day, banned it from the White House. And there were serious issues involved. In late 1897, McKinley's consul in Cuba, Fitzhugh Lee, reported that radical extremists were positioned to take over the anticolonial insurrection there. Americans could be killed and their property destroyed. McKinley realized also that Spain, declining fast as a global power, could never bring stability to Cuba. He sent the battleship *Maine* to Havana to ensure protection for U.S. citizens and their property. When it blew up and sank in the harbor (most likely from an internal explosion), the resulting anti-Spain passions in America rendered war inevitable. But there was another consideration in McKinley's mind that he didn't reveal publicly—his desire to acquire the Philippines from Spain as a forward base for America's growing Pacific fleet.

It was a short and glorious war for the Americans—"a splendid little war," as Secretary of State John Hay described it. Historian Walter LaFeber called it the "easiest and most profitable war in [U.S.] history." In May 1898, Admiral Thomas Dewey destroyed Spain's Pacific fleet at Manila Bay without any loss of American life. A similar naval action at Santiago de Cuba destroyed Spain's Atlantic fleet, while ground forces on the island vanquished the Spanish resistance. It was all over within three months, with only 385 combat deaths. Subsequent peace talks brought the Philippines, Guam, and Puerto Rico under American dominion, while Cuba came under U.S. control and Hawaii was soon added to the U.S. domain. Spain's global empire ended; America's was beginning.

This was a substantial presidential achievement, and it thrilled most of the electorate (though serious anti-imperial sentiments emerged). Thus, it would seem that the historians have slighted McKinley—perhaps (as in the case of Polk) because his war was driven by nationalist sentiments rather than humanitarian ones. Schlesinger Jr.'s 1996 survey, to take one example, places John Adams, Kennedy, Cleveland, Lyndon Johnson, and Monroe ahead of McKinley. Perhaps McKinley's constituency was closer to the mark.

Woodrow Wilson (failure): Wilson's war lesson is that military adventures abroad can devastate the home front. Wilson was an idealist whose reformist zeal came to the fore most powerfully in the realm of foreign policy. He often ignored geopolitical realities if they didn't conform to his moralistic worldview and dreamy perception of

WOODROW WILSON

A man of sanctimony, Wilson personifies the "split-decision presidents"—those whose successful first terms led to reelection and whose failed second terms ensured they would not be succeeded by a president of their own party. Few presidents were more discredited in voter eyes at the end of their tenure.

America as "the light which will shine unto all generations and guide the feet of mankind to the goal of justice and liberty and peace." This was the light that got America into World War I.

But he carefully avoided American involvement for more than two years following the onset of the European conflagration in August 1914. That was considered his greatest foreign policy triumph when he sought reelection in 1916. His electoral slogan—"He kept us out of war"—became the centerpiece of his campaign, and the Democratic convention that year was a full-throated celebration of Wilson's success in avoiding war.

This was no mean feat, given neutrality issues forced upon America by both Britain and Germany. Britain imposed a blockade to thwart all trade to the Central Powers and "starve the whole population [of

Germany]—men, women, and children, old and young, wounded
and sound—into submission," as Britain's pugnacious First Sea Lord,
Winston Churchill, brazenly declared. Meanwhile, the Germans in
February 1915 initiated submarine attacks designed to stop munitions
shipments to Britain and counteract the blockade.

Both of these policies severely strained America's effort to remain
neutral, and Wilson assiduously made his way through that thicket.
But ultimately he favored Britain. He not only observed the British
blockade but also allowed armed British merchant ships entry to U.S.
ports, which in turn fostered a flow of U.S. munitions to the Allied
Powers. At the same time, Wilson declared that Germany would
be held to a "strict accountability" for any American loss of life or
property from Germany's submarine attacks. This policy applied, said
Wilson, even if affected Americans were traveling or working on
British or French ships. He declined to curtail what he considered
Americans' "right" to travel on vessels tied to France or Britain.

Some Wilson advisers favored this approach because they wanted
America in the war against Germany. But Wilson was warned by
others, including Secretary of State William Jennings Bryan (who
resigned over the issue), that he faced a stark choice: Either adopt a
more evenhanded approach or accept the inevitability of war.

Wilson managed to get past the 1916 election, though just barely,
before this stark choice converged upon him. He collected 49.2 percent of the popular vote to 46.1 percent for his Republican opponent,
Charles Evans Hughes, and 3.2 percent for socialist Allan L. Benson.
"He kept us out of war" proved to be his political lifeline.

Within weeks of the election, however, the German government,
desperate to curb the British war-making machine before succumbing
to the British blockade, adopted a policy of unrestricted submarine
warfare against ships carrying goods to Britain or France. German
officials believed they could bring their enemies to their knees before
America could enter the war with enough force to tip the scales. It

was one of the great geopolitical miscalculations of the twentieth century.

Wilson promptly asked for a congressional declaration of war—and got it. Soon the scales *were* tipped against Germany, which consequently experienced not only defeat but a national humiliation. Before that could happen, however, Wilson's decision to lead America to war set in motion a series of domestic events that would destroy his political standing and ensure a Democratic presidential defeat at the next election.

The war transformed American society almost overnight as the reach of the national government expanded with a powerful force. The telegraph, telephone, and railroad industries were nationalized, along with the distribution of coal. The government undertook the direct construction of merchant ships and bought and sold farm goods. A military draft was instituted. Individual and corporate income tax rates surged. The government unfurled a massive propaganda campaign, and dissent was suppressed by the notorious Attorney General A. Mitchell Palmer, who vigorously prosecuted opposition voices under severe new laws.

The national economy, never strong under Wilson's leadership, flipped out of control. Inflation surged into double-digit territory. Real per capita Gross Domestic Product increased robustly with war production in 1918, but then turned downward dramatically, with no growth in 1919, a 2.24 percent decline in 1920, and a further 4.16 percent decline in Wilson's final budget year of 1921. A large migration of rural southern blacks into northern cities generated social upheavals that led to widespread urban riots. East St. Louis erupted in 1917 into a spree of violence that left 48 dead. The next year race riots in twenty-five cities killed more than 100. Labor upheaval also ensued, with 4 million workers on strike in 1919, including 300,000 coal miners. All this generated significant economic dislocations during Wilson's second term.

Wilson's political standing eroded further with a growing aware-ness among Americans that the president's war policies didn't stem from a sense of American national interest but rather from his vague commitment to all humanity. After America's entry into the war, the president frequently bragged that his country sought no national benefit from the turmoil of war. "What we demand . . . ," he said in a speech to Congress, "is nothing peculiar to ourselves. It is that the world be made fit and safe to live in. . . . All the peoples of the world are in effect partners in this interest." Wilson assured Germany, fol-lowing America's entry into the war, that any peace settlement would be based on his evenhanded "Fourteen Points." A just peace, he had declared, would be "a peace without victory." Then, after the belea-guered Germans accepted an armistice based on Wilson's assurances, the president proved impotent in his efforts to redeem those promises at the Versailles peace negotiations.

In fairness, he was up against some powerful nationalist forces, personified by France's relentless Georges Clemenceau and Britain's cunning David Lloyd George. At times Wilson managed deftly to maneuver against these men. But his effectiveness likely was under-mined by what may have been a minor stroke during the delibera-tions. And ultimately his dreamy notions of diplomacy undercut his influence.

"The single name most inextricably bound up with the Treaty of Versailles, and consequently with its failure," wrote historian Richard M. Watt in his book *The Kings Depart*, "was that of Thomas Wood-row Wilson." He added: "The [Wilson] dream of a world of happy peoples, each assembled into an entity of its own nationality and living in its own historical geographic location, were now seen [at the end of the Versailles negotiations] to have been imbecilic wishes which could not and would not come true."

Watt's judgment may be a bit harsh. But his critique accurately identifies the problems that often emerge with the kinds of dreamy sentiments embraced by Wilson: Inevitably they encounter the real world, where geography, power differentials, cultural passions, and national interest drive events. At Versailles, notwithstanding Wilson's naïve efforts (and perhaps in some measure because of them), many scholars and commentators have argued, Germany was crushed under the Allied boot with such harshness that a subsequent war became inevitable. *The Economist* has suggested that Versailles' harsh terms served to "ensure a second war." Not everyone agrees. In her probing history, *Paris 1919: Six Months That Changed the World,* Margaret MacMillan argues that "Hitler did not wage war because of the Treaty of Versailles." She adds that even if Germany had retained its old borders, maintained its military, and joined with Austria, Hitler "still would have wanted more"—including the destruction of Poland, control of Czechoslovakia, and the Soviet conquest. Of course, this begs the question whether the politics of Germany in such an environment would have spawned Hitler's rise in the first place.

In any event, it seems clear that Versailles produced a world far different from the one Wilson envisioned when he led his country to war. In that aftermath, when he sought to get Senate ratification for America's membership in his cherished League of Nations, the weakened president was dealt a fearsome political blow at the hands of Senate Foreign Relations Committee Chairman Henry Cabot Lodge. The president's self-righteous refusal to compromise contributed to that defeat.

The result was that Wilson took on the appearance of a hapless leader no more capable of maintaining prosperity and domestic tranquility at home than he was of realizing his gauzy humanitarian vision abroad. Contributing to this image was the truly serious stroke that hit him at the height of the political battle over the League of Nations, which left the president debilitated and sent him into White House seclusion. So discredited was Wilson's party by November 1920 that the American people expelled Democrats from power with a rare decisiveness. Harding of Ohio, hardly a distinguished person-age, received fully 60.3 percent of the popular vote against James M. Cox of Ohio. In addition, Republicans picked up sixty-three House seats and eleven in the Senate. The country has seen few political repudiations of such magnitude.

Franklin Roosevelt (success): In November 1938, as German resurgence became increasingly ominous in Europe, Roosevelt convened his top military officials to address a problem—the huge gap between America's existing air strength and its needs should war come. Roosevelt wanted a plan for producing 10,000 planes in two years, with a productive capacity to churn out as many planes annually thereafter. The plan raised concerns among the military officers, who felt the president hadn't sufficiently accounted for the support elements needed to ensure the planes' effectiveness. But they all muttered their approval. Then Roosevelt, after reiterating his rationale, turned to the new head of the army's War Plans Division, Brigadier General George C. Marshall.

"Don't you think so, George?" he asked.

"Mr. President," replied Marshall, "I don't agree with that at all."

Many participants immediately concluded the general had just upended his own career. But within a year, with war clouds darkening, Roosevelt selected Marshall as army chief of staff—the man who would lead the looming military effort.

The incident reflects an intriguing dichotomy in Roosevelt's managerial approach. By the time of Marshall's appointment FDR had been in office six years, and his presidential style was well known. He was crafty and inscrutable with subordinates, though voluble in meetings. He slyly and mischievously set up rivalries among his people. He never let anyone know the depth of his thinking until the moment of decision. He managed by manipulation.

But that was not his approach with military leaders in war, where the blood of millions of young Americans was at stake. Now he would manage in an atmosphere of greater forthrightness all around. This doesn't mean he stopped fostering back-channel flows of information or that he observed assiduously the niceties of organizational structure. But the war president was more straightforward and direct than the domestic president, less inclined to leave ambiguities in his wake. "His military instructions, issued at numerous and critical points," writes military historian Eric Larrabee, "were in the main concise and final, contrary to his practice when the ebb and flow of politics was the determining factor."

Roosevelt's excellent military team, selected before the war, remained largely intact for the duration. He pulled to himself all broad strategic planning and felt no inhibitions in countermanding military decisions. Kent Roberts Greenfield, onetime chief historian of the U.S. Army, identified twenty-two Roosevelt decisions rendered "against the advice, or over the protests, of his military advisers." Greenfield also listed thirteen major military decisions instigated by Roosevelt on his own—including the firing of General Joseph Stilwell (a Marshall favorite) as commander of the China-Burma-India theater and the selection of North Africa as the site of the war's first Allied offensive. Roosevelt delegated day-to-day matters to his commanders and confined his management to ensuring their actions were consistent with his broad strategic vision. At times Marshall didn't see the president for up to a month or six weeks at a time (though he could always get access when needed through presidential confidant Harry Hopkins).

The Japanese attack at Pearl Harbor and Hitler's subsequent declaration of war against the United States naturally stirred Americans to a high pitch of war fervor. Roosevelt skillfully leveraged this sentiment by speaking to the American people candidly about the magnitude of the coming challenge and its geopolitical stakes. It was going to be a "long war," he declared, and a "hard war." He added: "Every man, woman, and child is a partner in the most tremendous undertaking of our American history." The enemy was aligned, he proclaimed, against "the whole human race." To underscore the coming transformation, he announced that "Dr. Win the War" was replacing "Dr. New Deal."

Such declarations inspired the country and fortified it for the president's planned "total war." It was America and Britain that organized most effectively for this total war, while the more autocratic German and Japanese nations proved incapable of doing so. Hence, Roosevelt unleashed what was probably the greatest surge of military construction in history. By war's end America had turned out nearly 6,000 merchant ships, 1,556 naval vessels, 299,293 aircraft, 634,569 Jeeps, 88,410 tanks, 6.5 million rifles, and 40 billion bullets. Historian David M. Kennedy called it a "stupendous Niagara of numbers," and it proved decisive.

The president's war record was not entirely unalloyed. It could be argued that his policy of forcing an unconditional surrender on Germany allowed the Soviets to conquer nearly all of Eastern Europe and threaten the West with a mortal danger; a clearer understanding of the Soviet challenge might have averted the worst of the Cold War. Even accepting that policy and the resultant Soviet expansion westward, some have argued that Roosevelt naïvely underestimated the aggressiveness of Soviet intentions, apparently thinking he could "handle" Soviet leader Joseph Stalin through cajolery and his force of personality. And of course history has condemned Roosevelt's internment of Japanese Americans on grounds of domestic security.

Nevertheless, by the election of November 1944 it appeared that the Allies were well on their way to victory in both the Pacific and European theaters, and the economy was booming from massive munitions production. The electorate, concluding the president had met the profound challenge of the time, gave him his fourth presidential victory, with 53.4 percent of the popular vote to 45.9 percent for New York Governor Thomas E. Dewey.

Harry Truman (war president through inheritance, failure): It's pain-

ful to see the word "failure" next to the name of Harry Truman, consistently ranked by historians as Near Great. The disparity, of course,
reflects the disparity between his two presidential terms. His highly
successful first term included his actions to end decisively the war he
had inherited upon becoming president in April 1945. He effectively
matched wits with Stalin at the Potsdam conference in the summer
of 1945, playing the hand dealt him by the Allies' military positioning at war's end. Though he bowed to Stalin's stubbornness on some
issues (notably, recognition of some Eastern European countries that
eventually slipped under Soviet domination), he left Potsdam with
the wartime alliance intact, with German reparations set at a reasonable magnitude, with German rehabilitation in prospect, and with the
restoration of Italy (a key goal) in sight. Later, Truman's decision to
employ atomic weapons against Japan, however agonizing it was in
the president's private moments, concluded the Pacific war abruptly.

But Truman's handling of the Korean War was a stumble, beginning even before the war started. Truman and his top advisers,
concluding the West's communist enemies sought expansion not by
war but through campaigns of infiltration and subversion, cut military
spending to $13 billion for fiscal 1951 from some $14.4 billion the
previous year. They reasoned that the tools of war were unneeded in
a competition of political intrigue, and the United States could save
money by not building those weapons. Then in early 1950, Truman's
secretary of state, Dean Acheson, suggested the Korean Peninsula lay
outside the U.S. "defense perimeter."

Those policy prescriptions didn't hold up in June 1950 when
the communist North, the Democratic People's Republic of Korea,
invaded the Western-aligned regime of Syngman Rhee, known as
the Republic of Korea. Truman abruptly changed course. He fired
Defense Secretary Louis Johnson, architect of the military build-
down, and placed Korea immediately inside the country's defense
perimeter. Truman committed U.S. troops to a combined United

Nations military effort and got General Douglas MacArthur named as commander of U.N. forces.

But the arrival of American troops—two army infantry divisions, the First Cavalry, and a regimental combat team—only slowed the enemy advance. Over the next six weeks the invading army moved south, pinning the defending forces into the Pusan Perimeter, a 5,000-square-mile rectangle in the southeast corner of the peninsula. Their backs to the sea, U.N. forces managed to halt the communist advance, but their position was precarious. It looked as if Pusan might become an American Dunkirk.

Then, in a brilliant amphibious landing at Inchon in September 1950, MacArthur split the North Korean forces in half, cutting off the southern troops from their supply lines and forcing the northern armies into a headlong retreat northward.

But the tide turned once again as China, now under communist rule, threw 300,000 battle-tested troops against the American and South Korean armies that were beginning what they thought would be the war's mop-up operation. The Allied forces pulled back, eventually establishing a defensive perimeter about five miles south of the 38th parallel, the old dividing line between the two Koreas. It was a devastating military defeat and an even more devastating psychological blow for the nation. The result was a protracted, painful stalemate. Many in official Washington and around the country feared the Soviet-Chinese combine would force the West into either a strategic retreat or a world war.

For the next two years officials in Washington struggled with a war they could not win, could not walk away from, and could not afford to lose. In Tokyo, General MacArthur chafed at the restrictions placed on his forces and began a political offensive against Washington's "limited war" concepts, which prevented him from carrying the conflict into the enemy's "privileged sanctuary" north of the Yalu River. After the general's activity veered into insubordination, the controversy exploded in April 1951 when Truman fired MacArthur. It was a necessary decision, and a courageous one given the general's powerful popularity among many Americans, but it unleashed a tidal wave of political opposition that undermined the president's political standing.

That was the situation when Truman's Democratic Party next faced the voters in November 1952 and Truman's approval ratings warned against any reelection campaign. The party itself, under nominee Adlai Stevenson, relinquished the presidency after a twenty-year incumbency that had, until then, generated approval and appreciation from the American people. There is no doubt that the Korean stalemate contributed to the political reversal.

Dwight D. Eisenhower (war president through inheritance): Contemplating that stalemate during the 1952 election campaign, Eisenhower ran on the slogan "I shall go to Korea." Upon getting elected, he personally traveled there to negotiate an end to the war. In the process he slyly left an impression that failure in the talks likely would induce him to deploy tactical nuclear weapons. In getting a settlement, Eisenhower renounced all-out victory and accepted a communist North Korea—results that agitated conservatives within his party and some hawkish commentators. Columnists Joseph and Stewart Alsop, staunch Cold Warriors, derisively labeled the result a "false peace."

But behind this outcome was a much larger strategic perception that deserves attention because it was to bedevil subsequent presidents. By the time of Truman's 1948 election victory, the West's tense struggle with Soviet Russia had passed into a new global challenge. The first phase, the struggle for Europe, was marked by Truman's signature successes in checking Soviet advances in Greece and Turkey, the salutary impact of the Marshall Plan, the Soviet failure in Berlin, the decline in communist control of European trade unions. All had contributed to a "hair's breadth" victory for the West, which earned for Truman his elevated standing in history.

Eisenhower took power in the midst of the new Cold War phase, marked by two East Bloc salients. First, the Soviets, frustrated in Europe, now sought to undermine the West at its weak and vulnerable colonial flanks, initially in the Far East but eventually elsewhere. Their aim was to attack the West by unraveling its positions in various troublesome and dangerous regions. By Eisenhower's time China had gone communist and joined the Soviet Union in an ominous anti-Western alliance. America remained pinned down in Korea. Other tests were anticipated in places such as Vietnam, Laos, Egypt, Iran, Cuba, and Central America. Second, the Soviets would seek to consolidate their positions throughout their own empire—concentrating on armaments and strengthening their hold on the satellites—as a means of girding themselves for the protracted conflict.

America had embraced the challenge of countering communist expansion in these far-flung trouble spots, but Eisenhower saw the danger in manning the barricades of this vast global defense perimeter. The Soviets could sap American strength by causing flare-ups at places and times of their choosing, thus keeping Western interests off-balance and on the defensive. Besides, it wasn't clear Americans would accept overseas combat missions when the opposition was operating merely in stealthy insurgencies rather than direct military action. As Secretary of State John Foster Dulles told Joseph Alsop early in the Eisenhower years, "We can't get Americans to fight for these areas, if there is no direct aggression—just penetration and infiltration."

Eisenhower viewed this vast perimeter defense as a fool's game, as reflected in the Korean quagmire and the turmoil it caused in domestic politics. So he decisively cut the country's losses in Korea and worked intently to avoid other such geopolitical traps. That particularly meant staying out of Vietnam even after the defeated French were forced into a negotiated settlement at Geneva that divided the country into two parts, a communist North and a Western-allied South. Eisenhower did not want to get bogged down in an Asian land war, and his policy of "massive retaliation"—using the threat of nuclear retaliation to keep communist regimes in check—was designed in part to avoid such quagmires. He did avoid them while also thwarting the spread of communism, and it isn't surprising that later historians would mark his administration as a foreign policy success. But the Cold War doctrine of maintaining a vast global defense perimeter against communist aggression remained intact. Neither Eisenhower nor anyone else could come up with a viable alternative.

Lyndon Johnson (failure): Johnson inherited that defense perimeter strategy and followed it straight to Vietnam. His Oval Office taping system captured the agony that descended upon him as he grappled with the Vietnam conundrum. "The more I stayed awake last night thinking about this thing," Johnson told McGeorge Bundy, his national security adviser, in May 1964, "the more . . . it looks like to me we're gettin' into another Korea. . . . I don't think it's worth fightin' for and I don't think we can get out. And it's just the biggest damn mess."

The problem was that the country's Cold War strategy implied a commitment to defend the global perimeter, and Vietnam clearly was on that perimeter. To abandon Vietnam could undermine the country's overall Cold War effort—which, as Johnson perceived, was politically untenable. Indeed, the imperative of defending the vast Cold War perimeter had been the country's strategy throughout John Kennedy's administration, fully embraced by many Kennedy advisers retained by Johnson, most notably Defense Secretary Robert McNamara, Secretary of State Dean Rusk, and National Security Adviser Bundy. These men had contributed significantly to the Vietnam situation inherited by Johnson, and it was fraught with peril.

Kennedy had bolstered U.S. arms shipments to South Vietnam and had increased the number of U.S. military advisers to 16,700 from 685. He locked his country into the fate of South Vietnam with his complicity in a coup against its leader, Ngo Dinh Diem, which led to Diem's death in the fall of 1963, just three weeks before Kennedy's

own death. Some have argued that Kennedy, unlike Johnson, would
have avoided the Vietnam trap, as reflected in the fact that before
his assassination he had ordered the recall of some thousand advisers.
But it isn't clear what political or diplomatic motives lay behind that
decision, and in any event it was rendered before the Diem killing
transformed the Vietnam situation into a predicament from which
America couldn't easily extricate itself.

Johnson instantly perceived the fateful implications of this "damn
mess," as he called it. His concern is reflected in a bizarre request he
made of his old friend and mentor, Democratic Senator Richard Russell of Georgia. In early 1964, Johnson asked Russell to make a bold
Senate speech condemning the Vietnam commitment and urging
withdrawal. The president hoped that would provide sufficient cover
for an exit. But Russell, who saw the coming quagmire as clearly as
Johnson, preferred to keep his concerns private.

So Johnson forged ahead. Many historians have suggested that
Vietnam was an unwinnable war, that the problem was not in the
execution but in the concept that a superpower such as the United
States—even given all of its military might—could gain sway over
events in that far-off land. Perhaps. But Johnson's greatest mistake
was accepting the military strategy developed by Defense Secretary
Robert McNamara and his Vietnam commander, General William
Westmoreland. They embraced a war of attrition, a resolve to kill so
many Vietnamese communists that the sponsoring regime in North
Vietnam would "cry uncle" and negotiate a settlement. The problem
was that this "body count" strategy could never overcome North
Vietnam's ability to throw manpower and matériel at the conflict. The
strategy was doomed from the start.

The illusions undergirding the strategy hit the American consciousness with a shattering force with the communist Tet offensive
of January 1968, which unleashed 70,000 troops on American command posts and other strategic targets. The American counteroffensive

proved devastating, killing some 37,000 communists to just 2,500 Americans killed. But the display of communist capability after four years of war destroyed the country's appetite for a conflict that now looked hopeless. Within two months Johnson, the lion of American politics, announced his retirement from the game.

Richard Nixon (war president through inheritance): Nixon came to power with Vietnam lingering as a cancer upon the body politic. Viewing military victory as impossible and defeat as unthinkable, he initiated a retreat—a slow, deliberate military withdrawal in the face of enemy fire. The inherent dangers of this Great Retreat—the greatest military withdrawal in American history—were accentuated by the nature of the Vietnam deployment and the domestic antiwar fervor. In Vietnam the ratio of support troops to combat troops was two to one, and Nixon concluded he must bring home the combat troops first, to reduce casualties and calm the home front. In doing so he left the remaining support troops vulnerable to a communist attack such as the Tet offensive that had destroyed Johnson's Vietnam policy and his presidency.

Hence, Nixon placed himself in a predicament of epic proportions. His military challenge was to calibrate a risky maneuver in Vietnam, which could lead to disaster in the field and just as easily lead to political crisis at home. And his political challenge was to manage an unstable domestic scene, which could engulf him at home and upset his military calibrations in Vietnam.

Throughout his first term Nixon wended his way deftly through this political and military thicket—moving when possible to place the antiwar movement on the defensive, carefully marshaling support from the "Silent Majority," bringing home his troops in carefully calculated increments. The effort almost unraveled when he approved a military assault into Cambodia to destroy communist sanctuaries there and thwart a looming enemy offensive that could have devastated his diminishing military presence in the South. The incursion

was necessary militarily. American troops captured vast stores of matériel and held up some 12,000 North Vietnamese troops in the infiltration pipeline.

But at home it nearly destroyed his plan. Campuses across the nation exploded, the country's intellectual leaders attacked viciously, and his ability to keep the antiwar movement off guard disintegrated. Yet he pressed ahead, and slowly the plan began to work. The South Vietnamese army improved, the country grew more stable, and negotiations with the North appeared increasingly hopeful. Ultimately, Nixon negotiated a settlement with Hanoi that ended the hostilities, returned American prisoners of war, and gave South Vietnam a chance to survive on its own. A major foreign policy calamity was averted—at least for a time.

Nixon's Vietnam gamble represented impressive presidential leadership both as commander in chief and as steward of the nation. Ultimately, his effort to save South Vietnam proved unavailing, as the South fell to the communist North about a year after he left office. But a close reading of that era's history indicates Nixon's Watergate travail weakened his political standing and that of his successor, Gerald Ford, to such an extent that the antiwar forces in Congress were able to undermine presidential efforts to protect the peace settlement and enforce its terms. Beyond that, Nixon's long Vietnam retreat had broader implications for his foreign policy in the Far East, which became a highly significant legacy of that tragic figure, to be explored in the next chapter.

George H. W. Bush (success): When Iraq's Saddam Hussein conquered the tiny oil sheikdom of Kuwait in the summer of 1990, Bush sent an expeditionary force of 540,000 troops to the region. The troops arrived in increments designed to, first, deter an Iraqi invasion of Saudi Arabia; then to repel such an invasion if it occurred; and finally to expel the invader from Kuwait if Congress approved. In the meantime, Bush pushed for United Nations approval for such a military action, which came on November 29. Then the president asked for congressional approval to unleash his army and liberate Kuwait. In the January votes, only ten Democratic senators supported the president, while two Republicans abandoned him. In the House, three Republicans voted no, while Democrats split 179 to 86 against Bush. The primary Democratic argument was that the administration should give economic sanctions a chance to force Saddam out of Kuwait before using military action.

But within the Bush circle the focus centered on oil and geopolitical reality, as distilled by Director of Central Intelligence William Webster in a meeting with the president and his top advisers a few days after the invasion. With his Kuwaiti incursion, said Webster, Saddam had taken control of 20 percent of the world's oil reserves. If he moved just a few miles more into Saudi territory, he could grab another 20 percent. "He'll have easy access to the sea from Kuwaiti ports," Webster declared. "Jordan and Yemen will probably tilt toward him, and he'll be in a position to extort the others. We can expect the Arab states to start cutting deals. Iran will be at Iraq's feet. Israel will be threatened." In short, concluded the country's top spy, Saddam Hussein would become the preeminent figure in the Persian Gulf.

Bush refused to let that happen, and the driving force in his decision-making was the balance of power in a crucial corner of the world. Bush got United Nations support and pulled together a coalition of some twenty-six nations to support his enterprise. Then on January 17, 1991, he unleashed his air force. After Bush destroyed Iraq's command and control centers and devastated Saddam's troops, he sent in his ground forces. They wrapped up the operation in four days. Iraq suffered an estimated 100,000 combat casualties, while U.S. combat deaths numbered only 148.

It was a tidy piece of geopolitical action, deploying overwhelming force to minimize risk and restore equilibrium to a crucial strategic locale. Bush took some criticism for not conquering Iraq and deposing

Saddam. But the electorate, based on the polls, seemed to agree that it was best to avoid the cultural strife this would have unleashed in the heartland of Islam.

If there is merit in my argument that the electorate's contemporaneous judgment should be given weight in assessing our presidents, there is no area where this is more pertinent than in matters of war and peace. When it comes to domestic policy, particularly economic policy, the voters watch their presidents closely. Anything related to jobs and their plentitude, or their diminution, is monitored on an ongoing basis. But on foreign policy the voters are more inclined to delegate decision-making to their chief executives—who, it is assumed, understand the complexities of the world far better than the voters. Even when the commander in chief attempts to lead the nation to war, the electorate generally accepts that judgment and rallies to the cause.

But this delegation of authority comes with a powerful proviso: Don't mess it up. When it comes to the expenditure of blood, the American people expect the rationale of war to hold up; they expect honesty in that rationale; they expect a benefit to the nation from the sacrifices involved; they expect effectiveness in the war effort; and they demand victory within a reasonable time span. When those things aren't in evidence, the voters terminate the delegation of authority and force a change in policy—and perhaps personnel—at the next election.

That's why the decision to go to war remains any president's most politically dangerous decision—as it should be. The people own the office. And there is no escape from the force and unsentimental severity of America's presidential referendum politics.

8

SPLIT-DECISION PRESIDENTS

In early March 1968, some weeks before Wisconsin's Democratic presidential primary, U.S. Postmaster General Lawrence O'Brien traveled to Milwaukee to deliver a campaign speech for his boss, President Lyndon B. Johnson, who was battling the political insurgency of Minnesota Senator Eugene McCarthy. O'Brien had sent out a group of advance men ahead of time to ensure the hall would be teeming with people, mostly postal workers. Part of his speech was captured on the television news, which prompted Johnson to call O'Brien at his hotel. The conversation unfolded essentially as follows:

LBJ: How does it look in Wisconsin?

O'BRIEN: Mr. President, I'll give it to you straight. You're gonna get clobbered.

LBJ: But you had a big, enthusiastic crowd out there—I saw it on
          television.

O'BRIEN: Yeah, but that was a put up job—I had advance men and postal
          people. I didn't want to talk to an empty hall. I passed your
          headquarters and McCarthy's on my way back to the hotel, and
          yours was closed and his was swarming with kids.

LBJ: Clobbered?

O'BRIEN: Clobbered.

By month's end Johnson announced that he wouldn't seek another
presidential term. He gave a high-sounding rationale for his stunning
decision, but in reality his aim was to avoid the stark humiliation
bearing down on him like a dreadnought heading toward Jutland.

That capped one of the most precipitous political falls in American presidential history. Less than three years earlier, at the close of
1965, Johnson maintained a rare mastery over the country's politics.
There wasn't any civic force that could say him nay on the bold plans
he had set before the nation. In the previous election he had scored
one of the most decisive presidential victories in history, collecting
61 percent of the popular vote against the hapless Republican challenger, Barry Goldwater. What's more, following the 1964 elections,
Johnson's Democratic Party held 295 House seats to just 140 for the
Republicans, while 68 of 100 Senate seats belonged to Democrats.

And now his administration was in shambles, his long and illustrious career brought down by kids flocking to Wisconsin to rally
around "Clean Gene" McCarthy's antiwar mutiny.

What happened? Johnson failed the test I call "longevity of
success"—successful stewardship over two full terms. Extended success
is requisite to passing the corollary test of highest electoral attainment—
two terms followed by party succession. As the electorate makes its unsentimental assessments as determined by the Founders—in four-year

increments—it excludes all considerations except the president's performance in the concluding term. He may have been brilliant in the previous term, but that counts for nothing in the referendum system. Every presidential term stands or falls on its own.

It's in that context that we now explore the national leaders I call "split-decision presidents"—those who impressed the voters in one term but failed to do so a second time; in other words, two-term presidents who didn't maintain party control of the White House after their second terms. There are seven of them—Wilson, Truman, Eisenhower, Johnson, Nixon, Clinton, and George W. Bush. In some instances, the variation in their two terms is considerable; in others, slight. But, in all events, the voters responded to the second term by expelling the president's party and embracing the opposition. Referendum politics reigned.

In most cases we see also a flaw of leadership that catches up with the incumbent over time, precipitating a decline in presidential effectiveness. We saw how Grant's managerial aloofness contributed to the scandals that hounded his second term and fostered his lassitude in the face of economic travail. For Johnson it was hubris.

In looking at the split-decision presidents, we already have explored the varied success levels between Truman's two terms, with the observation that history and the electorate both probably had it right in their separate assessments. Discussion of Clinton and George W. Bush will be deferred to the final chapter, which explores the performance of presidents whose tenures in office are too recent for serious historical perspective. That leaves, within this group, Wilson, Eisenhower, Johnson, and Nixon.

Woodrow Wilson: The former Princeton president and New Jersey governor was a man of high intellect and considerable erudition on the intricacies of American government. But he was consumed with feelings of sanctimony, a sense that he was not only right on most things but right because of a moral superiority. This is not a trait that fosters political effectiveness. Presidents who shared it included John Quincy Adams, a one-term president; James Polk, whose pietism produced unnecessary political difficulties; Jimmy Carter, also a one-termer; and George W. Bush, a split-decision president. In all instances their tendencies toward sanctimony hampered their ability to deal effectively with other political players and maneuver tactically through the political vortex of their times. For Wilson, this trait contributed to diplomatic and domestic misfires that rendered his second term a failure, at least in the judgment of the electorate.

It also was coupled with his strong sense of idealism. Unlike Johnson, obsessed with the accumulation and exercise of power for its own sake and for personal glory, Wilson felt a need to encase his political aims in a larger structure of meaning, a framework of elevated sensibility. Thus, in domestic policy, he was a thoroughgoing progressive, which meant he advocated using the power of government to protect citizens from corporate abuse and to distribute wealth more widely throughout society. Hence he continued the Theodore Roosevelt tradition, popular with the electorate at that time.

He was elected in 1912 with just 41.8 percent of the popular vote, while Theodore Roosevelt received 27.4 percent under the Progressive Party banner and William Howard Taft, the Republican incumbent, collected 23.2 percent. Although a minority president in the popular vote, he deftly fashioned a new coalition pulling together progressives from both parties, including many GOP followers of Theodore Roosevelt. That strategy yielded a highly successful first term.

His primary domestic aim was tariff reductions. Progressives saw high tariffs as providing unfair preferences for special interests, particularly the despised trusts that held a powerful grip on the American economy. He got the legislation he wanted from the House, but when it languished in the Senate, he succumbed to his self-righteous tendencies. He lashed out at opposition lobbyists with such abandon that it nearly upended his effort, as members of both parties castigated his

apparent inability to distinguish between illegality and traditional political behavior. But the setback proved fleeting, and the Senate passed
the legislation in the fall of 1913. It was a major accomplishment.

Next Wilson put forth a proposal to create a government-managed
central bank that would serve as repository for federal funds and an
agency for ensuring currency stability. By year's end the Federal
Reserve System was created. He then got enactment of a graduated
income tax. "There is nothing in life that succeeds like boldness," said
an exultant Wilson, "provided you believe you are on the right side."

The next year he pushed through Congress the seminal Clayton
Antitrust Act, which curbed anticompetitive business practices and
created the Federal Trade Commission. This prompted the influential
Saturday Evening Post to hail the president as "the biggest Democrat
in the country—the leader and the chief." It praised his mastery of
issues and "persistency and unfailing tact" in dealing with a fractious
Congress.

Still, economic difficulties plagued Wilson's early tenure, as GDP
declined nominally in 1913. The following year unemployment hit
double digits, and bank failures increased by 50 percent. In the 1914
elections, opposition Republicans gained sixty-one House seats. But
by 1915 the economy revived, growing by 6 percent, and Wilson
continued his domestic policy program. Before the end of his first
term he had signed legislation to provide federal loans to farmers,
establish workmen's compensation, regulate child labor, and require
an eight-hour workday for railroad employees.

Wilson's idealism came to the fore most powerfully in the realm
of foreign policy. As we have seen, his internationalist outlook centered not on American national interests but rather on universal ideals
that transcended the interests of any country and also historic notions
of global balance of power.

The limitations of this outlook became apparent in his relations
with Mexico after Victoriano Huerta emerged as the country's strong-

man leader in February 1913. Wilson despised Huerta and wished to foster the competing governmental claims of his rival, Venustiano Carranza, whom he saw, not entirely accurately, as an idealistic reformer like himself. The president sent American troops to occupy the Mexican port city of Veracruz following an incident involving the arrest of some American seamen. The provocation hardly justified such action, and most Mexicans were outraged, Carranza no less than Huerta. Wilson promptly withdrew the troops but not before 19 Americans and 126 Mexicans had died in the incident.

The episode had "aspects of *opera bouffe*," as one Wilson biographer suggested. Later, when guerrilla forces under a rebellious military leader named Francisco "Pancho" Villa lashed out against U.S. citizens on both sides of the border, killing 36 Americans, Wilson sent an army of 4,000 troops into Mexico to hunt down the elusive rebel. He was never captured, and relations between the two countries deteriorated badly before the troops were withdrawn after some eleven months in country.

Notwithstanding these indecisive adventures, Wilson retained widespread adulation from his countrymen on international matters largely because of his greatest foreign policy triumph—keeping America out of the Great War that had consumed Europe beginning in August 1914. That accomplishment, coupled with his bold domestic initiatives, brought him his 1916 reelection victory. Wilson's first-term performance commanded widespread respect and appreciation throughout the country.

His second-term performance, as we have seen, was a mess. And the mess emerged largely through his resolve to get America into the European war. The electorate came to believe that Wilson's rationale for American involvement didn't hold up as events undermined his idealistic pronouncements. America lost its zest for international adventurism. Meanwhile, deterioration in the country's domestic health brought on by the war proved politically devastating. The electorate

turned on Wilson with a vengeance, manifested in the 1918 midterm
elections and in the Republicans' landslide presidential victory in
1920. No doubt the president's political remoteness, as he struggled
with the stroke that had brought him low, contributed to the country's
perception of his second-term performance. Even allowing for that,
it's difficult to avoid the conclusion that Wilson's second term was a
clear failure.

And yet the historians have rewarded Wilson with extraordi-
narily high ratings—fourth in both Schlesinger Sr. polls, and sixth
in Porter, Neal, and Murray-Blessing. He drops down to eighth in
Schlesinger Jr.'s 1996 survey and slips further to eleventh in the *Wall
Street Journal*'s 2005 poll. This mismatch between the electorate's
judgment and history's is all the more curious when one compares
Wilson to, say, Harry Truman. Both faltered in their second terms, but
Truman's first term was characterized by numerous actions of sweep-
ing historical dimension. It can be fairly said that he saved Western
Civilization from Russian Bolshevism, poised on the doorstep of
Europe with 1.3 million Soviet and client-state ground troops. Thus
it can be argued that both history and the electorate were correct in
their Truman assessments.

It's more difficult to make that case with Wilson, whose first
term, while certainly successful, hardly brought forth historical break-
throughs in either domestic or foreign policy. On the domestic side,
the progressive Wilson followed a course already set by Theodore
Roosevelt during his presidency half a decade earlier. And his war
policy was repudiated by the electorate at the earliest opportunity.
Wilson's first-term record doesn't rise to such a level of success as to
supersede, or even blunt significantly, the failures of his second term.
The voters had it right; the historians seem off the mark.

Dwight D. Eisenhower: Eisenhower's temperament and personality were about as different from Wilson's as it was possible to be
(though they did share a passion for golf). Possessing no dreamy

DWIGHT D. EISENHOWER

Never included among the Greats, Eisenhower is consistently adjudged a Near Great. Dismissed by some as a status quo plodder during his tenure, he now is viewed as a masterly political maestro who directed America smoothly through turbulent times. His first term was more successful than his second.

idealism or high-minded sensibility, Eisenhower dwelt in the real world, unencumbered by self-righteous sentiments of the kind that animated Wilson. Also, whereas Wilson possessed the complex brain of an intellectual, Eisenhower's mind was not cluttered by abstraction or philosophical musings. His view of an intellectual was "a man who takes more words than necessary to tell us more than he knows."

Eisenhower's effectiveness lay in his ability to see the world through the cold eye of realism and get to the heart of any matter quickly and effectively, stripping away extraneous issues. This trait served him well during his leadership of Allied forces in World War II, and it guided him also in his presidency. But, while Eisenhower's mind operated efficiently in tactical and strategic thinking, it did not include a visionary component. As president, he was not likely to perceive, or even search for, opportunities to alter the course of American history.

Capitalizing on his standing as war hero and Truman's second-term failures, Eisenhower captured the presidency with 55 percent of the vote in 1952, at a time of severe Cold War tensions and the Korean War stalemate that had sapped Truman's political standing. Operating in the mode of his military-command background, he broke down the job into discrete challenges and then attacked them one by one—Korea, the Cold War, the economy, Roosevelt's lingering New Deal.

On Korea, Eisenhower brought together a potent combination in his willingness to negotiate a settlement and his hint that failure in the talks could induce him to employ tactical nuclear weapons. History will never know whether he actually would have done so, just as Eisenhower himself probably didn't know. But the suggestion was credible, and it seemed to work.

Eisenhower demonstrated his resolve by dismissing the advice of those who wanted to press for victory on the ground. Eisenhower saw insufficient prospects for that to justify such a magnitude of American deaths. He also showed toughness in dealing with South Korean President Syngman Rhee, another advocate of continuing the fight and a darling of many conservative Republicans. Rhee was told bluntly that his views on the issue didn't count for much in the new administration.

On the Cold War, Eisenhower's nonideological temperament steered him away from the politically provocative rhetoric of hardline Republicans. He refused to repudiate the 1945 Yalta Agreement among Roosevelt, Churchill, and Stalin, which was widely denounced as selling out the freedom of Eastern Europe. While the president completely embraced Truman's commitment to preserving the freedom of Western Europe, Eisenhower sought to balance that with the country's fiscal health. He struggled to hold down defense spending even at the expense of generating political rancor from members of his party.

Eisenhower saw clearly, as Stephen E. Ambrose explained in his biography, that unlimited war in the nuclear age had become unimaginable, while limited war was likely unwinnable. As a military man, he had an aversion to letting American boys die for the mere purpose of maintaining a stalemate. This led him to see the threat of nuclear warfare as the great equalizer in thwarting Soviet incursions against Western interests. The prospect of "massive retaliation," in this view, would keep would-be communist aggressors in check. He also fully embraced covert actions by stealthy CIA operatives to thwart communist expansionism.

These approaches held down defense costs and bolstered Eisenhower's pursuit of what he considered sound fiscal policies, with federal budgets balanced or close to balanced. He parried Republican calls for tax cuts, insisting the budget first had to be in surplus. But, as a political pragmatist without ideological inclinations, he made no effort to dismantle Roosevelt's New Deal. Indeed, he pushed for modest expansions in Social Security, unemployment compensation, and aid for housing, health, and education. He also supported a small increase in the minimum wage. He accepted the New Deal as an established part of American life and sought to operate within the framework left by twenty years of Democratic rule. At the same time, he curbed the regulatory zeal often seen during the Roosevelt and Truman years and pushed for tax policies designed to stimulate business investment. His biggest domestic push was the interstate highway system, which he initiated in 1956.

Throughout his first term Eisenhower presided over modest but consistent economic growth following a short and shallow recession early in his term. Inflation remained negligible. Americans felt a strong sense of economic well-being, with car ownership rising to 77 percent of U.S. households in 1960 from just 60 percent in 1952.

On foreign policy he showed restraint in keeping the country out of Vietnam as the French position there deteriorated in 1954. When advisers advocated strikes against China to thwart any Vietnam involvement, Eisenhower rejected the concept of "preventive war." Asked about it at a news conference, he said, "I don't believe there is such a thing; and, frankly, I wouldn't even listen to anyone seriously that came in and talked about such a thing."

There were no serious scandals during Eisenhower's first term and no civic disruptions of any magnitude. Eisenhower capped his first term by maneuvering diplomatically against Britain, France, and Israel when they sought to manufacture a Middle East crisis to create a pretext for the seizure of the Suez Canal from Egypt. With the election looming, some advisers feared negative political fallout from this move against U.S. allies, but Eisenhower said principle trumped national friendships. He added he didn't think the voters would toss him out for such a decision, "but if they did, so be it."

They didn't. Eisenhower was reelected with 57.4 percent of the popular vote to just 42 percent for Democrat Adlai Stevenson. Based on the Lichtman-DeCell 13 Keys formula, only a single key turned against the Republican incumbent. That was the one denoting whether the president had produced a major domestic policy accomplishment. His tendency to manage the status quo, rather than creating new national directions, left him without such an achievement.

But that status quo mentality caught up with Eisenhower in his second term, perhaps accentuated by a mild stroke suffered in late 1958. Again, he scored no major domestic policy accomplishment, but he also brought about no major foreign policy achievements. Meanwhile, the Soviet Union's launch of its Sputnik satellite in October 1957 generated widespread fears that the United States was falling behind the Soviets in space and weapons technology. This led to the so-called Missile Gap warning zealously pushed by columnist Joseph Alsop and Senator John Kennedy in the 1960 campaign. It was a false claim, as Kennedy quickly discovered upon becoming president. In the meantime, though, these warnings generated discomfort among many Americans over Eisenhower's austere defense budgets. The 1960 U-2 spy plane incident, in which Eisenhower was caught in a public lie about America's involvement, eroded his standing further. That negative fallout increased when the episode led to cancellation of a much-touted summit meeting between Eisenhower and Soviet Premier Nikita Khrushchev scheduled for later that spring.

The economy faltered during the second term. Real per capita Gross Domestic Product remained flat in 1957, then declined 2.6 percent in 1958. Unemployment hit 7 percent in 1958, the highest level since the Great Depression. After a strong rebound performance in 1959, the economy again slipped into recession in the campaign year of 1960. Fully nine of the Lichtman-DeCell keys turned against the Republicans that November, and the GOP standard-bearer, Richard Nixon, lost narrowly to Democrat John Kennedy in the presidential election. Eisenhower became a split-decision president.

Still, the disparity between the performances of his two terms wasn't particularly wide, certainly nothing like the differentials seen in the presidencies of Wilson, Truman, Lyndon Johnson, and Nixon. Perhaps that accounts for the slim margin in the 1960 presidential election. It could be argued that Eisenhower was a strong status quo president at a time when that was what the country wanted. But the voters, in their dispassionate way, render their decisions every four years with a cold, unblinking eye. Many Americans loved and appreciated Eisenhower, but he wasn't on the ballot in 1960, and his second-term performance wasn't quite sufficient for Republican White House retention.

The historians are not wrong in crediting him with managing the country well during a difficult and dangerous era. The *Wall Street Journal*'s 2005 survey ranked him eighth among all presidents. Judged against the contemporaneous voter assessment, that may be a bit high.

Schlesinger Jr.'s 1996 poll had him at fourteenth, just below McKinley and ahead of Kennedy. That may be a touch too low. But both rankings seem within the range of credible debate in the presidential Rating Game.

Lyndon Johnson: Assuming office at the death of John Kennedy in November 1963, Johnson seized almost total sway over the nation's politics. He brought to fruition the entire Kennedy agenda, augmented by his own substantial ambitions. In February 1964, Johnson pushed through Congress the Kennedy tax cuts, setting off a 4.3 percent increase that year in real per capita Gross Domestic Product (and 5 percent the following year). In June, Congress enacted the landmark Civil Rights Act designed to protect minorities from discrimination, the most far-reaching civil rights legislation since the 1860s. Later in the year he fostered passage of his Equal Opportunity Act, linchpin of his "Great Society" vision of combating poverty.

"Taken together," wrote Lichtman and DeCell, "the Keynesian tax cuts, the civil-rights bill, and the war on poverty constituted the most significant domestic-policy innovation since the New Deal." Johnson continued his legislative blitz in his second term, getting enactment of the Voting Rights Act of 1965, Medicare and Medicaid, and a host of direct-benefit programs in areas such as housing, education, and nutrition.

This irrepressible political force emanated from an irrepressible political figure. Johnson was a big man whose mountainous guile was waved around as a display of potency and vigor designed to subdue lesser men. His repertoire of manipulation included deft displays of cajolery, bluster, menace, flattery, thoughtful gift-giving, and subtle political threats wrapped in lighthearted smiles. His instinct was toward big thoughts and big ambitions, all aimed at bringing attention and glory to himself. Many Americans concluded by the end of 1965 that the presidential office had met its match in this unstoppable politician.

But within a year Johnson's apparent fortress of political power crumbled. In the 1966 midterm elections, his party lost forty-seven House seats and three Senate seats. Just seventeen months later, after that conversation with Larry O'Brien, the proud president announced his retirement. His human flaw was hubris, a conviction that he could command forces far beyond the capacity of any president. Ultimately, his voracious presidential ambitions collapsed under their own weight.

By 1966 many elements of Johnson's presidency had dissolved. First his war in Vietnam became practically synonymous with the word "quagmire"—a war that seemingly can't be won and from which the country can't extricate itself. By the end of 1967 the president had dispatched 485,000 troops to Vietnam, with another 55,000 on the way, and military deaths had exceeded 20,000. Officials were telling Johnson it would take years, and another 120,000 troops, to quell the insurgency in South Vietnam and stem the communist infiltration from the North. In the meantime, the growing antiwar movement at home was tearing at the fabric of American society.

What's more, the war's costs led to curtailments in Johnson's Great Society, which contributed to a sense of dashed expectations among the poor, particularly blacks. That contributed to a surge of black militancy and urban riots. The 1964 riots in the Watts area of Los Angeles led to 34 deaths and some thirty-five million dollars in property damage. More riots followed the next summer in thirty-eight cities, including Chicago, Cleveland, Milwaukee, Atlanta, and Phila-delphia. The upheaval severely undercut white support for Johnson's Great Society initiatives. By 1967 urban summer riots had become a routine element of American society, an apparent reality that gener-ated powerful anxiety and anger among middle-class Americans. Six days of ghetto riots in Newark, New Jersey, claimed 26 lives and destroyed much of the inner city. A few weeks later Detroit erupted in the country's worst civil disturbance since the wartime race riots there in 1943. These developments, coupled with growing numbers of increasingly destructive antiwar demonstrations on the nation's campuses, signified that Johnson couldn't deliver one of the foremost requirements of any president—domestic tranquility.

The economy continued to grow through Johnson's second term, but fiscal pressures emerged from the president's "guns and butter" policy of funding both the Vietnam War and his domestic agenda. Inflation began to surge, with the consumer price index rising 13 percent between 1964 and 1968—more than two and a half times higher than the inflation rate of the previous four years. Federal deficits were rising, and Johnson began pressing for an unpopular income-tax surcharge that threatened to slow or halt growth rates.

All this, but particularly the emotion-laden war issue, brought forth opposition in the 1968 Democratic primaries—a sure sign that Johnson's presidential standing was slipping to dangerous levels. The independent campaign of Alabama's former governor George Wallace posed a further threat to the incumbent party. Based on the Lichtman-DeCell 13 Keys formula, fully eight keys turned against the Democrats, and the voters chose Republican Richard M. Nixon over Democrat Hubert H. Humphrey, Johnson's vice president, in the November election.

History's judgment credits Johnson's presidential successes and also condemns his failures. As noted earlier, he entered the surveys rather high in the historians' assessment—eleventh in Porter's 1981 poll and thirteenth in Neal's survey of the same year, then tenth in the Murray-Blessing poll of 1982. But from there he fell to sixteenth in Schlesinger Jr.'s 1996 poll and eighteenth in the *WSJ* survey of 2005. Perhaps Robert J. Caro's multivolume biography of the man, which rendered a rather unsavory portrait of a politician thoroughly self-absorbed and consumed with naked ambition, contributed to the slippage. In any event, his failures as well as his triumphs have shaped his place in history.

Richard M. Nixon: This president's tenure is marked by one of

the country's greatest reelection victories (61 percent of the popular vote in 1972) followed by the most ignominious political fall in
American history. What was the flaw that generated such a disparate
presidential record? We know from the man's White House tapes that
he harbored venomous attitudes toward his political opponents and
wished them ill far beyond any normal political sentiment. He also
didn't operate on the basis of any reservoir of fundamental political
principles but rather moved in various ideological directions based on
political expediency. Though he called himself a conservative, he never
sought to govern as one. And he allowed himself to be drawn into
a cover-up of the Watergate burglary at an early stage, which sealed
his political fate while exposing his flawed character.

All contributed to his tragic fall. He took office in the midst
of a national crisis. The Vietnam War continued with no end in
sight—and with casualties growing by the month. Campus unrest was
reaching new levels of violence and property destruction. Inner-city
riots the previous year, following the assassination of civil rights leader
Martin Luther King, raised fears among many Americans that severe
racial tensions had become endemic in society. Mounting inflation
threatened the economy.

I have presented earlier my interpretation of Nixon's Vietnam
strategy as essentially a retreat, conducted under harrowing military
circumstances in the country of war and ominous civic turmoil at
home. Nixon's aim was to extricate America from the Vietnam quagmire while bolstering the country's Asian presence. Hence he never
talked of winning the war; he spoke of "ending the war and winning
the peace."

Nixon's Vietnam retreat should be considered in the broader context of his grand geopolitical vision, as reflected in the brilliant article
he wrote for *Foreign Affairs* magazine in October 1967. Entitled
"Asia After Viet Nam," Nixon's piece foreshadowed a new Cold War
strategy based on significant developments in the geopolitics of Asia.

These included the growing tensions between Communist China and the Soviet Union; the rise of economically progressive nations in "non-communist Asia," including Japan, Hong Kong, Singapore, Taiwan, South Korea, and Malaysia; these nations' lingering concerns about the threat from China; and America's desire to retreat from the role of "the world's policeman."

All this posed an opportunity for America to work with these rising Asian nations to fashion a collective regional defense posture against a menacing China while also trying to lure China out of its "angry isolation." The rising tensions in China-Soviet relations provided a promising opening to this new policy. "Taking the long view," wrote Nixon, "we simply cannot afford to leave China forever outside the family of nations, there to nurture its fantasies, cherish its hates and threaten its neighbors. . . . Thus our aim, to the extent that we can influence events, should be to induce change. The way to do this is to persuade China that it . . . cannot satisfy its imperial ambitions, and that its own national interest requires a turning away from foreign adventuring and a turning inward toward the solutions of its own domestic problems."

Nixon's article presaged his later overture to China and also helped prepare China intellectually for that overture when it came. But, in the meantime, it was crucial that he prevent a communist victory in Vietnam. Otherwise, as Nixon understood, America's Asian presence would have been severely attenuated. And without a clear American commitment to the region, the rising noncommunist nations likely wouldn't have been emboldened to resist the Chinese giant; and China wouldn't have been emboldened to break decisively with the Soviet Union.

The profound significance of this geopolitical chess game was that it finally broke America's Cold War need to defend that vast global defense perimeter, at least insofar as Asia was concerned. By pulling together the rising noncommunist states of Asia and bringing

RICHARD NIXON

Here was a truly tragic figure who brought to his presidency a rare brilliance and boldness, particularly in foreign policy, that left an indelible mark upon the country and the world. But his flaws, magnified horrendously under the crucible of presidential pressure, destroyed his presidency and himself.

China back into the world as a responsible player, Nixon began a process of bolstering stability throughout Asia—and, in the process, diminished the threat of America being pulled into endless wars in the region.

This was brilliant foreign policy. Unfortunately, Watergate ultimately intervened to nullify much of the Vietnam portion of this grand vision. But the vision remained intact—and its vestiges remain with us today (although the growth in China's economic and geopolitical power, which began with Nixon's overture, seems destined to usher in a new Asian era within a decade or so).

Nixon began his reelection year of 1972 with his triumphal trip to Beijing, which brought a dramatic flair to his subtle foreign policy maneuverings. That was followed by a trip to Moscow, where the president leveraged his new relationship with China to pressure the Soviets to accept two arms-limitation agreements. He also brought home a commercial pact that included the sale of American grain to Russia, which didn't hurt his later effort to cadge votes from the U.S. Farm Belt.

On the economy, Nixon initially accepted tight monetary policies designed to combat inflation. But as the election approached, he abandoned all pretense of fiscal conservatism and brought forth a new economic plan that included substantial deficit spending, wage and price curbs, and a currency devaluation through the suspension of dollar convertibility into gold. It worked, at least for the short term, boosting Gross Domestic Product in 1972 by 4 percent and enhancing the president's reelection prospects.

The result was the landslide victory over Senator George McGovern of South Dakota, but it was all downhill from there. The Watergate mess destroyed his presidency, but other problems emerged as well, some stemming from the preoccupation with the burgeoning scandal but others flowing from faulty policy decisions. Nixon's first-term economic policies may have boosted the economy in time for his reelection, but they later generated intertwined inflation and unemployment on a fearsome scale. An oil embargo by the Organization of Petroleum Exporting Countries jolted the economy further. Gross Domestic Product declined by 1.5 percent in 1974, while inflation hit 11 percent. It took years for the country to recover from Nixon's economic schema. By that time Nixon was long gone, borne aloft by Marine One from the White House South Lawn in August 1974, and then shipped off to exile in California.

In retrospect, it is clear that the seeds of Nixon's fall were sown in his first term, but the voters had no way of discerning that at the time. It's safe to say history will never warm to the man. There may be occasional defenders bent on shocking the nation's historical sensibilities with elaborate arguments on why he deserves better. But I suspect he's locked into his current space—dead last in the Schlesinger Jr. poll of 1996, third from the bottom in Murray-Blessing, thirty-second in his most favorable placement, in the *WSJ* survey of 2005.

My own view is that the best we can say about him is that his Great Retreat from Vietnam brought to the fore his worst impulses as well as his best. Mingled with the courage and brilliant calibrations of that difficult policy were his tendencies to question his opponents' motives, to pity his beleaguered self, to seek destruction of those he considered his enemies. That may be the true tragedy of Richard Nixon—that his greatest achievement contained the seeds of his own destruction and set his place in history for all time.

9

LEADERS OF DESTINY

"A statesman," Charles de Gaulle said, "may be determined and tenacious, but if he does not understand the character of his time, he will fail." The general was talking about the leadership trait called political perceptiveness—the capacity to develop a thorough and accurate understanding of the civic concerns, angers, hopes, pressures, and forces swirling through the nation and around it. This may seem like a common attribute among politicians, but few possess it in finely honed form. It is one of three fundamental qualities needed for the highest success in presidential politics. Another is vision—the capacity to visualize a new national direction and a significantly changed country. Finally, there is the more vague quality of political adroitness—the ability to harness those political forces to move the country toward the vision.

These criteria were identified by historian Henry Adams, who wrote that the American president resembles a ship commander at sea: "He must have a helm to grasp, a course to steer, a port to seek." The beckoning port represents his vision of America. The course he steers represents his ability to comprehend all the elements that must be leveraged or circumvented to reach his destination—weather, wind, tides, other vessels, underwater boulders, land contours. And the helm represents control over the vessel.

The presidents who possessed all three of these attributes inhabit the country's political pantheon. I call them Leaders of Destiny, and they all met three fundamental requirements of presidential greatness. First, they all passed the highest test of the electorate—two terms (or partial terms) followed by party succession. Second, they have resided consistently near the top of the historians' rankings. And, finally, they all transformed the country's political landscape and set it upon a new course.

The Leaders of Destiny are (in order of service) Washington, Jefferson, Jackson, Lincoln, Theodore Roosevelt, and Franklin Roosevelt.

These men set the direction of American history. Other presidents managed the country's civic affairs, effectively or otherwise, but they could not lead it away from the general direction set by the latest Leader of Destiny. The nation is not fickle, lurching hither and thither based on political whims. It moves forward inexorably based on an underlying logic of politics, as set down by the presidential greats and embraced by the electorate for significant periods of time.

Each president of such quality created a new political landscape, and succeeding presidents generally operated within the constraints and opportunities of that landscape—until it could be reshaped by the next Leader of Destiny. Eisenhower wisely made no effort to repeal or even seriously blunt Franklin Roosevelt's New Deal, despite bitter complaints from conservatives within his Republican Party. He knew that such an effort could not have succeeded because the nation remained in the Roosevelt era, even without Roosevelt. Not only would he have unleashed political havoc but also would have insulted the electoral majority, which had supported FDR's presidency over more than a dozen years.

This suggests that not every president, no matter how brilliant or forceful, can be a presidential great, any more than all the firs in the forests around Puget Sound can be the same height. There are times when the country needs or wants a new direction and times when it doesn't. The first test of presidential leadership is to divine which is the case and govern effectively within that context. Among presidents, the Leaders of Destiny were the ones who saw the national need or desire for a new direction and then managed to lead the country along that uncharted course.

George Washington: The challenge facing the first president was to set the nation upon a path that could sustain its viability for centuries. Even small missteps in the nation's earliest days could have had huge consequences. Washington steered the course with brilliance and political sensitivity. The Framers had fashioned the outlines of the new nation in large measure knowing the enterprise would be placed in the hands of this most able of its statesmen. Washington rose to the occasion through his actions and also through his persona.

Throughout his career Washington had cultivated the image of a man who transcended small conflicts and disputes and sought to personify the profound precepts and aspirations of his country. During the Constitutional Convention, which Washington presided over at the behest of the delegates, everyone knew his presence lent seriousness and weight to the proceedings. As they fought, with occasional bursts of intensity, over the elements of the new government, the presiding officer expressed hardly a word. He knew this demeanor, mixed with his well-earned stature as the First Man of America, would serve his ambition to become the first president and bolster his effectiveness in that role.

GEORGE WASHINGTON

Adjudged by nearly all academic polls as history's greatest or second-greatest president, Washington shaped the American presidency through a brilliant combination of prudence, boldness, and a willingness to walk away from power at an appropriate time.

As president, he continued to transcend the sectional and political divisions of his day in order to give the Republic time to take root in the new Constitution. Washington's challenge was to consolidate power sufficiently to move the nation beyond the fecklessness of the Articles of Confederation while at the same time assuring Americans that they needn't fear this governmental consolidation.

To nurture confidence in the new system and engender a sense of national unity, he toured the nation extensively. He firmly protected the prerogatives of the federal government vis-à-vis the states, but he demonstrated a careful deference toward Congress, even eschewing the presidential veto except in the single instance when he felt a measure violated the Constitution. When an antitax revolt, the Whiskey Rebellion, erupted in western Pennsylvania, Washington

demonstrated the primacy of federal protection by summoning mili-
tias from surrounding states to subdue the rebellion. He traveled to
Pennsylvania to oversee the military preparations and left only after
the revolt evaporated in the face of the president's resolve.

In foreign policy he governed by an outlook that was crucial to
the Republic's early success—avoid permanent entangling alliances
that would embroil the country in conflicts unrelated to its national
interests. Hence, America maintained neutrality in the ongoing European wars that disrupted Atlantic shipping during those decades. It
wasn't always easy, but it gave the new republic time to develop into a
global power. At the same time, Washington tended to favor Britain
over France in the geopolitical wars that emerged during that long
European rivalry. This became particularly apparent with the signing
of John Jay's famous treaty with Great Britain, designed to settle issues lingering from the Revolutionary War. These included Britain's
refusal to remove troops from America's northwestern territories and
U.S. reluctance to compensate British creditors for prerevolutionary
debts (mostly owed by southern planters). Jay's treaty required removal
of the British troops, but on commercial matters it accepted the
prewar debts and solidified Britain's commercial dominance over Atlantic trade. That ignited a backlash from anti-Federalists, who were
sympathetic to France and who felt the treaty's multiple concessions
undermined America's national interests. Nevertheless, the president
managed to get his treaty ratified by the Senate.

Washington aligned himself with the emerging Federalist movement also on domestic policy. The Federalists favored investing federal
power in national elites capable of ensuring civic stability in the new
nation. The guiding force behind this outlook was Treasury Secretary
Alexander Hamilton, who fashioned a plan for handling the daunting
national debt left from the Revolution. Aimed at restoring the country's public credit, the plan involved consolidating foreign, federal,
and state debt into a single pool, then selling the debt at discounts to

speculators willing to bet on the American future. He also proposed a national bank to manage this flow of capital and maintain currency stability.

It was a brilliant plan, and it worked. But it generated intense hostility from emerging anti-Federalist factions who saw a dangerous concentration of power in this debt consolidation and national bank. Virginia's governor warned Washington that Hamilton's plan would lead to either "the Prostration of Agriculture at the feet of Commerce, or a change in the present form of Federal Government, fatal to the existence of American liberty."

Washington supported Hamilton and helped shepherd a compromise version through Congress. The anti-Federalists now had a cause, and soon they would have a champion—Thomas Jefferson, who resigned from Washington's Cabinet to marshal opposition forces, sometimes deployed with vicious abandon. Thus did the first big political fault line emerge in America—the Hamiltonians vs. the Jeffersonians. On one level it was between those who wanted important financial decisions to be guided by an enlightened elite versus those who wanted the nation's financial affairs to be directed by ordinary citizens. It also reflected an ongoing tension between southern agrarianism and the emerging manufacturing sectors of the North. Washington's Federalism continued to dominate the nation as his vice president, John Adams, succeeded him. But Adams's presidential tenure was cut short at one term by the emergence of the man from Monticello.

Thomas Jefferson: Tall, clever, elegantly turned out, Jefferson conducted himself, in the words of Abigail Adams, "with a grace, dignity, and ease that leaves Royal George [of England] far behind him." Scintillating in small groups and one-on-one encounters, he often faltered before large crowds, becoming ill at ease and lacking eloquence. He hated conflict and appeared accommodating and placatory even with his political adversaries. But he excelled at developing stealthy

schemes designed to outmaneuver his rivals, and he developed a reputation as scheming and duplicitous. "When dealing with his peers, he
was inept," historian Forrest McDonald wrote, "but when he was the
master of his circumstances, he had no peers."

Jefferson saw more clearly than others the opportunity posed by
the new political fault line emerging in America, and he set about,
in the observation of Henry Adams, to grasp the helm, steer a new
course, and get to port. In doing all three successfully, he became the
next presidential Man of Destiny, elected in 1800, then reelected four
years later and succeeded by his favored candidate, Madison, who also
served two terms.

Jefferson's vision was of a nation that pushed aside the kind of
budding governmental aristocracy favored by the Federalists—a powerful federal government run by men accustomed to leadership. He
desired a smaller federal government more attuned to the interests
of ordinary folk—farmers, laborers, mechanics, artisans—and less
inclined to supersede the rights and prerogatives of the states. He
opposed Hamilton's federally chartered bank, for example, as representing a dangerous concentration of power. And he was aghast at the
Federalists' Alien and Sedition Acts during the John Adams administration. He foresaw a new party emerging from the anti-Federalist
ferment manifest in a series of feisty Democratic societies, clubs, and
polemical publications that had sprouted up during Washington's
presidency. This vision soon became the new Democratic-Republican
Party that was his creation.

Under the banner of this fledgling institution, Jefferson crafted
a brand of politics that would drive the country in new directions.
Never again would the Federalists win a presidential election. Now the
most potent political catchphrases would be: small government, strict
construction of the Constitution, states' rights, hard money, reduced
taxes, less intrusion into the lives of citizens. Jefferson's administration
would speak for "the rational, self-improving, independent man who

could be counted on to take care of himself and his family if only intrusive institutions were removed," as historian Joyce Appleby put it.

Jefferson's vision was expressed in his first message to Congress. He vowed to abolish all internal federal taxes and reduce federal expenditures and personnel. He attacked a system in which, "after leaving to labor the smallest portion of its earnings on which it can subsist, government . . . consume[s] the residue of what it was instituted to guard." Hamilton, aghast, said this attack on Federalism should "alarm all who are anxious for the safety of our government, for the responsibility and welfare of our nation." But John Quincy Adams, whose father had just lost the presidency to Jefferson, understood these political initiatives well. They are, he lamented, "all popular in all parts of the nation."

Jefferson governed as he had promised. He eliminated internal taxes, cut the size of government, reduced the national debt. He brushed aside Hamilton's concept of selling federal lands at robust prices in order to fill government coffers, pay down the national debt, and invest in infrastructure projects such as roads, bridges, and canals. Jefferson sold the lands to ordinary Americans at modest prices based on his vision that the West would fill up with independent-minded farmers reveling in their land ownership and opportunity for self-betterment. He was confident that these yeoman folk would build up the nation from below.

Jefferson placed his small-government philosophy aside when he encountered a rich opportunity to purchase from France the entire Louisiana Territory, thus doubling the size of the country. It wasn't clear there was a constitutional foundation for such a purchase, but the vision of a burgeoning nation extending to the Pacific Ocean proved too enticing. The president seized the opportunity, accepted the jeers of "hypocrisy" from Federalists, and promptly dispatched an exploratory team to map the territory.

Like any president, Jefferson suffered some setbacks while in

office. His embargo against shipping to France and Great Britain, aimed at ensuring America's neutrality in the ongoing European hostilities and discouraging those countries from seizing U.S. ships, severely curtailed U.S. trade without altering the behavior of either country. His first-term vice president, Aaron Burr, became a fugitive from justice when New York authorities issued an arrest warrant for him following his killing of Alexander Hamilton in a duel. After his term as vice president, Burr, now disenchanted with the course of his political career, moved to the West and led an elaborate scheme to detach western territories from U.S. control. He was tried for treason and acquitted despite Jefferson's active efforts in behalf of conviction. Burr brought serious political embarrassment to Jefferson during his presidency.

But the Jeffersonian outlook dominated the political debate through the eight-year presidency of his chosen successor, Madison. Although Madison departed slightly from Jefferson in accepting modest protective tariffs and reestablishment of the national bank, he embraced Jeffersonian principles in vetoing legislation for national infrastructure improvements, in governmental restraint, and in his rhetoric. And Jefferson's general opposition to an expansive federal government would become a recurrent political theme in American politics.

The force of the Jeffersonian vision of small government and strict construction began to wane during the Monroe presidency. The Federalist Party was dead by this time, but the Democratic-Republicans now found themselves divided between the pure Jeffersonians and a new breed that wanted to resurrect some of the old Federalist notions (without, however, any Federalist aristocracy). The leader of this movement was Kentucky's Henry Clay, whose philosophy of governmental activism included federal programs and policies he considered essential to American progress—federally funded roads, canals, and bridges; high tariffs; federal land sales at high prices. Monroe

embraced some of these notions, such as a national bank, increases in protective tariffs, canals and roads for military and commercial uses, and a national university. The result was a new political schism in American politics. "Everything is scattered," said Supreme Court Justice Joseph Story in 1818. "Republicans ... are as much divided against themselves as the parties formerly were from each other." This became particularly intense after the election of John Quincy Adams, who called himself a Democratic-Republican but governed more in the vein of his Federalist father.

Andrew Jackson: The Adams-Clay alliance brought forth a relent- less force of opposition in the figure of Jackson, the next Leader of Destiny. Jackson leveraged the Jeffersonian ethos into something even more powerful and transformed the nature of American politics.

After he lost to Quincy Adams in the 1824 presidential election, Jackson perceived that there were subtle but powerful changes occur- ring in American politics. In the nation's early decades, presidential elections were in the hands of state legislators and other local men of prominence, who selected electors who selected the president. The people themselves were excluded from the process. Property restric- tions also served to limit voter involvement. Responding to a wave of populism in the burgeoning West, some states began choosing electors by popular vote and eliminating property requirements. This created, for the first time, a mass electorate, and a candidate who could reach these new voters could blow away the opposition. Jackson understood this. Adams and Clay missed it.

Jackson, as we have seen, abhorred concentrated power in Wash- ington, which he believed would be captured inevitably by irresponsi- ble elites and turned against ordinary citizens. His campaign message in 1828 was: They're trying to take away your democracy, but I will get it back for you. Thus did Jackson marshal the political force of ordinary Americans—the "humble members of society," as he called them—to dispatch Quincy Adams and capture the White House.

As we saw in Chapter 2, Jackson opened up American politics and moved the country a considerable distance toward democratic ideals. His Democratic Party became the country's dominant political force.

As a nationalist, Jackson embraced the idea of America's westward expansion, but he moved with caution when Texas won its independence from Mexico through force of arms. He recognized the new regime, as did many European nations, but he made no move to bring Texas into the federal union. He feared that a conflict with Mexico, which refused to recognize Texas independence, would complicate or upend his other pressing goals. It was left to James Polk to press forward with big expansion policies a decade later—annexation of Texas, accumulation of most of Oregon (encompassing the states of Washington, Oregon, and Idaho, and parts of Montana and Wyoming), and acquisition of large expanses of land in what is now the American Southwest and California. Polk's policies were Jacksonian in origin.

Polk's expansionist accomplishments brought a fearsome new intensity to the cankerous slavery issue, as the nation grappled with the question of what to do about that doleful institution in the new territories. Soon this intractable issue would engulf the Union, then destroy it.

Abraham Lincoln: The man who saved the Union from this destruction was, of course, Lincoln, and this profound achievement has placed him at the most hallowed location in the nation's presidential pantheon. He was "undeniably a great man," says Thomas A. Bailey, "... in spirit, in humility, in humanity, in magnanimity, in patience, in Christlike charity, in capacity for growth, in political instincts, in holding together a discordant political following, in interpreting and leading public opinion, and in seizing with bulldog grip the essential idea of preserving the Union." But Bailey points out numerous instances when Lincoln could have handled specific challenges of the secession crisis with greater deftness or appropriateness, particularly regarding his willingness to trample the Constitution in order to save

ABRAHAM LINCOLN

A political genius nearly always ranked as the country's greatest president, Lincoln perceived the world more acutely than others and subdued a crisis that nearly crushed him and his country. He saved the Union, freed the slaves, and gave birth to the Republican Party, which guided America through the industrial era.

it. He suspended habeas corpus in defiance of a ruling by Chief Justice Roger B. Taney that only Congress had the right to do that in wartime. (The Constitution ensures the habeas corpus privilege "unless when in Cases of Rebellion or Invasion, the public safety may require" suspension, and Taney, presiding over the relevant circuit court, ruled against the administration in a particularly nettlesome case. Later, after the passions of war had subsided, the Supreme Court ruled in favor of Taney's position.)

Lincoln also shuttered newspapers that opposed his policies, closed the mail to opposition publications, arrested newspaper publishers, threw northern civilians into military prison camps, and created military tribunals to try civilians (without the constitutional right to a jury trial) who had discouraged people from enlisting in Union armies. One antiwar congressman, Ohio's Clement Laird Vallandigham, probably Lincoln's most vociferous critic among antiwar "Copperheads," was arrested by an army general, taken to a military prison, and tried by a military commission. Sentenced to imprisonment for the war's duration, he later was exiled to the South and eventually made his way to Canada.

It should be remembered, though, that mobs in Baltimore stoned Union soldiers on their way to defend Washington and then cut off telegraph and rail service to the capital. If Lincoln had not placed Baltimore under military rule, Maryland likely would have seceded and Washington would have been an island in the Confederacy. The crisis of the Union certainly was unprecedented.

We will look at Lincoln largely in the context of Henry Adams's three requisites of greatness: a helm to grasp, a course to steer, a port to seek. As the 1850s unfolded and the issue of slavery in the territories became increasingly inflammatory, the arguments of northern abolitionists and southern fire-eaters took on greater force. The country desperately needed compromise, and two very different concepts came from two Illinoisans—Stephen A. Douglas and Abraham Lincoln. Douglas's solution was "popular sovereignty"—allowing the territorial legislatures to decide the slavery question for themselves. This was the underpinning of his 1854 Kansas-Nebraska Act, which allowed the new territories of Kansas and Nebraska to settle the issue within their borders. But in addition, as noted earlier, it repealed the Missouri Compromise, which had allowed Missouri to enter the Union as a slave state but had also, for some three decades, outlawed slavery north of latitude 36°30'.

The Kansas-Nebraska Act enraged moderate northerners by opening previously free territory to the possibility of slavery. It unleashed the events of "Bleeding Kansas," the violent conflict that attended that territory's struggle to decide its slavery policy. It nullified the presidency of Franklin Pierce, who had endorsed the legislation. It destroyed Douglas's Democratic Party in the North. In the South it obliterated the Whig Party, which had largely opposed Douglas's Kansas-Nebraska bill. It later vaporized the Whigs entirely as many anti-Douglas and antislavery voters coalesced into the new Republican Party. Ultimately, it dashed Douglas's presidential ambitions.

Lincoln took a different tack, finely crafted to correlate with the growing feeling in the nation that the status quo was untenable. He acknowledged the constitutional protection of slavery where it existed and insisted he had no wish or right to interfere with that. But he stood foursquare against its spread to any other states or territories. In accepting his party's nomination for Illinois senator in 1858—against Douglas—he attacked the Kansas-Nebraska Act for fanning passions on the slavery issue rather than calming them, as their advocates had promised. "Under the operation of that policy," Lincoln declared, "that agitation has not only, *not ceased*, but has *constantly augmented*. In *my* opinion, it will *not* cease, until a *crisis* shall have been reached, and passed." Then, drawing from Scripture, he spoke one of his most famous lines: "'A house divided against itself cannot stand.'" He explained: "I believe this government cannot endure permanently half *slave* and half *free*. I do not expect the Union to be dissolved—I do not expect the house to *fall*—but I do expect it will cease to be divided. It will become *all* one thing, or *all* the other."

This breathtaking candor helped get Lincoln known nationally, and it reflected a crucial element of his civic genius—his understanding of the power of political rhetoric that stings and disarms with its stark realism. His depiction of the situation facing America as crisis descended upon it, coupled with the moral sensibility he brought to the slavery issue, positioned him to squeeze out his 1860 presidential victory with less than 40 percent of the popular vote against three other candidates—northern Democrat Douglas, southern Democrat

John C. Breckinridge, and John Bell of the Constitutional Union Party, which emerged in 1860 as a political habitat for former Whigs and some southern Democrats dedicated to preserving the Union.

What was Lincoln's vision for America at the time of his election? That is the intriguing question. Clearly, his central aim was to save the union, as he made powerfully clear in his famous letter to Horace Greeley, dated August 25, 1862, in response to an editorial in Greeley's *New York Tribune* that questioned Lincoln's slavery policies. "My paramount object in this struggle *is* to save the Union, and is *not* either to save or destroy Slavery. If I could save the Union without freeing *any* slave, I would do it; and if I could save it by freeing *all* the slaves, I would do it; and if I could do it by freeing some and leaving others alone, I would also do that." Then, reflecting a broader vision, he added: "I have here stated my purpose according to my view of *official* duty, and I intend no modification of my oft-expressed *personal* wish that all men, everywhere, could be free."

Lincoln understood that a Union victory would bring with it emancipation, and clearly he welcomed that outcome. But he remained cautious during the war. He reversed actions of Union army commanders who freed slaves by military edict in Border States still in the Union. He willingly took intense political heat from abolitionists in doing so because he feared those actions would stir dangerous dissension and perhaps violence in the crucial Union slave states of Kentucky, Tennessee, Maryland, and Delaware. And he issued his own Emancipation Proclamation only "after much pulling and hauling, as an act of sheer military necessity," as Thomas Bailey puts it, noting that the Proclamation freed no slaves anywhere (it applied only to slaves in the seceding states). But Lincoln supported a Thirteenth Amendment abolishing slavery, and that outcome clearly became part of his vision as the war progressed.

Lincoln couldn't find his solution in the Constitution, which protected slavery in those states where it had existed at the time of the Constitution's ratification. So he reached back to the Revolutionary War era. Historian Garry Wills and conservative intellectual Willmoore Kendall argue that Lincoln's Gettysburg Address fostered a new concept drawn from language in the Declaration of Independence that brought equality forward as a fundamental element of the American ethos. Wills, in *Lincoln at Gettysburg*, calls Lincoln's interpretation of the nation's founding a "correction of the spirit" in America. He adds that it rendered "feckless" any attempts by historians and commentators to go back before Lincoln for lessons on the essence of the United States. America's embrace of the Gettysburg Address, writes Wills, transformed the country. "Because of it, we live in a different America." He calls this Lincoln legacy "one of the most daring acts of open-air sleight-of-hand ever witnessed by the unsuspecting."

Kendall, on the other hand, calls Lincoln's effort to rewrite the Constitution "heretical." The nation's founding document, he argues, was not the Declaration, which was never ratified by the people as a solemn commitment to a set of underlying governmental principles for generations to come. That document was the Constitution, written not "four-score and seven years" before Lincoln's Gettysburg "sleight-of-hand," but rather just two-score and sixteen years before. And that document dedicated the nation not to notions of equality (or the political egalitarianism of our time) but, writes Kendall, to "Union, Justice, Domestic Tranquility, the Common Defense, the Blessings of Liberty." In any event, there's no question that the powerful events of 1861 to 1865, and Lincoln's efforts to manage them, left the country fundamentally changed in ways that would guide its history forever afterward, and this change certainly included new views of equality. Further, there's no question that Lincoln captured this in his greatest showpiece of spare and penetrating eloquence.

More than any other president, Lincoln left behind a nation transformed. And his new Republican Party would be the country's dominant political force during the difficult Reconstruction period and throughout the remainder of the nineteenth century. Stunning developments were transforming the country and its governing party. Rapid industrialization brought the rise of big corporations, internal migrations from farms to cities, and the emergence of a large, urban working class. These in turn spawned plenty of civic problems—intermittent financial panics, worker exploitation, stock market abuse—but the country seemed little inclined to address them, so consumed was it with regional passions still flowing from the bloody years of war. Ultimately, they would have to be addressed, which meant the country would need a new Man of Destiny.

Theodore Roosevelt: The new era began with the new century, which brought dramatic developments in both domestic and foreign policy. The man who personified this new direction—and became that new Leader of Destiny—was Theodore Roosevelt, who saw the need for a new American vision, crafted that vision, and successfully brought it to the fore. He carefully managed his political career to foster his Leadership of Destiny.

In foreign policy America pushed beyond its continental boundaries and went into the world in search of power and influence. Roosevelt embraced this bold policy of imperialism, but he didn't initiate it. His predecessor, McKinley, led America into the Spanish-American War and brought forth the territorial acquisitions that would thrust the nation to the status of global power, even though McKinley wasn't driven by a clear-eyed vision. Upon assuming office, he declared, "We want no wars of conquest.... We must avoid the temptation of territorial aggression." Subsequently, he was carried by events more than he was a maker of events. Roosevelt, on the other hand, saw war, almost any war, as a vehicle for American greatness.

When McKinley hesitated to exploit Cuban insurrections against Spanish rule as a casus belli, Roosevelt dismissed him as being "soft as a chocolate éclair." When an explosion sank the U.S. battleship

Maine in Havana harbor, McKinley could hesitate no longer. Though there was never any solid evidence that Spain sabotaged the ship, the incident inflamed America and rendered war inevitable. Within four months the United States destroyed Spain's Atlantic and Pacific fleets, then moved quickly to extract Puerto Rico, Guam, and the Philippines from Spanish dominion. For good measure the country then acquired Hawaii. It was, declared the *Washington Post* enthusiastically, "an imperial policy!"

No one personified this imperialism more robustly than Theodore Roosevelt, a hero to the nation after his bold, almost reckless charge up "San Juan Hill." When he became president seven months into McKinley's second term, Roosevelt built up America's military capacity, particularly its naval forces on two oceans. He announced to the world in word and deed that America had arrived upon the global scene, to be taken seriously. Over time he crafted a concept of non-colonial imperialism—extending America's commercial and military reach without trying to subdue other peoples around the world. As TR biographer Kathleen Dalton wrote, "He finally recognized that Americans had no patience for doing the slow work of imposing colonial rule on unwilling subjects." He became, she adds, "a transitional internationalist figure between the diplomacy of imperialism and the generation ready to create a League of Nations to forestall war."

It was in domestic policy that Roosevelt was truly innovative, as noted in Chapter 5. In shaping the concepts of progressivism into a successful governing philosophy, he resurrected for a new century the politics of Henry Clay—the idea that certain concentrations of federal power were necessary to maintain the country's prosperity and ensure the well-being of its people. In doing that, Roosevelt set the country on a new course and opened up fresh governing approaches— including his trust-busting initiatives, creation of the Interstate Commerce Commission, and legislation to foster safety in the country's food supply and drugs. His chosen successor, William Howard Taft, embracing the TR sensibility, sponsored expansion of federal health inspections, extended government regulations to telephone and telegraph companies, and established a federal agency of mine safety. He helped enact a corporate income tax and fostered passage of the Sixteenth Amendment, authorizing personal income taxation. All this was made possible by Roosevelt's transitional leadership. Roosevelt, regretting his decision not to seek a second full term, soon became disenchanted with his protégé and attacked him as being hopelessly "stand pat" and beholden to corporate interests. Running against Taft in 1912 as a third-party "Progressive," he split the Republican vote and handed the presidency to Democrat Woodrow Wilson.

Wilson carried forward Roosevelt's brand of politics—until he ran it into the ground through the failure of his second term. By the time the country was finished with Wilson, internationalism and domestic progressivism were in eclipse. There they remained through the decade of the twenties—until the emergence of the Great Depression.

Franklin Roosevelt: In the crucible of that Depression, the next Leader of Destiny arrived—the Democratic Roosevelt, TR's distant cousin, who embraced the brand of politics fashioned by his namesake and built it into a governing edifice of immense proportions. FDR's standing in the presidential pantheon is beyond dispute. Consistently ranked within the top three by historians, he also not only passes the highest electoral test—two terms and party succession—but actually got himself reelected three times, his longevity of success unparalleled. His impact on the American Republic is rivaled only by that of Washington and Lincoln.

Roosevelt became president at the height of a crisis surpassed in the country's history only by the Civil War. Economically, America was on its knees. Real per capita Gross Domestic Product had contracted by nearly a third. Foreign trade had collapsed. Some 83 percent of shareholder value in the stock market had vanished. Unemployment soared to nearly 23 percent. Crop prices dropped

FRANKLIN D. ROOSEVELT

Ranked consistently by historians as the third-greatest president, FDR transformed the country and the world. His "longevity of success"—maintaining the voters' loyalty and support over a long period—is unmatched in American history, and he stands tall among the presidential "Leaders of Destiny."

to levels below what was needed to provide a bare subsistence for farmers, who heated their homes by burning corn they couldn't sell. Many lost their land to banks that were themselves on the brink of failure. The social fabric of the nation began to unravel as unemployed Americans desperately flocked to soup lines, scavenged for food, and hoveled in tarpaper shanties.

The new president confronted this national emergency with a buoyant demeanor that instilled optimism and resilience. His spirit and penchant for vigorous action proved infectious throughout much of the country. As historian Mark Leff has noted, the most famous line from his first inaugural speech—"The only thing we have to fear is fear itself"—was "on one level absurd." The country had plenty to fear in that season of uncontrolled economic contraction. But coupled with his declaration that "this nation asks for action and action now," Roosevelt's powerful admonition conveyed a confidence in the future that spread across the land.

It is fair to say FDR entered the presidency without a clearly developed idea of how to confront the crisis. His was an administration of "bold, persistent experimentation," as he put it during his first campaign, explaining that the aim was "to take a method and try it; if it fails . . . try another. But above all, try something." That defined his leadership.

Amid panicked fund withdrawals from banks across the country, Roosevelt closed the nation's financial institutions as Washington officials hurriedly crafted an emergency banking measure. Then in his first "fireside chat" to the American people he explained the complex policy in understandable terms. By the time the banks reopened (70 percent were back in business within a month), the panic was over. And Roosevelt was well on his way toward his "First Hundred Days" of legislative activity—the National Industrial Recovery Act, the Agricultural Adjustment Act, the Glass-Steagall Act creating the Federal Deposit Insurance Administration, creation of the Public Works Administration and the Tennessee Valley Authority. Later there would be Rural Electrification, the Wagner Act establishing new rules in collective bargaining, and Social Security.

The keystone to all this was the consolidation of power in Washington. Roosevelt embraced a crisis strategy of experimentation, but his experimentation consistently fit the progressive impulses of Theodore Roosevelt and Woodrow Wilson. He viewed a newly powerful federal government as the necessary agency of economic renewal. But, importantly, he also saw the federal consolidation of power as a positive good in itself. Unlike Lincoln, who aggrandized federal power to wage his war while carefully avoiding actions that would vest that power into the future, Roosevelt was to leave behind a thoroughly entrenched federal establishment. The Jackson-Clay tension that had

animated political discourse through most of American history—
power consolidation versus diffusion of power—suddenly tilted heavily toward Clay's view and then stretched far beyond anything ever
seriously contemplated before.

A result was the emergence of new national constituency groups
beholden to Roosevelt's party and thus intensely dedicated to it—
workers flocking to unions under the Wagner Act, senior citizens
mobilized by Social Security, farmers appreciative of agricultural
subsidies, artists and intellectuals stirred by the Works Progress Administration, and rural Americans focused on the prospect of cheap
electrical power. This was a significant political development in America—"special interests" fostered by federal policy-making—and precisely the kind of development that Jefferson and Jackson had sought
to prevent. There was an elitist element to this push to establish a
vast federal bureaucracy of officials—essentially a new governmental
elite—empowered to direct events in multiple areas of American life.

It has been argued by Roosevelt critics that none of this actually
succeeded in ending the impact of the Great Depression, which lingered in America until the country's entry into World War II finally
charged the economy. In her 2007 book, *The Forgotten Man: A New
History of the Great Depression,* Amity Shlaes suggests that Roosevelt
and his people never really understood the underlying causes of the
economic collapse because they were so bent on blaming businessmen
and capitalist elements, denounced by FDR as "economic royalists"
fostering a "new despotism" and "economic slavery." Schlaes argues
that Roosevelt's attacks on business created a climate of uncertainty
that discouraged private-sector enterprise and thus prolonged the
Depression. Indeed, Roosevelt's second-term economic policies (including substantial tax increases coupled with curtailments in federal
spending) led to a second severe economic downturn—the "Roosevelt
Recession," as it was called—that gripped the nation beginning in
1937. The historian James MacGregor Burns, a Roosevelt admirer,

has suggested: "Roosevelt's fumbling and indecisiveness during the recession showed his failings as an economist and a thinker."

That's probably a fair assessment. But Roosevelt amassed a creditable record in getting the economy moving in the right direction and leading the country out of the slough of despair. Lichtman and DeCell, in their *13 Keys to the Presidency,* point out that, by all indices of voter assessment, Roosevelt actually gave the country what it wanted. During his first term, Gross Domestic Product soared by 7 percent a year, manufacturing production increased by 50 percent, and unemployment dropped to 10 percent from nearly 23 percent. Employing the Lichtman-DeCell formula, only one of thirteen keys—the one denoting a major foreign policy achievement (hardly an FDR priority in those times)—turned against Roosevelt when he went before the voters in 1936.

This impressive performance continued through Roosevelt's second term, as the president turned to Keynesian pump-priming and boosted defense spending to reverse the Roosevelt Recession and move the economy upward once again. By the last two years of his second term, the economy was again expanding at 7 percent a year, and the voters rewarded FDR with a 54.7 percent victory in 1940.

By this time, however, the voters had curtailed Roosevelt's efforts to expand his New Deal into fresh areas of American life. They particularly recoiled at the president's 1937 "Court Packing Scheme," in which he sought to alter the balance of political power on the Supreme Court, which consistently had ruled his initiatives to be unconstitutional. Roosevelt's plan to expand the number of Court justices proved to be a turning point. Congress rebuffed this power grab severely, and Roosevelt lost further standing with the electorate due to the 1937–38 economic downturn. The electorate expressed its displeasure in the midterm elections of 1938, in which the Democrats lost seventy-one House seats and six in the Senate.

However, as war engulfed Europe and as Japan increasingly destabilized Asia, Roosevelt brought his visionary bearing to this new challenge. Though his primary motivation for getting into the war was to save Britain from the mortal threat posed by Germany, his broader vision encompassed America as a major world force, allied always with Britain, which was standing alone before the menace of Nazi Germany. Though willing in his crafty way to dress up his policies in the language of Wilsonian idealism, his thinking was driven first and foremost by a concept found at the heart of the old British system, the balance of power.

As long as conservative isolationism dominated American public opinion, as it did right up to Pearl Harbor, Roosevelt couldn't take overt actions to move America onto the world stage. But he sought in every way possible to help Britain and to nudge his country to war. He passed diplomatic secrets to friendly reporters. He pushed Japan into a position of near desperation—and forced an inevitable confrontation—by barring imports of raw materials to that country in 1940, then expanding the embargo to oil in 1941. And, as Robert Shogan writes in his book *Hard Bargain,* Roosevelt almost certainly violated the U.S. Neutrality Act in 1940 by making destroyers available to Britain in a deal that transferred to America property in Canada and the West Indies for U.S. naval bases. Roosevelt negotiated the deal in secret and never asked for congressional authority. When it later became public, Roosevelt blithely called it a *"fait accompli"* and rebuffed reporters' questions about it. Asked whether Congress should have been consulted, he defiantly replied, "It is all over; it is all done." Critics attacked Roosevelt for conducting his stealthy maneuver behind Congress's back. Michigan's Republican Senator Arthur Vandenberg called the deal "the most arbitrary and dictatorial action ever taken by any President in the history of the United States." But the president ignored his critics and casually let the storm pass.

In the end, war came, and Roosevelt was given an opportunity to lead America into a global role of fostering world stability with balance-of-power diplomacy. He embraced the nationalist vision of his distant cousin—the exercise of American power for American interests, including global stability. He was a brutal realist whose vision was of a postwar Anglo-American alliance that would pick up where the British Empire had been fading out, a kind of noncolonial, benign imperialism. America was well on its way toward that new world role at the time of Roosevelt's death in April 1945.

Roosevelt's twelve-year presidency truly transformed America, in foreign affairs no less than in domestic life. Roosevelt created a new political landscape that held sway in American politics for more than four decades. Eisenhower, as noted earlier, made little effort to chip away at the New Deal landscape. Then, under John Kennedy and Lyndon Johnson, the country saw a resurgence of the old FDR philosophy, manifested primarily in Johnson's Great Society and other domestic initiatives as well as in his Cold War commitment to prevent a communist takeover of South Vietnam. Most of the old Roosevelt coalition—urban immigrants and their offspring, big-city bosses, organized labor, farmers, intellectuals, Jews—pulled together for this last hurrah for the politics of the New Deal.

Then the old coalition began to unravel. Johnson's civil rights initiatives led to the departure of the Democratic South. The Vietnam quagmire turned off young people and intellectuals. Immigrants, Jews, and labor groups nervously raised questions about "quotas" in hiring and promotions emanating from the Democrats' civil rights policies. New strains of social-issue liberalism chipped away at the old coalition. It was clear a new political landscape would have to emerge to supplant the old Roosevelt hegemony. But the country seemed to be lurching in search of it. Nixon's "southern strategy," designed to pull the solid South into the GOP fold, enhanced the GOP position in presidential elections, but his administration was destroyed by Watergate—and probably didn't have much prospect of generating widespread popular enthusiasm anyway. A few years later Carter's presidency fell through a lack of vision and leadership. He talked to the nation in language suggesting the country's feeling of national listlessness needed to be addressed by the people themselves, rather than by himself as their leader.

The Carter failure led to the emergence of Ronald Reagan, who established a new course for America and generated a new optimism. Reagan was one of only four twentieth-century presidents who met the highest standard of contemporaneous voter assessment—serving two terms or partial terms and maintaining party succession. It could be argued also that he changed the political landscape. But history has yet to render a clear judgment on his place in the presidential pantheon.

The Leaders of Destiny were flawed in various ways. Washington could never get used to the vehemence of the opposition his policies generated in the political discourse he had done so much to set in motion. Jefferson could be underhanded and even nasty in his political dealings. Jackson often displayed an impetuous streak and a raging temper, and he seldom managed to keep his many grudges from influencing his political actions. Lincoln may have exceeded necessity in suspending constitutional guarantees in his pursuit of a Civil War victory. Theodore Roosevelt was too self-absorbed and excitable to develop strong political relationships; he "shattered his party's unity," as biographer Kathleen Dalton puts it, in pushing for legislation to regulate interstate railroad rates. Franklin Roosevelt's penchant for manipulating the people around him led to frequent dissembling, and he was not above skirting the law in pursuit of goals he considered paramount.

But these were visionary presidents. They understood the character of their times, in Charles de Gaulle's parlance, far better than others of their era. They all led their country successfully to the destination of their vision. They are the tall firs in the forest of American history, rising above all others and serving as landmarks by which the nation set its course through its long experiment in self-government. In the process they also won the approval of their fellow countrymen at election time—and eventually the highest accolades of succeeding generations.

Part IV

REPUTATIONS
IN FLUX

10

REPUBLICAN RESURGENCE

In 1976, after Ronald Reagan lost his bid for the Republican presidential nomination at the party's Kansas City convention, the California politician digressed a bit with his family on his most haunting disappointment. What he really wanted to do as president, he lamented, was to sit down with Soviet leader Leonid Brezhnev and negotiate with him in a way never before tried by an American president. He would allow Brezhnev to determine the size of the table and other ceremonial niceties, said Reagan, and he would let the Soviet leader unfurl his familiar list of U.S. concessions needed to ensure cordial relations between the two nations. "I was going to listen to him for maybe twenty minutes," Reagan said wistfully, "and then I was going to get up from my side of the table, walk around to the other side, and lean over and whisper in his ear, 'Nyet.'"

Reagan's diplomatic fantasy reflected a fundamental reality of his

RONALD REAGAN

Ridiculed and dismissed by many upon his election, Reagan proved more adept than his critics anticipated or wished to acknowledge. He restored national confidence, pulled the country out of an economic morass, and unleashed forces that led to the Soviet collapse. His stock is on the rise.

political persona—his utterly unconventional view of the world and prospects for changing it. No other politician of stature in America would have dared conceive of such a diplomatic approach to the Soviets in that epoch of Cold War tension. But Reagan not only conceived it; he actually did it. Just ten years after his 1976 Kansas City defeat and that wistful fantasizing, President Reagan sat down with Soviet leader Mikhail Gorbachev to work out a broad arms-limitation agreement. When Gorbachev insisted there could be no progress in the talks until Reagan abandoned his antimissile defense program, Reagan replied by saying in essence—with all due diplomatic refinement—"Nyet."

In domestic affairs no less than in foreign policy, Reagan brought to the White House in January 1981 a political outlook and vision of the future that were highly distinctive. Most analysts believed his agenda of cutting taxes and shrinking government would be shredded by the political establishment. But the new president took on the establishment and won.

Was he a Leader of Destiny, according to this book's criteria for such a designation? I believe he was. But the question is premature, because one criterion is consistently high rankings by history, and the polls of historians have accorded him no such standing (though there are signs they may be moving in that direction). But he clearly meets the other two criteria—highest assessment from his constituency (twice elected and succeeded by a man of his own party); and success in transforming the nation's political landscape and setting it upon a new direction. Reagan's legacy can be illuminated perhaps by considering his presidency in conjunction with that of his vice president and successor, George Herbert Walker Bush. The success and historical standing of the two men offer a study in contrasts.

Reagan assumed the presidency amid dire economic circumstances. The week of his inauguration, *Newsweek* announced from its cover: "The Economy in Crisis." Inside, it declared that the new president was about to "inherit the most dangerous economic crisis since Franklin D. Roosevelt took office." Unemployment was at 7.4 percent. The Gross Domestic Product had declined 1.5 percent the previous year. The prime interest rate stood at a commerce-crunching 21 percent, and inflation, the thief of financial value, exceeded 13 percent. As economist Walter Heller put it, "What the Great Depression was to the 1930s, the Great Inflation is to the 1980s."

Further, the country seemed hapless in the face of Soviet adventurism in Angola, Central America, and Afghanistan. In Iran, fifty-two American hostages had languished in captivity for 444 days. People wondered if the country was losing its edge, and some questioned whether the presidency even worked anymore.

Four years later, when Reagan sought reelection, inflation was under 4 percent. The country had experienced nearly twenty-five straight months of economic growth—"the strongest in thirty-four years," as the president proudly proclaimed—including a campaign-year growth rate in real GDP of 6.2 percent. The economy generated 7.3 million new jobs in two years. As *Time* put it, "Ronald Reagan can now boast of having engineered one of the most stunning economic turnarounds in U.S. history." What's more, Reagan's sunny buoyancy stirred in Americans a new optimism about their country's future. The president was reelected with 58.8 percent of the vote, losing only Minnesota and the District of Columbia in the Electoral College.

At the next election, when Vice President Bush sought the presidency, real GDP growth had averaged nearly 3.4 percent a year during Reagan's second term. Inflation had averaged just over 3 percent. Unemployment was down to 5.5 percent, the lowest level in fourteen years. In foreign affairs the traditionally hawkish Reagan had established a congenial relationship with Soviet leader Gorbachev that had yielded a breakthrough agreement involving nuclear missiles in Europe. Further arms-reduction deals appeared likely, and prospects for harmony between the superpowers looked bright. Despite the enveloping and debilitating Iran-Contra scandal and ongoing budget deficits, voters gave Bush a 53.4 percent victory.

Reagan's standing with voters and his record would seem to assure his place in history. But that is not what we see in many historians' polls. While some recent surveys suggest a warming trend, Reagan remains a polarizing figure. This was manifest in Arthur Schlesinger Jr.'s 1996 poll, which ranked Reagan down the charts at twenty-five. This came from academics who generally disapproved of his priorities, particularly his efforts to shrink government and his across-the-board tax reductions (though he also raised taxes in targeted ways on a number of occasions). The result was relegation to the Low Average circle, along with such relative nonentities as Chester Arthur and Benjamin Harrison. There is also the extensive poll of some 750 historians conducted from 1988 to 1990 by the team of Robert K. Murray and Tim H. Blessing. The results placed Reagan in the Below Average category, between Zachary Taylor and John Tyler.

The Murray-Blessing survey encompassed nineteen pages and 164 questions. Some 18 percent of respondents considered Reagan "a flat failure," while 44 percent ranked him Below Average. Only 1 percent considered him Great, while 20 percent rated him as either Above Average or Near Great.

The authors note that during Reagan's presidency the nation experienced "one of the longest and largest [economic] expansions in American history." And yet only 17 percent of respondents considered Reagan largely responsible for the favorable economic numbers, and 35 percent felt he deserved little credit for them. Regarding Reagan's tax-cut initiatives, a huge majority (89 percent) believed the country's wealthier Americans already were undertaxed when Reagan took office (though the top rate was 70 percent). Fully 66 percent believed the economic advances of Reagan's tenure had little benefit to anyone other than "the top sectors of American society." "In short," write Murray and Blessing, "it appears that the majority of historians do not believe that Reagan can claim credit for the economic advances of the 1980s, and a substantial number would redefine the meaning of the term 'economic advance' as applied to the Reagan years."

The negative sentiments were equally strong on social and cultural issues. When asked about Reagan's desire to have the courts apply a strict construction to the Constitution, only 20 percent approved while 57 percent strongly disapproved. Nearly 90 percent felt that welfare and social programs were underfunded during Reagan's presidency. Murray and Blessing sum up: "Reagan stands accused of racism, sexism, flawed judicial policies, underfunding of social and domestic programs, and creating and ignoring the homeless—a range of accusations to rival those leveled at any other president's domestic program."

In matters of foreign policy, Reagan fared slightly better, with 42 percent considering his summits with Gorbachev as sound and 56 percent saying the president generally handled those negotiations well. Still, a majority dismissed the idea that Reagan's military buildup had any appreciable impact in getting Soviet leaders to move toward those policies.

Reagan got a measure of credit for leadership ability and for improving the national morale, but 92 percent considered him intellectually unqualified for the presidency, and 54 percent considered him unqualified in terms of both intellect and experience.

The authors suggest that "to some extent Reagan's accomplishments were prejudged, that an academic bias against his conservative philosophy and a distaste for what many perceived as Reagan's simplistic approach to issues predetermined the low rating outcome." They add: "Some liberal bias undoubtedly did exist." They posit, however, that it takes about a generation for a president's place in the rankings "to achieve a stable resting place," and Reagan's standing could improve over time.

In suggesting that presidential assessments should take into account the contemporaneous judgment of the electorate, I don't argue that the voters are never wrong. When they are, they generally apply a corrective at the next election. Hence, length of support for a president usually describes length of success (in the voters' judgment) and would point to a presidency that shouldn't be dismissed in historical terms. A better approach would be to examine the pressures and forces at the time of a president's ascendancy to understand why the electorate supported him, often overlooking his limitations and failings in consideration of larger perceptions.

That is the approach adopted by Richard Reeves in his tough-minded but evenhanded book *President Reagan: The Triumph of Imagi-nation,* which sought to look at events during the Reagan presidency through the perspective of the president himself. Reeves dismisses the notion that Reagan was some kind of zombie politician manipulated by his staff. "Amazing things, good and bad, happened in the 1980s," he wrote, "because President Reagan wanted them to happen." True, he often was weak on detail, and his tenure was marked by numerous blunders. But generally he accomplished what he wanted to accomplish by getting the American people on his side. "His personal popularity remained remarkably high in the years after the recession of 1982," Reeves says, "even though a majority of Americans disapproved of what he was doing in driving the country deep into debt, fighting little wars in Central America, secretly selling arms to Iran, or refusing to acknowledge the lethal spread of AIDS across the nation." Indeed, he had the highest approval rating upon leaving office of any president of the second half of the twentieth century (63 percent).

Throughout his political career, Reagan demonstrated a notable perception of how political rhetoric could guide events. This was manifested in a particular political transformation in Reagan's outlook between his failed 1976 nomination fight against President Gerald Ford and his successful 1980 presidential run. In 1976, both Ford and Reagan embraced the party's austerity economics—balanced budgets first and foremost as a sign of fiscal responsibility. When Reagan's economics was joined to his longtime resolve to scale back government, the result was a certain rhetorical shrillness—a relentless attack on "welfare queens" and "the collectivist, centralizing approach" of "Big Brother Government." There wasn't much positive in his rhetoric of that time.

Within the next four years a powerful tax revolt emerged: California's Proposition 13 assault on state property taxes; the rise of New York's Representative Jack Kemp as a high-profile advocate of "supply side" tax cuts; and congressional action, over President Jimmy Carter's ardent objections, to slash capital gains taxes. Alone among the major Republican politicians vying for the 1980 GOP nomination, Reagan tailored his message to these new developments. Political opportunity no doubt played a role. But the new tax message fit neatly into his view that the federal government needed to be trimmed down and rendered less intrusive in Americans' lives. His message became less shrill as he focused on the highly resonant themes of economic growth and entrepreneurial energy.

Reagan also understood a social development that offered political opportunity—the suburbanization of America. With demographic changes, political dominance had shifted from the cities to the suburbs. Urban forces, which had held sway over American politics for a century, favored programs that funneled resources into the cities to combat the great urban ills—poverty, crime, illegitimacy, later AIDS. Those were precisely the problems that stirred suburban Americans to flee the cities. Hence they opposed the old redistributionist programs in favor of limited taxation and government efforts focused on basic services—schools, roads, health care, environmental protection. They wanted sustained economic growth. But they tended to be more liberal than hard-line Republicans on social issues such as abortion and gay rights.

Reagan's campaign message and his later governance were tailored to these suburban sentiments (except on environmental issues). And, although he maintained his base by dispensing red-meat rhetoric on social issues, he did little to translate that rhetoric into actual policies that could prove highly divisive. His message contributed significantly to his ongoing popularity, even as the declining urban forces and their supporters in the media and academia attacked what they considered a heartless and intellectually bankrupt political approach. It turned out that Reagan's perception of the realities of American politics was more penetrating than many people understood at the time.

Did Reagan put forth any kind of vision worthy of the name?

Reeves argues that Reagan was not a man of vision so much as a
man of imagination—"and he believed in the past he imagined." As
I came to see Reagan's vision during my years covering his economic
proposals in Congress, then his reelection campaign, then his White
House, I concluded he looked backward and forward at the same
time. Looking back, he sought to restore the country to the political
framework of Jefferson and Jackson—smaller government; strict interpretation of the Constitution; opposition to consolidation of power
in Washington on the grounds that such power entrenchments always
lead to corruption and intrusions into the private lives of citizens.

Reagan's opponents naturally considered this outlook retrograde,
but in reality his outlook matched the ongoing political tension between the politics of Henry Clay, embraced and leveraged with such
brilliant forcefulness in the twentieth century by Franklin Roosevelt,
and the politics of Andrew Jackson, which Reagan sought to resurrect.
Like Jackson on the issue of land sales or low tariffs or the Bank of
the United States, Reagan sought to move governmental institutions
out of the way so ordinary Americans could push the country forward
through hard work and entrepreneurial enterprise.

But Reagan also looked forward into a dawning era that
Americans were just beginning to perceive—the postindustrial future of high technology. While most of his political adversaries of
both parties—most notably his 1984 Democratic opponent, Walter
Mondale—seemed stuck in the industrial era, Reagan's message reso-
nated with those who understood that economic forces unleashed by
entrepreneurs were moving the country into the high-tech future,
with burgeoning knowledge and service industries.

During the 1984 campaign, one top Mondale staffer declared to
a reporter that the campaign would be "the last great class-struggle
election in America." He was wrong. It was rather the first truly
postindustrial campaign in America. To be sure, Mondale put forth
the traditional class-struggle rhetoric, attacking the opposition party

as having a heart "found on Wall Street" and a soul "found in the country club." But it didn't resonate against Reagan's Jacksonian declaration that "America doesn't need . . . a heavier tax burden. America needs more high tech to modernize heavy industry. We need more take-home pay, more investment, more innovation and more jobs." Reagan's growth themes trumped the class-struggle undercurrents of Mondale's industrial-era politics.

Finally, Reagan possessed the political adroitness to take the country a far distance toward his vision. His administration nearly sputtered in its first two years when the country experienced a deep recession brought on by Federal Reserve Chairman Paul Volcker's effort to squeeze inflation out of the economy. But Reagan stood by Volcker despite heavy political headwinds, and when the Fed policies worked, he was positioned to take credit for the spurt of economic growth that ensued.

In the meantime, Reagan pushed through Congress major legislation on taxes and spending, in all instances corralling significant numbers of Democrats in the Democratic-controlled House—twenty-nine Democratic votes to win his big 1981 budget battle and forty-eight in his House victory on his signature tax-reduction bill the same year. Regarding the later "tax reform" legislation of 1986, which reduced tax rates while eliminating tax preferences and transferred more of the burden to corporations from individuals, Reeves wrote, "And none of this, the most important tax changes since withholding was introduced during World War II, would have happened if Ronald Reagan had not been President."

The other element of Reagan's vision was the defeat of the Soviet Union, a prospect hardly anyone of consequence considered even remotely attainable. He began his presidency as a fierce Cold War hawk and made little effort to engage with his Soviet adversaries. His central aim was a military buildup in both conventional and nuclear weapons systems of such magnitude as to outstrip Soviet production

capacity—and force Kremlin leaders to acknowledge that they could not face down the United States. At one point about a year and a half into his presidency, when he realized he would never get from Congress the governmental curtailments he really wanted, he told an aide, "Screw it. I'm not going to spend any more time trying to get a budget out of this Congress; I am going to continue to build up the Department of Defense, so we can get the Soviets to the table. And we will take the blame for these deficits."

The result, as conceded years later by Soviet leaders, was the 1985 decision by the new Soviet general secretary, Gorbachev, to open up the Soviet system and work seriously toward more normalized relations with the United States. Reagan exploited the opportunity. After establishing cordial relations with Gorbachev, he entered into serious arms-reduction negotiations that yielded the elimination of intermediate-range missiles in Europe and eventually led to serious reductions in strategic missiles on both sides. Still, in spite of his relationship with Gorbachev, Reagan cast aside the counsel of most of his advisers in declaring publicly, at the Berlin Wall in June 1987: "Mr. Gorbachev, tear down this wall!" As Reeves wrote, "The speech was page three as news, but the moment was forever, played again and again and again on television all over the world."

Barely more than two years later the wall came down, and two years after that the Soviet Union dissolved. Gorbachev's regime couldn't withstand the competitive economic forces that had descended upon his country at the instigation of Reagan. Thus, Reagan merits a significant portion of the credit for the Cold War victory. As *The Economist* put it on its cover in 2004, above a photo of Reagan: "The man who beat communism."

Nevertheless, the second Reagan term was beset by major setbacks and a dangerous loss of momentum. The president's obsession with perceived communist inroads in Central America got him crosswise with the American people on his policy initiatives in that region—

and led him to abysmal judgment in the Iran-Contra episode that brought serious scandal to his administration. It involved clandestine arms sales to Iran that had a twofold purpose—to court presumed moderates in the government and to trade for American hostages held by Islamist extremists in Lebanon. The arms-sale proceeds were diverted illegally to the Nicaraguan "Contras" fighting that country's communist government. Reeves's day-by-day narrative of that political drama renders a poignant portrait of a man nearly lost in his own dream world. A president of lesser political standing might have been undone by the dark revelations that tumbled out, but Reagan managed to get through those final months and relinquish the presidency under a rainbow of popularity and appreciation from the majority of Americans.

Did Reagan alter the country's political landscape? Barack Obama thought so, as reflected in a statement he made in January 2008 to the editorial board of the *Reno Gazette:* "I think Ronald Reagan changed the trajectory of America in a way that Richard Nixon did not and in a way that Bill Clinton did not. He put us on a fundamentally different path because the country was ready for it." Reeves points out that both supporters and critics credited Reagan with having "rearranged American politics." Charles O. Jones, onetime president of the American Political Science Association, suggested during the Reagan presidency that the fortieth president and Franklin Roosevelt should be viewed as "the bookend presidents." He explained: "One pushed in the direction of more government, and trying to make the system work. This one is trying to make it work in the sense of less government. They're both radical, but in totally different directions."

Further, the reach of Reaganism extended well into the administration of Bill Clinton, who assumed office in 1993 with a resolve to govern from the left and, as he put it, to "repeal Reaganism." Independent voters turned on him forcefully at the midterm election, giving Republicans control of both houses of Congress for the first time in

four decades. Clinton's liberal agenda was dead in its tracks. It was the greatest political setback suffered by the Democratic Party in nearly fifty years. Clinton promptly tacked to the middle and deftly crafted a series of rolling coalitions that allowed him to govern effectively from the center-left. Abandoning any intent to repeal Reaganism, he announced instead that "the era of big government is over."

This suggests strongly that Reaganism remained the country's prevailing political force well into Clinton's presidency. Having fostered the so-called Reagan Revolution, American voters weren't yet inclined to abandon it.

It is true that Reagan left behind huge deficits; that Iran-Contra had tarnished his record for all time; that he never reduced the federal monolith as much as he intended or promised; that his antimissile defense system never became reality; that he steered the country away from programs designed to help the poor and disadvantaged. "There is . . . no doubt," writes Reeves, "that many Americans paid a high price for President Reagan's certainty." And he wonders about the "opportunity costs"—whether resources assigned to tax reductions and defense could have been better invested in such areas as education or health care.

That in turn raises a corollary question: whether, absent Reagan, a national leader would have emerged to lead the country in that different direction—and whether, in any event, that was where the country wanted to go. That probably is the fundamental question of Reaganism, and no doubt history eventually—on its own timetable—will provide an answer.

The story of Reagan's successor, H. W. Bush, is a sad tale in many ways. He was a good man and certainly well prepared for the job. No problems approaching crisis level occurred during his watch—no ongoing domestic disturbances or deep recessions or foreign debacles or serious scandals. He scored some significant triumphs, including

his Panama incursion to remove the corrupt and menacing Manuel
Noriega from his seat of power there; the Americans with Disabilities Act, which codified certain civil rights for handicapped persons;
and—most notably—his consummate military victory in the first Gulf
War. Further, the Soviet Union collapsed on his watch, and while
Reagan's policies contributed most to that outcome, Bush managed
the transition with measured deftness. Yet the voters turned him out
after a single term. Some historians and commentators have expressed
puzzlement over this. In a 2011 *New York Times* column entitled
"Bring Back Poppy," Thomas L. Friedman extolled the elder Bush's
presidency and lamented the passing of his brand of moderate and
"prudent" conservatism. He called Bush "one of our most underrated
presidents."

And yet if one accepts that the voters aren't fickle, then the 1992
election outcome must have some underlying logic. To explore that
logic we shall begin with a *Washingtonian* magazine piece written by
Ken DeCell in September 1992, just two months before the election
in which Bush was seeking a second term. Using the 13 Keys formula
developed by himself and Robert Lichtman, DeCell predicted that
Bush almost surely would be reelected. The president, said DeCell, appeared "likely to face the electorate with only four keys turned against
him—two short of the number necessary to predict his defeat."

Recall my admonition that such political formulas shouldn't be
applied too strictly or literally. In the case of the Lichtman-DeCell
keys, this is particularly so, given that some of them call for subjective
assessments. Still, they provide a good starting point for assessing the
H. W. Bush presidency. The four keys DeCell saw as turning against
Bush included: the "party mandate" key denoting that the incumbent
party failed to score a net gain of seats in the House of Representatives in the previous two congressional elections; the "long-term
economy" key, meaning real per capita economic growth fell short
of the mean growth during the previous two presidential terms; the

"policy change" key denoting that the president initiated no major changes in national policy; and the "incumbent charisma" key indicating the president lacked the kind of charisma that helps turn elections.

The significance of these keys could be summed up by saying that the GOP was beginning to lose political steam after nearly twelve years in office, that the economy was not growing sufficiently during Bush's term to sustain strong voter support, and that Bush seemed too much the status quo president, too willing to accept things as they were and not sufficiently willing to attack perceived domestic problems. (The charisma key, whatever its significance, wasn't something Bush could do anything about.) But, under this analysis, Bush still enjoyed sufficient standing to ensure his reelection.

What went wrong? For starters, at DeCell's writing, Texas billionaire Ross Perot had abandoned his independent presidential candidacy, but afterward he got back into the race and eventually collected 19 percent of the popular vote. That turned another key against the incumbent. Secondly, DeCell underplayed commentator Patrick J. Buchanan's intraparty challenge against Bush in the 1992 primaries; thus he didn't count against Bush the key focused on whether a serious contest emerges for the incumbent-party nomination. But Buchanan's challenge was serious. He pulled nearly 38 percent of the vote in the New Hampshire primary and went on to collect 2.9 million votes in subsequent contests. This was a stunning political rebuke to a sitting president. History warns that intraparty nomination battles and independent general-election challenges usually deliver powerful blows to incumbent presidents seeking reelection. They are signs of intrinsic political weakness. The question then becomes, what were the underlying gaps in Bush's performance that brought forth the Buchanan surge and Perot's rare level of success as an independent candidate.

First, a successful president needs a vision of the future. Bush not only lacked vision but defiantly refused to consider its importance. He once evinced irritation at me in an interview during his vice presidential years when I sought to get him to talk about how he would like to see the country's future unfold. He deflected the question numerous times as I sought to come at it from different angles, then he said with a tone of exasperation: "I know what you're trying to do here, Bob, and I'm not going to answer that question, so you might as well just move on." It was some time later, during the 1988 campaign, that he publicly dismissed any interest in "the vision thing."

That lack of vision contributed greatly to his one-term fate. He was an "in basket" president who dealt with what came his way but didn't seek to initiate much change. History suggests that dynamic and innovative presidents have a higher chance of reelection—and history's favor—than status quo executives. Bush was a status quo executive.

In addition to his stand-pat temperament, he seemed uninterested in the changed political landscape wrought by his predecessor. In much of what he did, Bush repudiated—consciously or not—the political populism that was the heart of the Reagan legacy.

As we have seen, Reagan's populism animated his presidency and gave it force. It contributed to his success among the so-called Reagan Democrats and younger voters—both crucial elements of his governing coalition. It helped fend off Democratic suggestions that his wealth and hoity-toity friends betokened an inability to understand the concerns and cares of ordinary Americans. It gave him credibility in saying that he spoke for the people.

It rested on two foundations: a faith in the ability of the people to order their economic affairs; and a distrust of institutional elites that controlled important economic matters and other aspects of people's lives. In policy terms this led to his call for cuts in income-tax rates, his push to eliminate special-interest tax breaks through the 1986 "tax reform" measure, his willingness in that 1986 tax bill to favor entrepreneurial businesses over large established corporations, his efforts in behalf of stable currency exchange rates. In rhetorical terms it gave Reagan a powerful message of economic growth and faith in a high-tech future loaded with opportunity.

Bush abandoned much of that. When I was covering the Reagan White House (and by extension the Bush vice presidency), I developed an impression that many Bush people considered Reagan to be essentially a bumbler whose bumbling ways would come to an end when they took over. His ways did come to an end when Bush pushed aside both the policies and the rhetoric of Reagan-style populism. He declined to position himself as a champion of working-class Americans beset by growing difficulties in making ends meet. His only serious growth issue was a call to cut capital gains taxes, an initiative he pushed with intermittent enthusiasm.

This had two serious consequences. First, he became vulnerable to Democratic allegations that he and his party were "elitist," a poisonous accusation in American politics. Second, by abandoning Reagan's growth policies and reneging on his pledge to resist tax increases, he fostered an economic erosion that beset the nation and undermined his standing with voters.

Reagan's critics have made much of his federal budget deficits, for good reason. But a careful look at the record reveals an interesting distinction between his record and Bush's on the deficit—and on the corollary matter of economic growth. Once Reagan got the country through the recession of his early tenure, he accumulated an average annual GDP growth rate of 3.86 percent. Bush's average annual growth rate was below 1 percent, including a negative 1.55 percent in the recession year of 1991. Those numbers, politically debilitating in themselves, also had a significant impact on the budget deficits of both presidents. You can't balance the budget with a stagnant economy.

It is true, of course, that Reagan's policies generated huge budget deficits in his early years—including a stratospheric high of 5.88 percent of GDP in the recession year of 1983. (It's interesting to note that Franklin Roosevelt's 1936 deficit reached nearly 5 percent of GDP. That fact gets lost in the overall success of his presidency.) But Reagan's deficit had been declining steadily as the economy took off in the years leading up to his last budget year of 1989—3.16 percent of GDP in 1987, 3.04 percent in 1988, and a fairly manageable 2.87 percent in 1989. The trend was good. Then under Bush, with the economy sputtering, the deficits rose again—up to 4.58 percent of GDP in his final presidential year of 1992. During that year also, unemployment rose to 7.4 percent, up from 5.3 percent in 1989. History suggests that, in political terms, the actual unemployment level is less important than whether it is rising or falling. For Bush this metric was moving in the wrong direction at election time.

I believe Bush's repudiation of Reagan-style populism and his failures on economic policy spawned Buchanan's nettlesome nomination challenge in 1992 and Ross Perot's independent-party incursion in the general election. Those in turn sealed Bush's fate as a one-term president.

Yet Bush's accomplishments merit acknowledgment. His passion was foreign policy, and he assumed office with stirring words that seemed to presage the fall of the Soviet Union and the end of the Cold War—developments that were to unfold during his presidency. "The totalitarian era is passing," he said in his inaugural speech, "its old ideas blown away like leaves from an ancient, lifeless tree." He foresaw "a world refreshed by freedom . . . for in man's heart, if not in fact, the day of the dictator is over."

The day of Panamanian dictator Noriega came to an end within Bush's first year as president, when he sent a force into that country to oust the strongman drug lord whose actions had threatened the safety of Americans there as well as U.S. interests in preserving access to the Panama Canal, set to be transferred to Panamanian control in a few years. It was a bold and clean military action. And his Gulf War initiative of 1991, described in Chapter 7, represented a tremendous presidential triumph, rendered all the more impressive for his refusal to conquer Iraq and get his country embroiled in the sectarian and ethnic strife that had beset that country for decades. The national exhilaration spawned by that victory buoyed Bush's approval rating to above 90 percent, a stunning level of support far outstripping anything seen in the history of presidential polling.

But in the end Bush's stand-pat temperament and middling economic performance brought him back to earth, and soon his poll numbers suggested he had entered a political danger zone. Historians have rendered an early verdict that seems consonant with the electorate's—twenty-fourth in Schlesinger Jr.'s 1996 survey and twenty-first in the *Wall Street Journal*'s 2005 poll. Those rankings might hold into the future, but they also could slip. They aren't likely to rise, because the George H. W. Bush record isn't one to stir the juices of history.

11

THE POST–COLD WAR
PRESIDENTS

In surveying the White House performances of the last three presidents, it's best to keep in mind Clinton Rossiter's judgment on Dwight Eisenhower when the thirty-fourth president was still in office—that he stayed too long, thought too small, and did too little. History, as we have seen, ultimately brushed aside that critique on its way to elevating Ike, in the last two surveys, to eighth and tenth on the list. History can't be rushed or manipulated. As Princeton's Sean Wilentz wrote during the George W. Bush presidency, in predicting a lowly historical ranking for the younger Bush, "No historian can responsibly predict the future with absolute certainty."

But we do have the electorate's contemporaneous judgment—the other serious index for gauging presidential performance. That can tell us something not only about the success level of a president but also about what history may ultimately conclude. And, after all, this *is* a rating game, and the rules of any game can be changed from time to time. We don't necessarily have to wait for history before engaging in the beguiling exercise of predicting its likely appraisal.

It is in that spirit that we now turn to the last three presidents—whose times in office were too recent for history to have rendered a serious judgment but whose activities in office are etched vividly in our consciousness. Having dealt with Reagan and George H. W. Bush in this way, I now turn to the post–Cold War presidents—Bill Clinton, George W. Bush, and Barack Obama.

Bill Clinton: When William Jefferson Clinton took office in January 1993, U.S. unemployment stood at 7.4 percent (one of the economic metrics that contributed to his victory over George H. W. Bush in the 1992 presidential referendum). Throughout his subsequent stewardship that metric declined, year by year, to 7.2 percent, 6.6 percent, 5.5 percent, 5.5 percent, 5.2 percent, 4.6 percent, 4.3 percent, and finally 4 percent in his last year in office, 2000. This is a remarkable statistical string—a steadily declining unemployment rate, with not even a slight year-to-year uptick throughout two presidential terms. It captures a central reality of Clinton's presidency: He presided over relatively good times and managed the country well.

Officially, Clinton was a split-decision president—reelected but unable to foster the election of a Democratic successor. But the voters gave his vice president, Al Gore, a narrow popular-vote victory in 2000, and the crossover of just a few Florida ballots that year would have handed Gore an Electoral College victory and placed Clinton in that definitional circle of electoral success—two terms and succeeded by his own party. Notwithstanding Gore's fate, Clinton must be classified as a largely successful president whose first term reflected a remarkable talent for political dexterity and whose second term, while solid, slipped just enough to open the way for a Republican succession.

BILL CLINTON

Not a great president but a good one, Clinton presided over robust times and proved adept at commingling his party's fundamental outlook with the country's mood. He lacked personal control, which led to a smarmy scandal, and he was unwilling to expend political capital in behalf of bold policymaking.

One of his political assets was his inherent likability. Even many of his opponents found it difficult to dislike the man, with his undisciplined earnestness and roguish charm. Amid the storied chaos of West Wing operations, the apparent self-indulgence, and the intermittent whiff of scandal, the president maintained political momentum, propelled by his manifest brilliance, his famous mastery of the details of governance, and the genuine anguish he displayed over the hurts and wants of fellow citizens. That likability quotient served him well when he came under a furious GOP attack in his second term, following revelations of his dalliance with Monica Lewinsky.

We have seen in the preceding chapter how Clinton sought initially to govern from the left—to "repeal Reaganism," as he put it. And it was noted that, following the Democratic debacle in the

1994 midterm congressional elections, Clinton deftly moved to the center. It is also noteworthy that he assumed the presidency with just a 43 percent mandate—reflecting his popular vote share in an election in which independent candidate Ross Perot collected 19 percent of the popular balloting. Hence, Clinton lacked a mandate for bold initiatives such as his big health-care effort. Presidents in that position must choose their battles carefully, investing political capital wisely in relatively small, low-risk initiatives. Then, as political capital accumulates with these multiple small victories, the minority president is positioned to make bigger investments, with bigger returns that then point to reelection. That's what Richard Nixon did effectively after his own 43 percent victory in 1968. And it's what Clinton finally did in the second half of his first term.

But he started out with an apparent resolve to tack left at a time when the country was not prepared to accept such an abrupt departure from the Reagan legacy. Although his first significant achievement fit into this overall commitment to activist government, it wasn't of such magnitude to stir serious political agitation. That was his signing, barely two weeks into his tenure, of the Family and Medical Leave Act of 1993, requiring employers to grant leaves of absence to employees who were seriously ill, had newborn or newly adopted children, or had to care for sick relatives. As journalist Ronald D. Elving wrote, "Just sixteen days after taking his oath of office, Clinton could claim to have enacted a significant change in social policy in keeping with the 'People First' theme of his campaign." He also scored a signal triumph—and revealed his free-market sensibility—with his North American Free Trade Agreement, securing open trade with Canada and Mexico.

But other initiatives did stir significant voter agitation. He introduced the high-voltage issue of gays in the military at a time when the country was not ready for such a policy approach. He installed as surgeon general a social-issue liberal with a passion for provocative statements that left many Americans outraged. Most significantly, he brought forth a huge health-care initiative that would have greatly increased federal intrusion into a large segment of the economy.

When the health-care initiative stalled in Congress, it proved a political embarrassment for the president. But it also became a turning point for his presidency. Shortly thereafter the voters handed him a major defeat by awarding both houses of Congress to the opposition Republicans. Clinton responded by fashioning a brilliant new political paradigm calculated to propel him through the thickets of divided government.

He expropriated carefully chosen Republican issues and gave his party a deftly calibrated center-left cast. The starkest example was his decision to sign the big welfare overhaul bill of 1996. No Democratic president since the Great Depression would have considered such an action. Also, some journalists noted at the time that many executive agencies seemed to be shifting their policies toward the right in a host of administrative decisions designed to blunt the force of the Republican Congress. But he also dealt a devastating blow to the Republican opposition over appropriations, when GOP stubbornness led to a governmental shutdown. That victory swelled his store of political capital.

To all of this we must add Clinton's notable success in the realm of economic policy—a "misery index" (unemployment and inflation rates added together) that was the lowest in nearly three decades; a robust 4.2 percent increase in GDP during the second quarter of Clinton's reelection year; a 1996 deficit of just 1.37 percent of GDP. All this contributed to his solid reelection in 1996, with 49.2 percent of the popular vote to 40.7 percent for Republican Bob Dole (and 8.4 percent for Ross Perot in his second independent presidential bid). This sprightly economic performance continued into Clinton's second term as high-tech developments produced significant productivity gains. Real per capita GDP growth through Clinton's second term averaged 3.25 percent (though the economy began to sputter a bit at the end of his presidency). With the economy growing and unemployment dropping, the persistent deficits of the Reagan-Bush years (and before) turned into consistent surpluses stretching from 1998 to 2001.

From 1995 onward, Clinton governed with an apparent appreciation for the fact that the country had seen no successful liberal president since voter sentiment forced Lyndon Johnson into retirement in 1968. Probably the greatest reason for this is that, unlike most European countries, the United States has never had a rigid class system. In Europe, class barriers and class sensibilities have nurtured a sizable voter segment that is strongly leftist, largely socialist, and sometimes quite angry. Though a minority, this segment exercises a strong pull on politics at all times and, in certain circumstances, can tip the balance of political power.

But in America's fluid system, most people at the base areas of the economic mountain maintain aspirations of climbing to higher elevations, and the class impulse thus has never spawned a permanently significant repository of socialist or even leftist sentiment. Of course, in times of severe economic travail, leftism can flourish, as it did during the Great Depression when Roosevelt railed against "the purblind rich," declaring defiantly that these people hated him—"and I welcome their hatred." With so many Americans feeling trapped economically, it worked (though it probably retarded the economic expansion by introducing uncertainty into business decision-making). And the recent Occupy Wall Street movement shows that harsh times often summon leftist sentiment within the populace.

But class conflict politics hasn't worked in recent U.S. history. Class warfare sentiments don't resonate sufficiently with the American people to form the core of a successful governing philosophy. And the country didn't hear much of that kind of rhetoric from Clinton during his presidency and certainly not during his reelection campaign in 1996.

All of this poses a question: Why didn't the voters respond to this solid record by giving the Democrats a sizable Electoral College victory in 2000? I see two likely reasons. First, there was the Monica Lewinsky scandal. Whatever one thinks about the impeachment of Clinton and the Senate effort to remove him from office (politically, they were monumentally stupid), the fact remained that such sordid revelations have an impact on significant portions of the electorate. And they probably should. One needn't be an off-putting moralist to believe that presidents should not debauch their office and lie about it under oath in the manner of Clinton, with his artful philosophical musings over the meaning of the word "is." The American people seemed perfectly willing to accept their president as a charming and politically effective rogue, but this represented more of a blot than some citizens were comfortable with.

Second, after building up his political capital with great political acumen through the last two years of his first term, Clinton, once reelected, seemed reluctant to invest this capital in anything very big or risky. It was as if his presidential ambition consisted mostly in his desire to be president. Even if, as I have argued, the American people weren't looking for a profound change in the political landscape, there were still opportunities for him to push major initiatives that could have left a significant mark upon history. There was the looming entitlement crisis that threatened to engulf the U.S. economy within a decade or so. There was the problem of al Qaeda, ensconced in its Afghan haven and posing an ongoing terrorist threat to American citizens and the country's interests. There was health care, botched in the first effort but perhaps susceptible now, with more political capital in the bank, to a new, bipartisan approach.

The Clinton tenure was marked not by large initiatives but by numerous smaller ones. He fostered and signed the Brady bill, which imposed a five-day waiting period for the purchase of handguns. He expanded the Earned Income Tax Credit, which provided subsidies for low-income workers. Banking was deregulated to a significant degree with repeal of the Depression-era Glass-Steagall Act. Taxes were raised on the wealthiest Americans but reduced for low-income workers and small businesses. Following the Republican takeover of Congress after the 1994 elections, the president accepted measures designed to curtail growth in federal spending.

In foreign affairs, Clinton served as peacemaker in fostering the so-called Dayton Accords, which largely ended bloody sectarian fighting in the war-torn Balkans. Later he successfully pushed for extensive NATO airstrikes against Serbia to force an end to Serbian dominance over the Albanian population in Serbia's Kosovo region.

The watchword for Clinton's second term was caution. In an "Editor's Note" to John Seigenthaler's brief biography of James Polk, Arthur Schlesinger Jr. posits that national crises have demonstrated sharp distinctions between presidents of mediocrity and of greatness—between Buchanan and Lincoln, for example, or Hoover and Franklin Roosevelt. He adds: "Still, even in the absence of first-order crisis, forceful and persuasive presidents—Jefferson, Jackson, James K. Polk, Theodore Roosevelt, Ronald Reagan—are able to impose their own priorities on the country." Clinton did not seek to impose his priorities on the country in any meaningful way. He managed the country and managed it well. For that he earned and received the appreciation of his fellow citizens, but it wasn't quite enough for party retention.

In Schlesinger Jr.'s 1996 survey, Clinton ranks twentieth; in the *Wall Street Journal*'s 2005 poll, twenty-second. Based on voter sentiment in Clinton's own time and his solid if uninspiring performance, it seems reasonable to expect that those rankings will rise over time. Some presidents now ranked above him likely will slip below. These could include H. W. Bush, Hayes, Taft, Van Buren, Lyndon Johnson, Monroe, and Cleveland. If there is justice (though in this instance there probably isn't), that list also might include Woodrow Wilson. In any event, it doesn't seem fanciful to suggest he could rise five or even six notches above his *Journal* ranking.

Whatever history has in store for Clinton, he seems resigned to the outcome, knowing that his contemporaries appreciated his personal charm, his manifest compassion, his solid stewardship, and his facile brilliance. As he said after leaving office, "I may not have been the greatest president, but I've had the most fun eight years."

George W. Bush: In 2003, President Bush, then two years into his tenure, was asked by journalist Bob Woodward about his place in history. "History," he replied. "We don't know. We'll all be dead." This is a remarkable statement from any president, suggesting a blithe attitude toward the job's magnitude and responsibility to posterity. Compare this insouciance, as historian Sean Wilentz did in a searing *Rolling Stone* piece on the younger Bush, with another president's observation on the subject. "Fellow citizens," said Lincoln, "we cannot escape history. We of this Congress and this administration, will be remembered in spite of ourselves. No personal significance, or insignificance, can spare one or another of us. The fiery trial through which we pass, will light us down, in honor or dishonor, to the latest generation."

Wilentz's *Rolling Stone* piece, appearing in the spring of 2006, with Bush still in office, posed a question: Was this president the worst ever? The Bush presidency, wrote Wilentz, appeared "headed for colossal historical disgrace," and there didn't seem to be anything Bush could do to forestall that fate. He added, "And that may be the best-case scenario. Many historians are now wondering whether Bush, in fact, will be remembered as the very worst president in all of American history."

In the 5,500-word analysis that followed, Wilentz presented a solid case, although some of his arguments and expressions sounded

GEORGE W. BUSH

Impulsive and full of bonhomie, the second Bush is likely to generate controversy through history. Historian Sean Wilentz thinks he may be the worst president of all, and his decision to invade Iraq will likely tar his reputation forever. After a moderate first-term success, he logged a second-term failure.

more like they emanated from the Democratic side of the U.S. House floor than from a dispassionate historical examination. Like his good friend Arthur Schlesinger Jr., Wilentz has nurtured a career combining rigorous scholarly pursuits with occasional vectors of partisan advocacy for Democratic causes. But the question deserves attention, and Wilentz poses it with verve and pungency.

Bush began his presidency with a burden—his 2000 victory emerged in the country's most hotly contested election since 1876, with the final outcome determined by a 5-to-4 Supreme Court decision. This naturally generated some lingering political animosity in the country. It can be argued that in the early months of his administration Bush worked effectively to establish the legitimacy of his presidency. But even early on it sometimes seemed that Bush con-

fronted weighty presidential decisions with the same blithe attitude
that characterized his answer about history's judgment. He often
appeared to have his eye fixed more on immediate outcomes than on
long-term consequence. In taking his country to war in Iraq, he failed
to meet the two fundamental tests of presidential war-making. One
was the Polk lesson: Ensure that no one can ever make an accusation
that the president dissembled with the American people in order to
get permission to spill American blood. The other was the Lyndon
Johnson or Harry Truman lesson: Ensure that the country doesn't get
bogged down in a war it can't win and can't end. Avoiding these
ominous pitfalls would have required a sober and solemn assessment
of all the risks and dangers of the enterprise, both military and political. There is little evidence that Bush conducted such an assessment
before his war decision.

In building an intellectual foundation for his war, Bush crafted a
rationale of necessity and a rationale of success. The former encompassed the reason why America needed to invade Iraq, and that reason
was twofold and interconnected: weapons of mass destruction and the
Iraqi government's flirtation with Islamic terrorists. The two together,
according to the Bush reasoning, constituted a major national and
global threat that required immediate action. It turned out, however,
that the weapons of mass destruction didn't exist, and the connection
with terrorists couldn't be established. Hence, the rationale of necessity collapsed after the invasion, and Bush was diminished in much of
public opinion for having crafted a rationale for war that was either
disingenuous or carelessly flimsy (I believe the latter).

The rationale of success is more complex. When presidents take
the country to war, they must present a depiction of victory—how
U.S. forces will meet the military challenge, how they will subdue the
enemy, how they will maintain control over the situation throughout
hostilities and afterward, how the president will avoid the kind of

geopolitical trap that ensnared Truman in Korea and Lyndon Johnson in Vietnam. To fashion his rationale of success, Bush reached back to the gauzy notions of Woodrow Wilson. As Wilson had sought to make the world safe for democracy, Bush would make Iraq hospitable to Western democratic institutions, and the resulting stability would ensure the success of the military enterprise—and serve as regional example and beachhead for similar Wilsonian initiatives throughout the Middle East.

This was—there is no kinder word for it—delusional. It rested on the idea that America could foster world peace by spreading throughout the world its democratic ideals, viewed widely in the West as universal. But they aren't universal. Particularly in the Middle East, many people consider American values to be an assault on their own cherished cultural sensibilities. And America's political and economic models are losing force in the consciousness of other peoples around the world. China, for example, competes with America not just economically and increasingly in the military sphere, but also in its view of the best approach to government. The China model is stirring interest and enthusiasm around the globe. As Stefan Halper of the University of Cambridge in England writes, "Given a choice between market democracy and its freedoms and market authoritarianism and its high growth, stability, improved living standards, and limits on expression—a majority in the developing world and in many middle-sized, non-Western powers prefer the authoritarian model."

Hence the Bush war policy was based upon an idle fancy, and the war's outcome bore little resemblance to what was advertised. There was no widespread welcoming of American military "liberators," as administration officials had predicted. There was no blossoming of peaceful democratic practices. There was no beachhead for further Wilsonian pursuits in the region. Instead, the American incursion detonated a wave of sectarian killing—and growing casualty rates for Americans as the U.S. military found itself trying to subdue the violence. The later Bush "surge" of additional troops didn't constitute a military success, as is sometimes argued, but rather amounted to a negotiated peace with the country's minority Sunnis, who had been devastated by the majority Shiite factions and needed American protection.

U.S. casualty rates declined thereafter, however, which helped diminish domestic opposition to the war. Still, the president's standing took a hit based on the collapse of both the rationale of necessity and the rationale of success, the chaos unleashed in Iraq by the American invasion, the strains placed on the American military, and the lingering military presence there without a clear sense of a worthy outcome.

Remember, though, that the American people judge their presidents largely in four-year increments, and by the time Bush faced the voters for reelection in 2004, not all of these negative factors had come fully into focus. What's more, the national economy was percolating nicely. Hence, there was no particular reason to turn Bush out of office, although the electorate wasn't about to give him much of a mandate. He collected only 51 percent of the popular vote and took the Electoral College contest by a mere thirty-five ballots.

On the economy, many Bush critics like to point out that real GDP growth averaged only about 2.1 percent a year during his eight years. True. But that misses the significance of referendum politics in presidential elections. Bush took office with a mild Clinton recession in progress, and hence his 2001 GDP growth rate was dismal (though he wasn't blameworthy)—just over 1 percent (which brings down his average percentage). But the economy picked up nicely in the next three years, with GDP expanding by a respectable 3.47 percent in the reelection year. That certainly helped propel him to his November triumph. We have since seen a hearty partisan debate over the impact of Bush's early tax-cut initiatives in helping to foster this growth. Democrats, including Wilentz in his *Rolling Stone* article, argue vehemently that there was no connection, while Republicans have insisted the link is clear. My own view is that, with the waning of the powerful productivity wave that helped fuel Clinton's growth performance, a tax stimulus was probably needed. But we needn't adjudicate that argument here because, in any event, the president always gets credit or blame for what happens on his watch. And Bush's first-term economic performance merited the appreciation it got from the voters.

It was during the second term that things fell apart. The folly of the Iraq war became increasingly clear, and Bush's credibility plummeted. The war sapped federal resources and threw the nation's budget into deficit. The president made no effort to inject any fiscal austerity into governmental operations, eschewing his primary weapon of budgetary discipline, the veto pen. His first budget director, Mitch Daniels (later Indiana governor), strongly urged a transfer of federal resources from domestic programs to the so-called War on Terror, much as Franklin Roosevelt directed such a transfer when he led the country into World War II. Bush rejected that counsel and allowed federal spending to flip out of control. The national debt, which was being steadily paid down under Clinton, shot back to ominous proportions. Meanwhile, economic growth rates began a steady decline, culminating in a negative growth rate in the 2008 campaign year.

Contributing to Bush's problems was a personality trait that hindered his ability to work with others in the political arena, particularly the opposition Democrats. He brought to his presidency a high level of sanctimony—an apparent conviction that he operated on a higher plane of rectitude than other politicians. Sanctimony, as noted earlier, is not a trait that contributes to smooth effectiveness in the political game, and sanctimonious presidents—Quincy Adams,

Polk, Wilson, Carter, and the second Bush—almost inevitably have found themselves isolated and beleaguered. All brought upon themselves unnecessary difficulties traceable to their self-righteous temperaments.

In Bush's case it was seen in his refusal to acknowledge any major mistakes, which made it difficult for him to change course when inevitable setbacks demanded flexibility. This rigidity not only kept him clinging to failed policies but also created the spectacle of the president issuing what conservative commentator William F. Buckley Jr. called "high-flown pronouncements" about plans and programs seen widely by others as hopeless. Worse, Bush's tendency toward sanctimony militated against the kind of compromises needed to lubricate the gears of government. Listening to naysayers helps politicians understand the forces swirling through the nation, but Bush demonstrated little interest in doing so. He tuned out the naysayers, whether from the other party or his own inner circle. "No other president," writes Wilentz, ".... faced with such a monumental set of military and political circumstances failed to embrace the opposing political party to help wage a truly national struggle."

It wasn't surprising, based on all this, that Bush's standing with the American people plummeted through his second term, that his approval rating in the Gallup Poll would drop to the lowest level of that of any president in thirty-five years, and that his party would be expelled from the White House at the next election. The key was the independent vote, which Bush split with his Democratic opponent, John Kerry of Massachusetts, in 2004, but which turned away from the Republicans four years later.

Does this mean Wilentz is correct, and history will relegate Bush to the very bottom of the presidential heap, lower even than Harding and Buchanan? Impossible to know. But, based on the contemporaneous voter assessments, the objective record, and what we know of history, it's difficult to see him even in middle-ground territory. History likely will view Bush largely as the voters did after eight years of his stewardship. And so it's probably just as well that he doesn't care much about the verdict of history.

Barack Obama: One thing we know about Obama: He really does not want to be a one-term president—however contented he may feel, in his most secure moments, with the accomplishments of his initial term. Despite whatever sincerity lay behind his expression to Diane Sawyer, it was inevitable that human nature eventually would prevail. No president allows himself to think the country would be better off without him at the helm. And no president wants the political and personal ignominy of a reelection defeat.

That is why we have seen Obama try to scramble back from the political territory he occupied at the time of the 2010 midterm elections, when the voters devastated his political standing with that "shellacking," as he put it. After the Republicans' House takeover, various commentators wondered whether the president would respond by adopting the so-called Truman model (defiant and pugnacious toward the GOP opposition) or the Clinton model (centrist, seeking to co-opt selected Republican issues). Initially, he opted for a kind of blended approach—taking on the opposition in sometimes stark language on some issues while avoiding direct confrontations when possible. More recently, though, Obama has embraced thoroughly the Truman pattern, reflected in his persistent attacks on opposition Republicans in Congress for their refusal to support his proposals to generate jobs in the American economy.

Implicit in that strategy was an apparent recognition that a one-term president tossed aside by the voters is unlikely to be tagged by history as a "really good president." Indeed, if he fails to win reelection, he will reside on the charts of history with such recent one-termers as Carter and H. W. Bush. And his first two years in office, marked by audacious leadership in pursuit of a liberal resurgence, will be viewed by historians as one of the great political miscalculations of our time. On the other hand, if he wins reelection, it will be because the American people concluded that they had redirected this president toward a more measured form of blended politics, in the vein of Bill Clinton after his own political drubbing in 1994.

A bigger question is whether this Truman strategy can work. As we have seen, Truman's attacks on the "Do Nothing Congress" probably didn't contribute much to his 1948 election, which turned more on his actual accomplishments in foreign policy and in moving the country successfully from a wartime economy to a peacetime economy. Similarly, Obama's fate will hinge on real-world factors affecting the lives of Americans and their country's standing in the world.

I should stipulate here that we really can't do justice to any effort to predict Obama's standing in history. Even as this is written, too much of his presidential story is yet to unfold, and too many questions about the man and his political instincts remain unanswered. Hence no such predictive effort will be seen here. What we can do is analyze his first three years in office with an eye toward assessing what they say about the president and the times in which he operated. That period was unquestionably a pivotal time in America, irrespective of Obama's ultimate political fate.

His early performance seemed to emanate from both his policies and his temperament. Obama took office in the midst of one of the country's greatest economic crises—the GDP in contraction, credit frozen, banks and other major corporations facing bankruptcy, business confidence shattered, consumers skittish. The prospect of a broad economic meltdown was real. The crisis demanded bold action, and Obama was a bold leader.

He pushed for a $787 billion stimulus program, mortgage assistance legislation, bailouts for large banks and other major corporations, and greater regulation of the financial industry. Whatever one may think about these initiatives (and they certainly generated controversy), they addressed the country's most ominous problems, and it can be argued that some of them likely helped stave off a possible economic cataclysm. But his early agenda went far beyond the economic crisis, to include other initiatives unrelated to it—the megalithic health-care overhaul, for example, and the "cap and trade" energy legislation. And his effort to address the housing bubble of personal debt led to a massive increase in the country's sovereign debt, with potentially ominous consequences in the future.

Added together, Obama's policies and programs amounted to the greatest drive for federal power consolidation since Lyndon Johnson's Great Society. His White House chief of staff, Rahm Emanuel, revealed the plan when he told the *Wall Street Journal*, "You never want a serious crisis to go to waste." That signaled a presidential ambition to leverage the economic emergency to reshape the American political landscape in the image of the country's frustrated liberalism. It also signaled a blithe attitude toward the public fisc, weighted down by a national debt projected to grow from $10.6 trillion on inauguration day to $16.2 trillion in 2012.

Obama, who likes to use the word "audacity," clearly saw himself as a presidential Man of Destiny. But history tells us that, while America's Leaders of Destiny always kicked up intense opposition, they also managed to build broad new reservoirs of support that mixed up the old flows of partisanship, demographics, and ideology. From Jefferson to Reagan, they all left behind new political coalitions based on new political alignments. Obama's bold governance didn't bring such new voters into his fold; instead, it stirred significant numbers of his election-day supporters to abandon him, at least for a time. Rather than uniting his party and dividing the opposition—a hallmark of any realignment president—he did the opposite, uniting the GOP and splitting his own ranks.

On the stimulus package, Obama probably should have insisted that the job of crafting it fall under his own auspices, with solid input from both parties. Instead, he turned the effort over to House Democrats, who predictably loaded the legislation up with pet programs long languishing in a legislative netherworld due to a lack of public support. Many had little or no stimulative effect. A more active leadership approach not only would have meant a greater focus on provisions to boost the economy but also would have helped redeem the president's campaign pledge to foster a new era of collaborative politics in Washington. His approach instead signaled that he harbored no serious intention to seek real change in the capital's political tone.

Obama's energy bill, which passed the House but died in the Senate, drove a wedge through his party. Some Democratic representatives who voted for it, particularly those who represented more conservative districts, found themselves vulnerable at election time to arguments that their votes could have harmed the economy when the country's economic health was its most pressing issue.

Finally, the president's demand that Congress pass his health-care overhaul in the face of widespread and intense voter opposition represents a level of political bravado rarely seen even in today's highly charged political environment. Never in memory has legislation of such magnitude been pushed through Congress without a broad coalition of support cutting across party lines—and never with reliance on parliamentary maneuvers that in previous times would have been considered unthinkable. The manner of its passage and the public reaction calls to mind the political firestorm that greeted enactment of the 1854 Kansas-Nebraska Act.

Thus do we see that much of Obama's policy formula simply wasn't in line with voter desires and sentiments. Perhaps, had his programs spurred a solid economic expansion and brought unemployment down to levels predicted by his economic advisers, the electorate eventually would have bought in to the grand Obama vision. Perhaps he then would have succeeded in his plan to transform the American political landscape and usher in a new era of political liberalism and governmental expansion. It does seem clear, after all, that the country is poised for a significant new direction within the foreseeable future. But what-ifs don't drive politics—or history.

Beyond policy, it appeared that some voters reacted also to elements of the president's political identity. He came across to some as something of an elitist, all too quick to blame his political woes on the people rather than himself. During the 2010 campaign, he sometimes dropped hints that he wasn't sure the voters saw the choices before them with much perceptiveness. "Part of the reason that our politics seems so tough right now, and facts and science and argument does not seem to be winning the day all the time," he told a group of citizens near Boston, "is because we're hard-wired not to always think clearly when we're scared. And the country is scared." This and similar comments left him open to allegations that he lacked the one crucial ingredient of electoral success—a faith and trust in the good sense of the electorate.

That's related to an element of his identity explored by writer Shelby Steele of Stanford's Hoover Institution in the *Wall Street Journal* during the 2010 campaign. Steele dismisses those who suggest Obama is somehow not truly *of* America but rather guided by outside influences—the African part of his heritage, perhaps, or his father's Islamic faith. No, says Steele, Obama is very much an American product, but a product of the 1960s counterculture, which forced the country to face up to many of the "flagrant hypocrisies" of its history, such as racism, imperialism, suppression of women, and puritanical sexual mores. But in doing that, the counterculture embraced a view of the country that Steele calls "bad faith in America"—a feeling that the country remains tainted by its past and needs redemption.

"Among today's liberal elite," writes Steele, "bad faith in America is a sophistication, a kind of hipness." And Obama's "great ingenuity" was his ability to generate political motivation—votes—from that sentiment and its corollary conviction that it represents an intervention against evil. The underlying problem here is that this approach forecloses the celebration of American greatness as a rationale for power. "It puts Mr. Obama and the Democrats in the position of forever redeeming a fallen nation, rather than leading a great nation." Whatever merit there is in the Steele perception, it seems that Obama became weighted down politically by perceptions that he really didn't understand, and perhaps didn't appreciate, the electorate—or, as Steele puts it, that he "seems not to trust the fundamental decency of the American people."

In political terms, it is difficult to view Obama's performance during his first three presidential years as a success. A Harris poll just before the 2010 elections placed his approval rating at a feeble 37 percent. The Democrats' loss of sixty-three House seats and six in the Senate represented an unquestionable voter repudiation of Obama's leadership. Election-day exit polls showed that fully 62 percent of respondents believed the country was on the wrong track. (A year later that ominous metric would hit 77 percent.) The independent vote split 56 percent for Republican House candidates against just 37 percent for Democrats. Two years earlier, Obama garnered 52 percent of this crucial vote versus 44 percent for his opponent, Senator John McCain of Arizona.

As the 2011 summer faded into autumn, President Obama and the country he led seemed to be in a beleaguered state. Unemployment continued above 9 percent. Economic growth had slowed to negligible levels, threatening to fall into negative territory. The stock market went jittery. The debt ceiling imbroglio exposed a looming financial crisis of frightening proportions. All this placed immense pressure on the president, whose job was to lead the country out of these interlocking difficulties. As the campaign year began, improvements could be seen in many of these areas. But it seemed fair to say the president flubbed his midterm exam and was severely admonished by his instructor. It remained an open question whether he would get passing marks on the final.

If history has yet to make definitive judgments on these most recent presidents, we do know the electorate's assessments (in Obama's case, a preliminary midterm assessment). And, since they are the presidents who linger most vividly in our memory, they present an illustration of how voter judgments operate on the office. It isn't capricious or random. Rather, a collective logic seems to emerge as the voters survey the scene and render their intermittent judgments. Looking at it carefully, we can see clear connections between presidential performance and voter response—between Clinton's initial two-year performance and the electoral rebuke he received in 1994; between Clinton's subsequent solid stewardship and his 1996 electoral reward; between George W. Bush's first-term performance and his thin re-election margin; between Bush's second-term failures and the firm rejection of his party at the next election. We can see also the nexus between Obama's early performance and the rebuff administered to his party in 2010.

It's difficult for many to see these connections as logical and reassuring because we are too invested in one party or the other. Hence when election results are adverse, many people cling to notions of voter ignorance or unfair campaign practices or elections being bought—just about anything to avoid recognition that they were simply on the wrong side while the voters actually had it right. Of course, history ultimately will sort it out, but history doesn't seem to be on the mark all the time. When it isn't, you can usually see a gap between history's assessment and what the voters were saying at the time. And when we remove ourselves from our partisan passions and look at the most recent presidents objectively, it becomes clear that, when history and the contemporaneous electorate are at odds, it's time to study the actions and expressions of the electorate. That's where the greater wisdom usually resides.

Conclusion

CLEAR AND PRESENT DANGER

At the end of one of his less satisfying days as president, Harry Truman gazed into his bourbon glass and growled to his friends, "They talk about the power of the presidency, how I can just push a button and get things done. Why, I spend most of my time kissing somebody's ass."

The president's plaint may not seem like a profound insight of political science. Yet it encapsulates the delicate interrelationships of power embedded in the American system by the Founders. The president enjoys vast powers that can be exercised, however, only by surmounting extensive constrictions. He (or she) may be the only politician who can claim to speak for all Americans—but must nevertheless deal with 535 others who speak persistently for smaller constituencies. If he doesn't bring to the office large doses of guile, persistence, deviousness, and will—in addition to all the other elements of effective leadership—he almost surely will fail.

This raises a question of whether the presidential office is so loaded down with encumbrances that it can't be sufficiently leveraged to forestall or deal with national crises. This is a pertinent question for our time because the country today faces such a crisis—or, put more accurately, a number of intertwined crises. There is the persistent dynamic of Islamic fundamentalism in the Middle East, focused on America as an enemy to be brought low through terrorist murder and societal disruption. There is the lingering economic stagnation that thwarts business investment and employment opportunity as income disparities widen in the country. There is the growing evidence that America's position in the world is facing progressive erosion, which in turn breeds looming geopolitical challenges. Most ominously, there is the country's precarious financial position stemming from governmental spending commitments (state, local, and federal) that threaten to engulf the national economy. Finally, there is the widespread loss of national confidence engendered by these other persistent or looming emergencies.

It seems reasonable to ask not just whether the presidency is sufficiently powerful to handle these intertwined crises but also why the American people and their president lacked the understanding and will to head them off in the first place. Indeed, as I was writing much of this book, particularly the passages extolling the electorate's collective judgment, I wondered if some readers might be saying, "Wait a minute! If the system works as well as this guy seems to think, why are we in such a mess?"

A fair point. But history reveals that the task of governing any nation is messy at best, that all nations inevitably stumble into crises, that tidy long-view wisdom most often gets clipped by short-term political concerns and whims. In theory, perhaps, dictatorships are better positioned to take the long view, identify looming crises before they become intractable, and render decisions ensuring smooth progress through history. And yet they never do. Human nature inevitably comes into play, and dictators end up aggrandizing their own position and that of their self-motivated loyalists at the expense of the broad populace—hardly a recipe for long-term wisdom in civic decision-making. And so we are left with Churchill's famous dictum about democracy being the worst form of government in the world—except for all the others.

As for the presidency, even many who have sung its praises have also faulted its limitations. Clinton Rossiter called the office "one of the few truly successful institutions created by men in their endless quest for the blessings of free government." But he also felt the president's powers were unequal to his responsibilities. Harold Laski, the British scholar, captured the paradoxical majesty of the office when he called it "both more and less than a king ... both more and less than a prime minister." Nevertheless, his influential study of the presidency reflected a positive disdain for the office, largely because he didn't think it invested its occupant with sufficient power to pursue all the grand civic schemes that his liberal sensibilities desired from government.

We must accept the reality that America, no less than other nations, inevitably will stumble into wars, domestic turmoil, economic travail, and other crises—many seeming in hindsight to have been products of folly and hence avoidable. Besides, how do we know when we have actually avoided a crisis? Did Eisenhower's resolve to keep U.S. troops out of Vietnam in the mid-1950s prevent a crisis of the kind that eventually engulfed LBJ's presidency a decade later? The question is unanswerable.

What we do know is that crises demand leadership, and in the American system that leadership can come only from the president. Somehow that presidential leadership has emerged in America when needed, although often not in time to actually prevent crises. The 1850s were a time when presidential leadership was woefully inadequate to the magnitude of the crisis that then engulfed the nation.

Another example is Coolidge's inability to foresee, and Hoover's conscientious but failed effort to combat, the Great Depression. We can add the deterioration in America's world position and in its domestic economy in the time of Carter. But in all instances men emerged who proved equal to the national challenge of the time, and eventually the country moved through its travail.

So will it be, I believe, with the current intertwined crises, which will be subdued through presidential leadership or not at all. I suspect the country soon will call up a new Leader of Destiny capable of leading it through the current transitional time of turmoil and trouble, of economic threat and global challenge, of high rancor and rhetorical abuse. And when he relinquishes power, after a great deal of political turmoil and emotion, he will bequeath to America a new era reflected in a new political landscape.

Perhaps that Leader of Destiny will be Barack Obama. He certainly is driven by a strong sense of destiny, as reflected in his respectful musings about the bold leadership of Reagan and his apparent determination to define his place in history through audacious decision-making. But he began his presidency with a resolve to take the country where it didn't want to go, and it seems unlikely, irrespective of his 2012 electoral fate, that he will be given a second chance to shape a new era for America. Hence it would appear more likely that the next Leader of Destiny remains on the horizon, unknown until he emerges at some point through the country's presidential referendum politics and then demonstrates his capacity through actual performance.

Perhaps that Leader of Destiny already is visible on the scene. History tells us that we seldom know what to expect when a new president is sworn in and begins to demonstrate his abilities or limitations through action. Lincoln was widely seen as a frontier bumpkin when he arrived in Washington (under cover of a disguise to thwart suspected assassins), and his secretary of state, William Seward, was preparing to fulfill most of the leadership requirements of the presidency in order to compensate for the real president's presumed inadequacies. Oliver Wendell Holmes Jr. famously suggested Franklin Roosevelt had "a second-class intellect, but a first-class temperament." (Although some have speculated that Holmes was really referring to Theodore Roosevelt, that isn't supported by the evidence; besides, it would seem more accurate to say TR had a first-class intellect and a second-class temperament.) Reagan was dismissed by many as a failed actor who lacked the brainpower necessary for presidential success.

What we can predict, based on how our system works, is that the next Leader of Destiny will meet the test of greatness by forging a coalition of support powerful enough to attack the intertwined crises of our time, then *will* attack them with adroit and effective decision-making. It will be messy; there will be strong opposition to the new direction; the crisis will seem hopeless. But in the end he or she will succeed. Then will come appreciation and adulation from growing numbers of Americans—and the reward of both reelection and party retention.

And then, in keeping with that great gift of the presidency bequeathed to us by the Founders, the name and legacy of this next Leader of Destiny will be entered into the Great White House Rating Game that forever runs parallel to American history. If the success is robust enough, I might even have to write a sequel.

Acknowledgments

I begin this expression of acknowledgment and appreciation with Simon & Schuster and the publishing house's well-known editor, Alice Mayhew. This is my third book under the imprimatur of this house and the editorial direction of this editor, and the association deepens with each effort. In particular did Alice on this occasion bring her sharp literary eye and extensive historical knowledge to bear in pushing for a manuscript as unassailable as possible. The faults are mine, but any merit herein must be considered a product in significant measure of her sterling efforts, for which I am appreciative.

As always I owe my gratitude to Philippa ("Flip") Brophy of Sterling Lord Literistic, Inc., who, in serving as agent for this project, grasped instantly what I sought to accomplish and proved effective in representing the concept. I also wish to thank two members of the Mayhew team at Simon & Schuster who assisted the project, Roger Labrie and Rachel Bergmann, as well as Gypsy da Silva, associate director of copyediting, and her meticulous team.

At the manuscript stage I sought counsel from three friends with ideal credentials for the task of catching mistakes and directing my thinking. These were David Shribman, editor of the *Pittsburgh Post-Gazette*, whose passion for history and mastery of the writing craft proved invaluable; Stephen Hess of the Brookings Institution and The George Washington University, whose long career as writer, thinker, and doer in the political and academic arenas has produced a vast store of valuable insight; and Donald A. Ritchie, the Senate historian, who produced four pages of edifying counsel and observation on the subject. My brother, Jack Merry, also read early chapters and offered advice.

The extended Merry family showered me with encouragement. Son Rob Merry and daughters Johanna Derlega and Stephanie Merry showed their usual penetrating interest and rah-rah spirit, as did son-in-law John Derlega and daughter-in-law Kristin Merry. Maisie and Elliott Derlega were mostly just distractions, though welcome in that role.

Finally, once again a special note of appreciation and affection to Susan Pennington Merry, mate and soulmate, who read chapters (or submitted to having them read to her); extended advice, criticism, and occasional praise; relieved me from household responsibilities; and generally buoyed my life through the project, as she has done in general for forty-two years.

Appendix A

ACADEMIC POLLS

SCHLESINGER SR. 1948 (N=55)	SCHLESINGER SR. 1962 (N=75)	PORTER 1981 (N=41)	CHICAGO TRIBUNE 1982 (N=49)
Lincoln	Lincoln	Lincoln	Lincoln
Washington	Washington	Washington	Washington
F. Roosevelt	F. Roosevelt	F. Roosevelt	F. Roosevelt
Wilson	Wilson	Jefferson	T. Roosevelt
Jefferson	Jefferson	T. Roosevelt	Jefferson
Jackson	Jackson	Wilson	Wilson
T. Roosevelt	T. Roosevelt	Jackson	Jackson
Cleveland	Polk	Truman	Truman
J. Adams	Truman	Polk	Eisenhower
Polk	J. Adams	J. Adams	Polk
J. Q. Adams	Cleveland	L. Johnson	McKinley
Monroe	Madison	Eisenhower	L. Johnson
Hayes	J. Q. Adams	Madison	Cleveland
Madison	Hayes	Kennedy	Kennedy
Van Buren	McKinley	Cleveland	J. Adams } tie
Taft	Taft	McKinley	Monroe } tie
Arthur	Van Buren	Monroe	Madison
McKinley	Monroe	J. Q. Adams	Van Buren
A. Johnson	Hoover	Van Buren	J. Q. Adams
Hoover	B. Harrison	Hayes	Taft
B. Harrison	Arthur	Taft	Hoover
Tyler	Eisenhower	Hoover	Hayes
Coolidge	A. Johnson	Carter	Ford
Fillmore	Taylor	Arthur	Arthur
Taylor	Tyler	B. Harrison	B. Harrison
Buchanan	Fillmore	Ford	Taylor
Pierce	Coolidge	Taylor	Carter
Grant	Pierce	Tyler	Tyler
Harding	Buchanan	Fillmore	Coolidge
	Grant	Coolidge	A. Johnson
	Harding	A. Johnson	Fillmore
		Grant	Grant
		Pierce	Pierce
		Nixon	Buchanan
		Buchanan	Nixon
		Harding	Harding

Sources

Arthur Schlesinger Sr.'s first poll through Murray-Blessing poll: cited in Robert K. Murray and Tim H. Blessing, *Greatness in the White House: Rating the Presidents from George Washington Through Ronald Reagan* (University Park: Pennsylvania State University Press, 1994), 16–17. Murray and Blessing give the following citations: *Chicago Tribune Magazine*, January 10, 1982, 8–13, 15, 18; report on results of David L. Porter poll, 1981 (in Robert K. Murray's possession); *New York Times Magazine*, July 29, 1962, 12–13, 40–41, 43; *Life*, November 1, 1948, 65–66, 68, 73–74.

Arthur Schlesinger Jr.'s poll: Schlesinger Jr., "The Ultimate Approval Rating," *New York Times Magazine*, December 15, 1996, 46.

WSJ Poll: James Taranto and Leonard Leo, eds., *Presidential Leadership: Rating the Best and the Worst in the White House* (New York: Free Press, 2005), 11–12.

MURRAY-BLESSING 1982 (N=846)	SCHLESINGER JR. 1996 (N=32)	WSJ 2005 (N=82)	LEGEND
Lincoln F. Roosevelt Washington Jefferson	Lincoln Washington F. Roosevelt	Washington Lincoln F. Roosevelt	☐ Great or 10 Best
T. Roosevelt Wilson Jackson Truman	Jefferson Jackson T. Roosevelt Wilson Truman Polk	Jefferson T. Roosevelt Reagan Truman Eisenhower Polk Jackson	▦ Near Great ▩ High or Above Average ▦ Average ▩ Low or Below Average ■ Failure or 10 Worst
J. Adams L. Johnson Eisenhower Polk Kennedy Madison Monroe J. Q. Adams Cleveland	Eisenhower J. Adams Kennedy Cleveland L. Johnson Monroe McKinley	Wilson Cleveland J. Adams McKinley Kennedy Monroe	
McKinley Taft Van Buren Hoover Hayes Arthur Ford Carter B. Harrison	Madison J. Q. Adams B. Harrison Clinton Van Buren Taft Hayes G. H. W. Bush Reagan Arthur Carter Ford	Madison L. Johnson G. W. Bush Taft G. H. W. Bush Clinton Coolidge Hayes	
Taylor Tyler Fillmore Coolidge Pierce	Taylor Coolidge Fillmore Tyler	J. Q. Adams Arthur Van Buren Ford Grant B. Harrison Hoover Nixon Taylor Carter Tyler	
A. Johnson Buchanan Nixon Grant Harding	Pierce Grant Hoover Nixon A. Johnson Buchanan Harding	Fillmore Johnson Pierce Harding Buchanan	

Appendix B

PRESIDENTS BY CATEGORY BASED ON VOTER RESPONSE

TWO TERMS OR PARTIAL TERMS SUCCEEDED
BY PRESIDENT OF THE SAME PARTY

Washington
Jefferson
Madison
Monroe
Jackson
Lincoln
Grant
McKinley
T. Roosevelt
Coolidge
F. Roosevelt
Reagan

EXPLAINERS:

Lincoln: elected, reelected, died in office, and his administration was succeeded by his own party

Grant: served two terms and was succeeded by a president of his own party, but only through a stolen election

McKinley: elected, reelected, died in office, and his administration was succeeded by his own party

T. Roosevelt: succeeded to partial term, elected in his own right, and his full term was succeeded by a president of his own party

Coolidge: succeeded to partial term, elected in his own right, and his full term was succeeded by a president of his own party

SPLIT-DECISION PRESIDENTS:
TWO TERMS OR PARTIAL TERMS BUT NOT SUCCEEDED
BY PRESIDENTS OF THEIR OWN PARTY

Wilson
Truman
Eisenhower
Johnson

Nixon
Clinton
G. W. Bush

EXPLAINERS:

Truman: Succeeded to partial term, elected in his own right, but not succeeded by a president of his own party

Johnson: Succeeded to partial term, elected in his own right, but not succeeded by a president of his own party

Nixon: Elected, reelected in a landslide, then resigned from office due to scandal

ONE-TERM PRESIDENTS OR PARTIAL-TERMERS DEFEATED FOR REELECTION

J. Adams
J. Q. Adams
Martin Van Buren
Grover Cleveland
B. Harrison
Taft
Hoover
Ford (succeeded to presidency at Nixon's resignation)
Carter
G. H. W. Bush

ONE-TERM PRESIDENTS OR PARTIAL-TERMERS WHO DIDN'T RUN AGAIN

Tyler (succeeded to presidency at death of W. H. Harrison; couldn't get his
    party's nomination for a presidential run in his own right)
Polk (announced he wouldn't seek reelection upon getting party's presidential
    nomination)
Fillmore (succeeded to presidency upon death of Taylor)
Pierce (rejected by party for renomination)
Buchanan
A. Johnson (succeeded to presidency at death of Lincoln)
Hayes

Arthur (succeeded to presidency at death of Garfield)
Cleveland (following second nonconsecutive term, rejected for party
  nomination)

ELECTED, SERVED PARTIAL TERMS, DIED IN OFFICE

W. H. Harrison
Taylor
Garfield
Harding
Kennedy

Notes

INTRODUCTION: THE GREAT WHITE HOUSE RATING GAME

PAGE

xiii *"It is difference of opinion"*: Mark Twain, *Pudd'nhead Wilson,* printed in *The Family Mark Twain* (New York: Harper & Row, 1972), 976.

xiii *" 'Ranking the Presidents' "*: Clinton Rossiter, *The American Presidency,* rev. ed. (New York: New American Library, 1960), 137.

xiv *"fun to play"*: Ibid., 155.

xiv *"must see what he sees"*: Harold J. Laski, *The American Presidency: An Interpretation* (New York: Harper & Brothers, 1940), 34.

xv *"rather be a really good"*: Quoted in Robert W. Merry, "The Myth of the One-Time Wonder," *New York Times,* February 14, 2010.

xv *"A better approach"*: Ibid.

xix *nine Greats and Near Greats:* Arthur M. Schlesinger Jr., "The Ultimate Approval Rating," cover story, *New York Times Magazine,* December 15, 1996.

xx Wall Street Journal *poll:* James Taranto and Leonard Leo, eds., *Presidential Leadership: Rating the Best and the Worst in the White House* (New York: Free

Press, 2005), 11–12. Subsequent references to rankings in this and other polls can be seen traced in Appendix I.

xxi *"miracle":* Quoted in Catherine Drinker Bowen, *Miracle at Philadelphia: The Story of the Constitutional Convention, May to September 1787* (Boston: Little, Brown, 1966), vii.

CHAPTER 1: THE JUDGMENT OF HISTORY

PAGE

3 *fifty-five experts:* Robert K. Murray and Tim H. Blessing, *Greatness in the White House: Rating the Presidents from George Washington Through Ronald Reagan* (University Park: Pennsylvania State University Press, 1994), 7. All details on the two Schlesinger polls, as well as other polls cited in this chapter, come from this source, as well as from Meena Bose and Mark Landis, eds., *The Uses and Abuses of Presidential Ratings* (New York: Nova Publishers, 2003), from the *Wall Street Journal* poll cited above, and from Schlesinger Jr.'s "The Ultimate Approval Rating" cited above.

3 *"The test in each case":* Quoted in Murray and Blessing, 7.

4 *"highly informed opinion":* Ibid., 8.

5 *Truman, who logged:* Alvin Stephen Felzenberg, *The Leaders We Deserved (And a Few We Didn't): Rethinking the Presidential Rating Game* (New York: Basic Books, 2008), 2.

6 *"took the side of progressivism":* Quoted in Bose and Landis, 5.

6 *history departments of thirty:* Thomas A. Bailey, *Presidential Greatness: The Image and the Man from George Washington to the Present* (New York: Irvington, 1978), 337 (originally published in 1966).

6 *"He will be remembered":* Rossiter, 171.

7 *"to measure the immeasurable":* Bailey, 35.

7 *"yardsticks":* Ibid., 262.

7 *Bailey placed the presidents:* Ibid., 267.

7 *Historical Society surveyed:* Murray and Blessing, 9.

7 *David L. Porter, surveyed:* Ibid.

8 *"leading historians and political scholars":* Quoted in ibid.

8 *Robert K. Murray:* Described in detail in ibid., 11.

8 *"[m]odern opinion research":* Ibid.

10 *"The Ultimate Approval Rating":* Schlesinger Jr., "The Ultimate Approval Rating." All details of this poll are taken from this article.

10 *"peculiarity":* Donald A. Ritchie, letter to the author, April 18, 2011.

11 *eighty-two respondents:* Taranto and Leo, Appendix II, "Survey Participants," 273. All details of the *Wall Street Journal* poll are taken from this source.

12 *"Our goal":* James Lindgren, in Taranto and Leo, Appendix I, "Methodology of Rankings," 250.

12 *"the American people clearly want":* Ron Faucheux, "Polls and Political Intelligence," Clarus Research Group, January 21, 2009.

12 *C-SPAN viewer poll:* "Historical Ranking of United States Presidents," Wikipedia, http://en.wikipedia.org/wiki/historical_rankings_of_united_states_presidents.

12 *2000 ABC News poll:* Ibid.

12 *2007 Rasmussen:* Ibid.

13 *91 percent:* Lindgren, in Taranto and Leo, Appendix I, 252.

14 *"The popularization":* Felzenberg, 1. Details of the Felzenberg rankings are all taken from this book.

15 *"the periodic publicity":* Ibid., 2.

16 *"in U.S. history":* Ivan Eland, *Recarving Rushmore: Ranking the Presidents on Peace, Prosperity, and Liberty* (Oakland: Independent Institute, 2009), 13. Eland's presidential assessments are taken from this volume.

16 *"thus beginning":* Ibid., 64.

17 *"thoughts of tearing down":* Ibid., 130.

18 *1,180 responses:* Quantified in Murray and Blessing, 16–17; Schlesinger Jr.; and Taranto and Leo, 273.

CHAPTER 2: THE VAGARIES OF HISTORY
PAGE

20 *eight printings:* Schlesinger Jr., *The Age of Jackson* (Boston: Little, Brown, 1945), copyright page (all 1945 and 1946 printings listed).

20 *six more:* Ibid.

20 *nearly 100,000 copies:* Douglas Martin, "Arthur Schlesinger, Historian of Power, Dies at 89," *New York Times,* March 1, 2007.

21 *"the basic distinction":* Schlesinger Jr., *The Age of Jackson,* 152.

21 *"I was an ardent young New Dealer":* Schlesinger Jr., "History and National Stupidity," *New York Review of Books,* April 27, 2006.

22 *"a childish, temper-prone teenager":* Jon Meacham, "Rocking the Vote, in the 1820s and Now," *New York Times,* October 24, 2010.

22 *"emotionally challenged":* Ibid.

23 *"The predicament of slaves":* Schlesinger Jr., "History and National Stupidity."

23 *"hopelessly absorbed":* Ibid.

24 *"Henry Adams was a New Englander":* Drew R. McCoy, "James Madison," essay in Alan Brinkley and Davis Dyer, eds., *The American Presidency* (Boston: Houghton Mifflin, 2004), 50.

24 *"Every chapter quivers"*: Elizabeth Stevenson, *Henry Adams: A Biography* (New York: Macmillan, 1956), 242.

24 *"Jefferson led to Grant"*: Ibid., 257.

25 *"The change from the Dunning and Bowers school"*: Schlesinger Jr., "History and National Stupidity."

26 *"No man of his time"*: Quoted in Daniel Walker Howe, "The Ages of Jackson," *Claremont Review of Books,* Spring 2009.

26 *"Every generation"*: Schlesinger Jr., "The Ages of Jackson," *New York Review of Books,* December 7, 1989.

26 *Indian attack every ten days:* H. W. Brands, *Andrew Jackson: His Life and Times* (New York: Doubleday, 2005), 61.

26 *2,037 dead:* Merry, *A Country of Vast Designs: James K. Polk, the Mexican War, and the Conquest of the American Continent* (New York: Simon & Schuster, 2009), 21.

26 *13 killed:* Ibid.

27 *"prudent system of expenditure"*: Andrew Jackson, Veto Message, Maysville Road Bill, May 27, 1830, reprinted in Glyndon G. Van Deusen, *The Rise and Decline of Jacksonian Democracy* (New York: Van Nostrand Reinhold, 1970), 171.

27 *"a corrupting influence"*: Quoted in Merry, *A Country of Vast Designs,* 31. (Quotes are from "notes" on the Maysville Road issue written by Andrew Jackson.)

28 *"hydra headed monster"*: Quoted in Robert Remini, *Henry Clay: Statesman for the Union* (New York: W. W. Norton, 1991), 397.

28 *"Distinctions in society"*: Andrew Jackson, Bank Bill Veto, July 10, 1832, reprinted in Richard E. Ellis, *Andrew Jackson* (Washington, D.C.: CQ Press, 2003), 169.

28 *"Please give my compliments"*: Quoted in H. W. Brands, "Andrew Jackson," chapter in Taranto and Leo, 46.

29 *"combative-rebellious"*: Quoted in Howe, "The Ages of Jackson."

30 *"an evil so great"*: Quoted in ibid.

30 *"primitive conditions"*: Quoted in "Frederick Jackson Turner," PBS, http://www.pbs.org/weta/thewest/people/s_z/turner.htm.

30 *"that coarseness and strength"*: Quoted in ibid.

30 *"the best which the new West could breed"*: Vernon L. Parrington, *Main Currents in American Thought,* Vol. II, *The Romantic Revolution in America 1800–1860* (New York: Harcourt, Brace & World, 1927), 140.

31 *"Jackson expressed the more enlightened"*: Marquis James, *The Life of Andrew Jackson* (Garden City, N.Y.: Garden City Publishing Co., 1938), 550.

32 *"Schlesinger preferred to avoid":* Howe, "The Ages of Jackson."

33 *"In doctrine the Jacksonians":* Schlesinger Jr., "The Ages of Jackson."

33 *"a great dream of economic development":* Ibid.

33 *"The continuing development":* Quoted in Merry, "Finance Panel Can Look Back: Jefferson, Jackson, and Lincoln," *Wall Street Journal,* May 6, 1986.

34 *"broken promises":* Quoted in Wikipedia, http://www.wikipedia.org/wiki/bury_my_heart_at_wounded_knee.

34 *lingered on bestseller lists:* Ibid.

34 *seventeen languages:* Ibid.

35 *"a fallen hero":* Robert Remini, *Andrew Jackson and the Course of American Democracy, 1833–1845,* Vol. III (New York: Harper & Row, 1984), 530.

35 *"Bear me out in it":* Quoted in ibid.

35 *"made a mockery":* Brands, *Andrew Jackson: His Life and Times,* 536.

35 *"a rebuke":* Jon Meacham, *American Lion: Andrew Jackson in the White House* (New York: Random House, 2008), 359.

35 *"The tragedy of Jackson's life":* Ibid.

35 *"He still lives":* Quoted in ibid., 361.

35 "He still lives": Ibid.

37 *only 39,490 votes:* Merry, *A Country of Vast Designs,* 110.

38 *aggregate ranking:* The polls are: Schlesinger Sr., 1948; Schlesinger Sr., 1962; Murray-Blessing, 1982; *Chicago Tribune,* 1982; Siena, 1982; Siena, 1990; Siena, 1994; Ridings-McIver, 1996; C-SPAN, 1999; *Wall Street Journal,* 2000; Siena, 2002; *Wall Street Journal,* 2005.

38 *inflamed by the Vietnam war:* Sean Wilentz, "Into the West: James K. Polk Engineered the Triumph of Manifest Destiny," *New York Times Book Review,* November 22, 2009.

39 *"condemned by history":* Quoted in Merry, *A Country of Vast Designs,* 474.

39 *"dubious beginnings":* Quoted in ibid.

39 *"that this is the War":* Ibid.

40 *"simply false":* Wilentz, "Into the West."

40 *"But in the end":* Merry, *A Country of Vast Designs,* 474.

CHAPTER 3: THE MAKING OF THE PRESIDENCY
PAGE

43 *"I believe," declared Hamilton:* Quoted in Bowen, *Miracle at Philadelphia,* 107.

44 *no one rose to dispute:* Ibid., 108.

44 *"as honest as an angel":* Quoted in ibid., 89.

44 *"never said a foolish thing":* Quoted in ibid.

44 *"nothing more than an institution":* Quoted in Forrest McDonald, "Forward to the Liberty Fund Edition," Charles C. Thach Jr., *The Creation of the Presidency, 1775–1789: A Study in Constitutional History* (Indianapolis: Liberty Fund, 2007), ix. (The Thach treatise was first published by Johns Hopkins Press, Baltimore, 1922.)

46 *Allan Nevins has noted:* Quoted in Thomas E. Cronin, "Presidential Term, Tenure, and Reeligibility," Chapter 3 in Cronin, *Inventing the American Presidency* (Lawrence: University Press of Kansas, 1989), 63.

46 *"intrigues and contentions":* Quoted in Thach, 86.

46 *"the people at large":* Quoted in ibid.

47 *"One great object of the Executive":* Quoted in ibid., 87.

47 *"Of all possible modes":* Quoted in ibid.

47 *"The Magistrate is not the King":* Quoted in ibid., 89.

49 *"advice and consent":* U.S. Constitution, Article II, Section 2.

50 *"Let him once win the admiration":* Quoted in Rossiter, 29.

CHAPTER 4: THE PRESIDENTIAL REFERENDUM
PAGE

52 *"Effective government":* Allan J. Lichtman and Ken DeCell, *The 13 Keys to the Presidency* (Lanham, Md.: Madison Books, 1990), 397.

52 *"It posits":* Merry, "Presidential Politics and the Big Picture," *Congressional Quarterly Weekly Report,* May 5, 1990.

53 *The keys include such questions:* Lichtman and DeCell, 7.

55 *"And surely there was no evidence":* Jack W. Germond and Jules Witcover, *Wake Us When It's Over: Presidential Politics in 1984* (New York: Macmillan, 1985), 552.

56 *"an attention span":* Ibid.

56 *"The electorate":* Merry, "The Political Outlook of Teddy White," *Congressional Quarterly Weekly Report,* September 9, 1989.

56 *"In the hands of Bush's hired guns":* Jack W. Germond and Jules Witcover, *Whose Broad Stripes and Bright Stars? The Trivial Pursuit of the Presidency* (New York: Warner Books, 1989), 446.

57 *"The men he had . . . reported":* Theodore H. White, *In Search of History: A Personal Adventure* (New York: Harper & Row, 1978), 4.

59 *"may give a dangerous turn":* Quoted in Cronin, "Presidential Term, Tenure, and Reeligibility," 71.

59 *"The love of fame":* Quoted in ibid.

59 *"might be compelled":* Quoted in ibid.

59 *"Let him be of short duration":* Quoted in ibid.

59 *"a general principle of human nature":* Alexander Hamilton, "Federalist No. 71: The Duration in Office of the Executive," reprinted in James Madison, Alexander Hamilton, and John Jay, *The Federalist Papers: The Classic Original Edition* (New York: SoHo Books, n.d.), 207.

59 *"corrupt his integrity":* Ibid.

60 *"deliberate sense of the community":* Ibid.

60 *"it does not require":* Ibid.

60 *"As, on the one hand":* Ibid., 208.

60 *"establish a dangerous influence":* Quoted in Cronin, "Presidential Term, Tenure, and Reeligibility," 75.

62 *two hundred constitutional amendments:* Ibid., 78.

62 *advocated by a number of presidents:* Ibid.

62 *"an antiseptic, apolitical presidency":* Larry J. Sabato, *A More Perfect Constitution: 23 Proposals to Revitalize Our Constitution and Make America a Fairer Country* (New York: Walker & Co., 2007), 86.

64 *"We stay in Berlin":* Quoted in Richard Reeves, *Daring Young Men: The Heroism and Triumph of the Berlin Airlift, June 1948–May 1949* (New York: Simon & Schuster, 2010), 30.

64 *five keys turned against Truman:* Lichtman and DeCell, 281.

65 *"misery index":* Merry, "Referendum Politics: Dole's Campaign," *Congressional Quarterly Weekly Report,* August 10, 1996.

65 *misery index had soared:* Ibid.

65 *"Ask yourself":* Quoted in ibid.

CHAPTER 5: THE JUDGMENT OF THE ELECTORATE
PAGE

67 *age forty-seven:* Suzanne Garment, "Stephen Grover Cleveland," chapter in Taranto and Leo, 111.

68 *a disparity that has occurred four times:* John L. Moore, Jon P. Preimesberger, and David R. Tarr, *Congressional Quarterly's Guide to U.S. Elections,* Vol. I (Washington, D.C.: CQ Press, 2001), 701.

68 *five of the thirteen keys turned against:* Lichtman and DeCell, 160.

69 *600,000 workers:* Ibid., 163.

69 *killed 8 police:* Ibid., 164.

69 *margin of defeat:* Moore, Preimesberger, and Tarr, Vol. I, 742–43.

70 *"the bloom had worn off":* Bailey, 29.

74 *jumped at the sound of a gun:* McCoy, "James Madison," essay in Brinkley and Dyer, 48.

75 *"peaceable coercion":* Ibid., 55.

75 *fifteen hours a day:* Ibid., 48.

76 *"era of good feelings":* Sean Wilentz, *The Rise of American Democracy* (New York: W. W. Norton, 2005), 182.

76 *183 electoral votes:* Moore, Preimesberger, and Tarr, Vol. I, 725.

77 *a single electoral vote cast against:* Ibid., 726.

77 *seized more than three hundred U.S. trading vessels:* David McCullough, *John Adams* (New York: Simon & Schuster, 2001), 486.

77 *tortured an American captain:* Ibid., 487.

78 *"Men who have been intimate":* Quoted in ibid., 493.

78 *At least fourteen citizens:* Gordon S. Wood, *Empire of Liberty: A History of the Early Republic, 1789–1815* (New York: Oxford University Press, 2009), 260.

78 *ten were convicted:* Ibid.

78 *"it is hard to imagine":* McCullough, *John Adams,* 506.

78 *"Nothing in particular":* Quoted in Wood, *Empire of Liberty,* 260.

79 *"The Radical Republicans":* David C. Whitney, *The American Presidents: Biographies of the Chief Executives from Washington Through Ford* (Garden City, N.Y.: Doubleday, 1975), 162.

81 *six hundred convictions:* William McFeely, "Ulysses S. Grant," essay in Brinkley and Dyer, 211.

81 *$15.5 million to the U.S. Treasury:* Michael Barone, "Ulysses Simpson Grant," chapter in Taranto and Leo, 98.

81 *55.6 percent of the popular vote:* Lichtman and DeCell, 130.

81 *four-fifths of the electoral ballots:* Ibid., 136.

81 *House majority to 65 percent:* Ibid.

81 *only three keys turned against:* Ibid., 30.

82 *nine keys had turned against:* Ibid., 137.

82 *51 percent of the popular vote:* Moore, Preimesberger, and Tarr, Vol. I, 657.

83 *Electoral College, 203 to 184:* Lichtman and DeCell, 142.

83 *a one-vote electoral victory:* Ibid., 142.

84 *"Though much of the public":* Sean Wilentz, "Who's Buried in the History Books?," *New York Times,* March 14, 2010.

84 *385 U.S. combat casualties:* Walter LaFeber, "William McKinley," essay in Brinkley and Dyer, 264.

85 *"Restorer and Liberator":* Quoted in Lichtman and DeCell, 122.

85 *"This morning":* Quoted in ibid., 121.

85 *"Then," they write, "for the first and, to date":* Ibid., 122.

86 *"Where defeat had loomed":* Ibid.

86 *54 percent of the popular vote:* Ibid., 228.

86 *58 percent of the popular vote:* Ibid., 236.

88 *230 million acres:* John S. McCain, "Theodore Roosevelt," chapter in Taranto and Leo, 125.

88 *"We stole it fair and square":* Quoted in Michael Barone, Grant Ujifusa, and Douglas Matthews, *The Almanac of American Politics 1980* (New York: Dutton, 1979), 52.

88 *"sixteen lions":* Quoted in Kathleen Dalton, *Theodore Roosevelt: A Strenuous Life* (New York: Knopf, 2002), 342.

88 *"far and away the worst":* Quoted in ibid., 323.

88 *56.4 percent:* Lichtman and DeCell, 191.

CHAPTER 6: THE STAIN OF FAILURE
PAGE

90 *"The Presidency of Warren G. Harding":* Paula S. Fass, "Warren G. Harding," essay in Brinkley and Dyer, 314.

91 *careless more than villainous:* Arthur Schlesinger Jr., "The Ultimate Approval Rating."

92 *"Harding was not a bad man":* Quoted in ibid.

92 *GDP growth in 1922 of nearly 14 percent:* Lichtman and DeCell, 229.

93 *"degenerated into a train wreck":* Richard Norton Smith, "John Quincy Adams," essay in Brinkley and Dyer, 42.

93 *eight keys turned against:* Lichtman and DeCell, 352.

93 *Academics at the time:* Merry, "History and Gerald Ford," *National Observer,* January 22, 1977.

94 *"I believe he can . . . sleep easily":* Quoted in ibid.

94 *"Nobody ever asked Coolidge":* Quoted in Stephen Goode, "Herbert Hoover—An Uncommon Man Brought Down by the Great Depression," *The World and I,* republished by High Beam Research, http://www.highbeam.com/doc/1G1-70461375.html.

96 *"Young Hickory":* Cynthia Crossen, "Franklin Pierce," chapter in Taranto and Leo, 73.

96 *He emerged in American politics:* Daniel C. Diller and Stephen L. Robertson, *The Presidents, First Ladies, and Vice Presidents: White House Biographies, 1789–1997* (Washington, D.C.: Congressional Quarterly, 1997), 51.

97 *collected 254 electoral votes:* Ibid., 52.

98 *"was superseded by the principles":* Quoted in David M. Potter, *The Impending Crisis, 1848–1861,* completed and edited by Don E. Fehrenbacher (New York: Harper & Row, 1976), 162.

98 *"a test of Democratic orthodoxy"*: Quoted in "Kansas-Nebraska Act," Wikipedia, http://en.wikipedia.org/wiki/kansas%e2%80%93nebraska_act.

98 *"had thrown the nation into turmoil"*: Allan Nevins, *Ordeal of the Union: A House Dividing, 1852–1857,* Vol. II (New York: Scribner, 1947), 121.

98 *"Douglas suddenly brought out"*: Ibid., 122.

98 *At the next election:* Election results in Potter, 175.

99 *four successive territorial governors:* Joel H. Silbey, "Franklin Pierce," essay in Brinkley and Dyer, 158.

99 *"By the time he left office"*: Quoted in Crossen, chapter in Taranto and Leo, 72.

101 *"I cannot rely upon his honest"*: Quoted in Merry, *A Country of Vast Designs,* 234.

101 *"great evils to the master"*: Quoted in Jean H. Baker, *James Buchanan* (New York: Times Books, 2004), 82.

102 *He had violated propriety:* Ibid., 84.

102 *"A constitution shall be submitted"*: Quoted in ibid., 97.

103 *"either removal or extensions"*: Ibid., 103.

103 *" 'like hogs' "*: Quoted in ibid., 104.

103 *house divided against itself:* Paul I. Wellman, *The House Divides: The Age of Jackson and Lincoln, from the War of 1812 to the Civil War* (Garden City, N.Y.: Doubleday, 1966), 405.

103 *New York's William Seward:* Characterized in Baker, 128.

105 *slave couple and their three children:* Eric Foner, "Andrew Johnson," essay in Brinkley and Dyer, 190.

106 *"fought the bravest battle"*: Quoted in ibid., 198.

106 *1926 case involving similar issues:* John Adler, "The Impeachment of Andrew Johnson: The Tenure of Office Act," andrewjohnson.com, http://www.andrewjohnson.com/02keypoliticalissues/thetenureofofficeact.html.

106 *Myers v. United States:* "Myers v. United States," answers.com, http://www.answers.com/topic/myers-v-united-states.

108 *Fordney-McCumber Tariff:* Edward S. Kaplan, "The Fordney-McCumber Tariff of 1922," EH.net, posted February 5, 2010, http://eh.net/encyclopedia/article/kaplan.fordney.

108 *top rate of 57 percent:* Jude Wanniski, *The Way the World Works: How Economies Fail—and Succeed* (New York: Basic Books, 1978), 119.

108 *Gross Domestic Product shot up to $85 billion:* Ibid.

108 *establishing quotas:* Fass, essay in Brinkley and Dyer, 319.

109 *"After his death"*: Francis Russell, *The Shadow of Blooming Grove: Warren G. Harding in His Times* (New York: McGraw-Hill, 1968), xiii.

109 *Russell sees something of a double standard:* Ibid., xiii.

110 *"Countries cannot permanently buy":* Quoted in Wanniski, 128.

111 *top rate of 63 percent:* Ibid., 141.

111 *"Hoover's last gift":* Ibid.

111 *gain of fifty-three seats:* Moore, Preimesberger, and Tarr, Vol. II, 1570.

111 *ninety-seven House seats:* Ibid.

111 *didn't crack 40 percent:* Lichtman and DeCell, 242.

CHAPTER 7: WAR AND PEACE

PAGE

117 *At seven o'clock:* Merry, *A Country of Vast Designs,* 428.

118 *"constantly wasting":* Quoted in ibid.

118 *"for my administration":* Quoted in ibid.

120 *"Mr. Madison's War":* McCoy, "James Madison," essay in Brinkley and Dyer, 56.

120 *efforts for a negotiated solution:* Samuel Flagg Bemis, *John Quincy Adams and the Foundations of American Foreign Policy* (New York: Knopf, 1949), 185.

121 *"Mexico," he declared, "has . . . shed American blood":* Merry, *A Country of Vast Designs,* 245.

122 *"no conflict":* Quoted in ibid., 249.

122 *"monstrous":* Quoted in ibid.

122 *13,780 American lives:* Ibid., 450.

122 *hundred million in U.S. dollars:* Ibid.

122 *600,000 square miles:* Ibid., 449.

122 *intense personal course of study:* Jean H. Baker, "Abraham Lincoln," essay in Brinkley and Dyer, 182.

123 *at the front on eleven occasions:* Ibid.

123 *55 percent of the popular vote:* Lichtman and DeCell, 117.

123 *"He was America's most underrated":* Fred Barnes, "William McKinley," chapter in Taranto and Leo, 120.

124 *McKinley, outraged by the yellow journalism:* Walter LaFeber, "William McKinley," essay in Brinkley and Dyer, 262.

125 *"a splendid little war":* Quoted in ibid., 264.

125 *"easiest and most profitable":* Quoted in ibid.

125 *385 combat deaths:* Ibid.

126 *"the light which will shine":* Woodrow Wilson, Address at Independence Hall, "The Meaning of Liberty," July 4, 1914, The American Presidency Project, http://www.presidency.ucsb.edu/ws/index.php?pid=65381.

126 *"He kept us out of war":* Quoted in Whitney, *The American Presidents,* 248.

126 *"starve the whole population":* Quoted in Patrick J. Buchanan, *A Republic, Not an Empire: Reclaiming America's Destiny* (Washington, D.C.: Regnery, 1999), 197.

127 *"strict accountability":* Quoted in August Heckscher, *Woodrow Wilson: A Biography* (New York: Scribner, 1991), 361.

127 *Americans' "right":* Ibid.

127 *49.2 percent:* Lichtman and DeCell, 211.

128 *Inflation surged:* Ibid., 220.

128 *no growth in 1919:* Measuringworth.com.

128 *decline in 1920:* Ibid.

128 *further 4.16 percent decline:* Ibid.

128 *48 dead:* Lichtman and DeCell, 221.

128 *killed more than 100:* Ibid.

128 *4 million workers:* Ibid.

129 *"What we demand":* Quoted in Richard M. Watt, *The Kings Depart: The Tragedy of Germany: Versailles and the German Revolution* (New York: Simon & Schuster, 1968), 29.

129 *"a peace without victory":* Heckscher, 424.

129 *may have been a minor stroke:* Margaret MacMillan, *Paris 1919: Six Months That Changed the World* (New York: Random House, 2001), 276.

129 *"The single name":* Watt, 13.

130 *"ensure a second war":* Quoted in MacMillan, 493.

130 *"Hitler did not wage war":* Ibid.

130 *"still would have wanted more":* Ibid.

131 *60.3 percent of the popular vote:* Lichtman and DeCell, 218.

131 *sixty-three House seats:* Moore, Preimesberger, and Tarr, *Congressional Quarterly's Guide to U.S. Elections,* Vol. II, 1569.

131 *eleven in the Senate:* Ibid.

131 *"Don't you think so, George?":* Quoted in Thomas Parrish, *Roosevelt and Marshall: Partners in Politics and War* (New York: Morrow, 1989), 18. The following anecdote comes entirely from this source.

132 *"His military instructions":* Eric Larrabee, *Commander in Chief: Franklin Delano Roosevelt, His Lieutenants, and Their War* (New York: Harper & Row, 1987), 2.

132 *"against the advice":* Quoted in ibid., 15.

132 *thirteen major military decisions:* Recounted in ibid.

132 *a month or six weeks:* Ibid., 25.

132 *"long war":* Quoted in ibid., 4.

132 *"Every man, woman, and child":* Quoted in ibid.

133 *"Dr. Win the War":* Mark H. Leff, "Franklin D. Roosevelt," essay in Brinkley and Dyer, 362.

133 *6,000 merchant ships:* David M. Kennedy, *Freedom from Fear: The American People in Depression and War, 1929–1945* (New York: Oxford University Press, 1999), 655. All numbers are taken from this source.

133 *"stupendous Niagara of numbers":* Ibid.

133 *"handle" Soviet leader Joseph Stalin:* Leff, essay in Brinkley and Dyer, 361.

133 *53.4 percent:* Lichtman and DeCell, 270.

134 *effectively matched wits:* Robert J. Donovan, *Conflict and Crisis: The Presidency of Harry S Truman, 1945–1948* (New York: W. W. Norton, 1977), 80. The Potsdam summation comes from this source.

134 *cut military spending to $13 billion:* Merry, *Taking On the World,* 182.

134 *"defense perimeter":* "The United States Enters the Korean Conflict," National Archives (originally published in *Social Education,* journal of the National Council for the Social Studies), http://www.archives.gov/education/lessons/korean-conflict/.

135 *300,000 battle-tested troops:* Merry, *Taking On the World,* 201.

135 *"limited war" concepts:* Ibid., 204.

136 *"I shall go to Korea":* Quoted in Steve Neal, *The Eisenhowers: Reluctant Dynasty* (Garden City, N.Y.: Doubleday, 1978), 302.

136 *"false peace":* Quoted in Merry, *Taking On the World,* 252.

136 *"hair's breadth":* Quoted in ibid., 180.

137 *"We can't get Americans to fight":* Quoted in ibid., 253.

138 *"massive retaliation":* Carl Solberg, *Riding High: America in the Cold War* (New York: Mason & Lipscomb, 1973), 312.

138 *"The more I stayed awake":* Quoted in Robert Dallek, *Flawed Giant: Lyndon Johnson and His Times, 1961–1973* (New York: Oxford University Press, 1998), 145.

138 *military advisers to 16,700:* Ibid., 98.

139 *recall of some thousand advisers:* Ibid.

139 *a bizarre request:* Ibid.

139 *70,000 troops:* Merry, *Taking On the World,* 457.

140 *killing some 37,000 communists:* "William Westmoreland: Biography," Spartacus Educational, http://www.spartacus.schoolnet.co.uk/vnwestmoreland.htm.

140 *ratio of support troops to combat troops:* Merry, "Our Greatest Retreat," *Wall Street Journal,* April 27, 1994.

141 *12,000 North Vietnamese troops:* Ibid.

141 *force of 540,000 troops:* "Desert Storm," u-s-history.com, http://www.u-s-history.com/pages/h2020.html.

142 *only ten Democratic senators:* Merry, *Sands of Empire: Missionary Zeal, American Foreign Policy, and the Hazards of Global Ambition* (New York: Simon & Schuster, 2005), 101. (All House and Senate vote totals come from this source.)

142 *20 percent of the world's oil reserves:* Indirect quote in ibid.

142 *"He'll have easy access":* Quoted in ibid.

142 *some twenty-six nations:* "Operation Desert Storm: Military Presence, Allied Forces," desert-storm.com, http://www.desert-storm.com/war/nations.html.

142 *100,000 combat casualties:* "Desert Storm," u-s-history.com.

142 *U.S. combat deaths numbered only 148:* Ibid.

CHAPTER 8: SPLIT-DECISION PRESIDENTS

PAGE

144 *LBJ: How does it look:* "L O'B," typed reporting notes by Stewart Alsop based on interview with Lawrence O'Brien, Stewart Alsop Papers, Special Collections, Boston University Libraries.

145 *61 percent of the popular vote:* Lichtman and DeCell, 323.

145 *295 House seats:* Moore, Preimesberger, and Tarr, Vol. II, 1570.

145 *68 of 100 Senate seats:* Ibid.

147 *41.8 percent of the popular vote:* Lichtman and DeCell, 204. (All 1912 vote totals cited come from this source.)

148 *"There is nothing in life":* Quoted in Heckscher, *Woodrow Wilson,* 316.

148 *"the biggest Democrat":* Quoted in ibid., 321.

148 *GDP declined nominally:* Lichtman and DeCell, 211.

148 *unemployment hit double digits:* Ibid., 213.

148 *bank failures increased:* Ibid.

148 *sixty-one House seats:* Moore, Preimesberger, and Tarr, Vol. II, 1569.

148 *growing by 6 percent:* Lichtman and DeCell, 213.

149 *19 Americans:* Heckscher, 328.

149 *"aspects of opera bouffe":* Quoted in ibid.

149 *killing 36 Americans:* Ibid., 388.

149 *army of 4,000 troops:* Ibid.

150 *1.3 million Soviet and client-state:* Richard A. Bitzinger, "Assessing the Conventional Balance in Europe, 1945–1975," *A Rand Note,* May 1989, 4–5, http://www.rand.org/pubs/notes/2007/n2859.pdf.

151 *"a man who takes more words":* Quoted in Bailey, *Presidential Greatness,* 338.

152 *55 percent of the vote:* Lichtman and DeCell, 290.

153 *"massive retaliation":* Described in Stephen E. Ambrose, *Eisenhower: Soldier and President* (New York: Simon & Schuster, 1990), 357.

153 *car ownership rising:* Ibid., 386.

154 *"I don't believe there is such a thing":* Quoted in ibid., 369.

154 *"but if they did":* Quoted in ibid., 425.

154 *57.4 percent of the popular vote:* Lichtman and DeCell, 300.

154 *a single key:* Ibid.

155 *declined 2.6 percent in 1958:* Richard Sutch and Susan B. Carter, eds., *Historical Statistics of the United States,* Millenial Edition, Vol. III (New York: Cambridge University Press, 2006), Table Ca9-19.

155 *Unemployment hit 7 percent:* Ibid., 3–84.

155 *nine of the Lichtman-DeCell keys:* Lichtman and DeCell, 310.

156 *setting off a 4.3 percent increase:* Sutch and Carter, Table Ca9-19.

156 *"Taken together":* Lichtman and DeCell, 330.

157 *lost forty-seven House seats:* Moore, Preimesberger, and Tarr, Vol. II, 1569.

157 *three Senate seats:* Ibid.

157 *485,000 troops:* "Vietnam War Allied Troop Levels, 1960–73," http://www.americanwarlibrary.com/vietnam/vwatl.htm.

157 *another 55,000 on the way:* Merry, *Taking On the World,* 436.

157 *military deaths had exceeded 20,000:* National Archives, "Statistical Information About Casualties of the Vietnam War," http://www.archives.gov/research/vietnam-war/casualties-statistics.html#year.

157 *another 120,000 troops:* Merry, *Taking On the World,* 435.

157 *led to 34 deaths:* Dallek, *Flawed Giant,* 223.

157 *thirty-five million dollars:* Ibid.

157 *riots followed the next summer:* Ibid., 322.

157 *ghetto riots in Newark:* Ibid., 412.

157 *Detroit erupted:* Ibid., 413.

158 *consumer price index rising 13 percent:* Sutch and Carter, 3–84.

158 *two and a half times higher:* Ibid.

158 *eight keys turned against:* Lichtman and DeCell, 334.

159 *61 percent of the popular vote:* Ibid.

159 *"ending the war and winning the peace":* Quoted by David Eisenhower, speech at the Nixon Center, Washington, D.C., January 7, 2011.

160 *"the world's policeman":* Richard M. Nixon, "Asia After Viet Nam," *Foreign Affairs,* October 1967, http://www.foreignaffairs.com.

160 *"angry isolation":* Ibid.

160 *"Taking the long view":* Ibid.

162 *boosting Gross Domestic Product in 1972 by 4 percent:* Sutch and Carter, Table Ca9-19.

162 *Gross Domestic Product declined by 1.5 percent:* Ibid.

162 *inflation hit 11 percent:* Sutch and Carter, 3–84.

CHAPTER 9: LEADERS OF DESTINY

PAGE

164 *"A statesman":* Quoted in Schlesinger Jr., "The Ultimate Approval Rating."

165 *"He must have a helm":* Quoted in ibid.

167 *eschewing the presidential veto:* Herbert Sloan, "George Washington," essay in Brinkley and Dyer, 11.

169 *"the Prostration of Agriculture":* Quoted in Joseph J. Ellis, *His Excellency: George Washington* (New York: Knopf, 2004), 205.

169 *"with a grace, dignity, and ease":* Quoted in Forrest McDonald, "Thomas Jefferson," chapter in Taranto and Leo, 27.

170 *"When dealing with his peers":* Quoted in ibid., 26.

170 *"the rational, self-improving":* Joyce Appleby, "Thomas Jefferson," essay in Brinkley and Dyer, 37.

171 *"after leaving to labor":* Quoted in Merry, "Finance Panel Can Look Back: Jefferson, Jackson, and Lincoln."

171 *"alarm all":* Quoted in ibid.

171 *"all popular in all parts":* Quoted in ibid.

173 *"Everything is scattered":* Quoted in Ronald P. Formisano, "James Monroe," essay in Brinkley and Dyer, 63.

173 *"humble members of society":* Andrew Jackson, Bank Veto Message, July 10, 1832, reprinted in Glyndon G. Van Deusen, 183.

174 *"undeniably a great man":* Bailey, 291.

177 *"Under the operation of that policy":* Quoted in Benjamin P. Thomas, *Abraham Lincoln* (New York: Knopf, 1952), 180.

178 *"My paramount object":* Lincoln letter, reprinted in Michael Gartner, ed., *Outrage, Passion, and Uncommon Sense* (Washington, D.C.: National Geographic, n.d.), 103.

178 *"after much pulling and hauling":* Bailey, 293.

179 *"correction of the spirit":* Garry Wills, *Lincoln at Gettysburg: The Words That Remade America* (New York: Simon & Schuster, 1992), 147.

179 *"feckless":* Ibid.

179 *"Because of it":* Ibid.

179 *"one of the most daring acts":* Ibid., 38.

179 *"heretical"*: Willmoore Kendall, "Equality: Commitment or Ideal?," *The Intercollegiate Review*, Spring 1989, 25. (The description of the Kendall point of view comes entirely from this source.)

180 *"We want no wars of conquest"*: Quoted in Merry, *Sands of Empire*, 76.

180 *"soft as a chocolate éclair"*: Quoted in ibid.

181 *"an imperial policy!"*: Quoted in ibid., 77.

181 *"He finally recognized"*: Dalton, *Theodore Roosevelt: A Strenuous Life*, 282.

181 *"a transitional internationalist"*: Ibid., 242.

182 *Gross Domestic Product had contracted:* Sutch and Carter, Table Ca9-19.

182 *83 percent of shareholder value:* Mark H. Leff, "Franklin D. Roosevelt," essay in Brinkley and Dyer, 350.

182 *Unemployment soared to nearly 23 percent:* Bruce Bartlett, "Are We About to Repeat the Mistakes of 1937?," nytimes.com, http://economix.blogs .nytimes.com/2011/07/12/are-we-about-to-repeat-the-mistakes-of-1937.

183 *"The only thing we have to fear"*: Quoted in Leff, essay in Brinkley and Dyer, 351.

183 *"on one level absurd"*: Ibid.

184 *"this nation asks"*: Quoted in ibid.

184 *"bold, persistent experimentation"*: Quoted in ibid.

184 *70 percent were back in business:* Ted Morgan, *FDR: A Biography* (New York: Simon & Schuster, 1985), 378.

185 *Amity Shlaes suggests:* Described in James Piereson, "The Forgotten Man by Amity Shlaes," *Commentary*, September 2007.

186 *"Roosevelt's fumbling"*: Quoted in ibid., 157.

186 *Gross Domestic Product soared by 7 percent a year:* Sutch and Carter, Table Ca9-19.

186 *manufacturing production increased by 50 percent:* Lichtman and DeCell, 254.

186 *unemployment dropped to 10 percent:* Bartlett, "Are We About to Repeat the Mistakes of 1937?"

186 *only one of thirteen keys:* Lichtman and DeCell, 252.

186 *expanding at 7 percent a year:* Sutch and Carter, Table Ca9-19.

186 *FDR with a 54.7 percent victory:* Lichtman and DeCell, 262.

186 *seventy-one House seats:* Moore, Preimesberger, and Tarr, Vol. II, 1570.

186 *six in the Senate:* Ibid.

187 *almost certainly violated the U.S. Neutrality Act:* Robert Shogan, *Hard Bargain: How FDR Twisted Churchill's Arm, Evaded the Law, and Changed the Role of the American Presidency* (New York: Scribner, 1995), 17.

187 *"fait accompli"*: Ibid., 239.

187 *"It is all over":* Quoted in ibid.

187 *"the most arbitrary and dictatorial":* Quoted in Richard M. Ebeling, "Book Review" (review of the Shogan book), *Freedom Daily,* August 1995, http://www.fff.org/freedom/0895h.asp.

189 *"shattered his party's unity":* Quoted in Merry, "Urban Cowboy: A Biography of Theodore Roosevelt Stresses His Adventurous Spirit," *New York Times Book Review,* October 27, 2002.

CHAPTER 10: REPUBLICAN RESURGENCE

PAGE

193 *"I was going to listen":* Quoted in Deborah Hart Strober and Gerald S. Strober, *Reagan: The Man and His Presidency* (Boston: Houghton Mifflin, 1998), 10. (Reagan quoted in oral history remarks from Michael Reagan.)

195 *"The Economy in Crisis":* Newsweek, cover, January 19, 1981.

195 *"inherit the most dangerous":* Harry Anderson, with Rich Thomas and Pamela Lynn Abraham, "The U.S. Economy in Crisis," *Newsweek,* January 19, 1981, 30.

195 *Unemployment was at 7.4 percent:* Merry, "The Reagan Revolution," chapter in *Congress and the Great Issues* (Washington, D.C.: Congressional Quarterly, 1996), 117.

195 *Gross Domestic Product had declined 1.5 percent:* Sutch and Carter, Table Ca9-19.

195 *prime interest rate:* George Church, reported by William Blaylock and Michael Moritz, "The Biggest Challenge," *Time,* January 19, 1981, 61.

195 *inflation, the thief:* Ibid.

195 *"What the Great Depression was":* Quoted in Anderson, with Thomas and Abraham.

195 *fifty-two American hostages:* Reeves, *President Reagan: The Triumph of Imagination* (New York: Simon & Schuster, 2005), 1.

195 *444 days:* Ibid.

196 *inflation was under 4 percent:* Ibid., 242.

196 *twenty-five straight months:* Ibid.

196 *"the strongest in thirty-four years":* Quoted in ibid.

196 *growth rate in real GDP of 6.2 percent:* Sutch and Carter, Table Ca9-19.

196 *7.3 million new jobs:* Reeves, *President Reagan,* 242.

196 *"Ronald Reagan can now boast":* Quoted in ibid., 213.

196 *58.8 percent of the vote:* Moore, Preimesberger, and Tarr, Vol. I, 684.

196 *3.4 percent a year:* Sutch and Carter, Table Ca9-19.

196 *just over 3 percent:* Ibid.

196 *Unemployment was down to 5.5 percent:* Ibid.

196 *lowest level in fourteen years:* Ibid.

196 *53.4 percent victory:* Moore, Preimesberger, and Tarr, Vol. I, 684.

197 *750 historians:* Murray and Blessing, 79.

197 *nineteen pages:* Ibid. All details and quotations related to the Murray-Blessing poll regarding Reagan are taken from the chapter in their book entitled "Historians Rank the Presidency of Ronald Reagan."

199 *"Amazing things":* Reeves, *President Reagan,* xvi.

199 *"His personal popularity":* Ibid.

199 *63 percent:* Ibid., xvii.

199 *"the collectivist, centralizing approach":* Quoted in Merry, "Growth Agent: Reagan Transformed," *Wall Street Journal,* September 13, 1985.

201 *"and he believed in the past":* Reeves, *President Reagan,* 8.

201 *"the last great class-struggle election":* Quoted in Merry, "The Post-Industrial Campaign," *Wall Street Journal,* October 3, 1984.

202 *"found on Wall Street":* Quoted in ibid.

202 *"found in the country club":* Quoted in ibid.

202 *"America doesn't need":* Quoted in ibid.

202 *twenty-nine Democratic votes:* Reeves, *President Reagan,* 74.

202 *forty-eight in his House victory:* Ibid., 77.

202 *"And none of this":* Ibid., 323.

203 *"Screw it":* Quoted in Strober and Strober, 48. (Oral history remarks from Michael Deaver.)

203 *"Mr. Gorbachev":* Quoted in Gil Troy, "Ronald Reagan," essay in Brinkley and Dyer, 482.

203 *"The speech was page three":* Reeves, *President Reagan,* 401.

203 *"The man who beat communism":* Cover headline, *The Economist,* June 12–18, 2004.

204 *"I think Ronald Reagan":* Quoted in "Reagan Era," Wikipedia, http://en.wikipedia.org/wiki/reagan_era.

204 *"rearranged American politics":* Reeves, *President Reagan,* 325.

204 *"the bookend presidents":* Quoted in ibid.

204 *"repeal Reaganism":* Merry, "Why the Tea Party Movement Isn't Going Away Anytime Soon," stratfor.com, September 17, 2010.

205 *"the era of big government":* Matthew Dickinson, "Bill Clinton," essay in Brinkley and Dyer, 513.

205 *"There is . . . no doubt":* Reeves, *President Reagan,* xvii.

205 *"opportunity costs":* Ibid.

206 *"one of our most underrated presidents":* Thomas L. Friedman, "Bring Back Poppy," *New York Times,* July 30, 2011.

206 *"likely to face the electorate":* DeCell, "Lucky George," *Washingtonian,* September 1992. The following discussion of Bush's standing comes from this article.

207 *collected 19 percent:* Moore, Preimesberger, and Tarr, Vol. I, 686.

207 *nearly 38 percent:* "United States Presidential Election, 1992," Wikipedia, http://www.en.wikipedia.org/wiki/united_states_presidential_election_1992.

207 *2.9 million votes:* Ibid.

208 *"I know what you're trying to do":* Author interview with G. H. W. Bush, autumn, 1985.

208 *"the vision thing":* "George H. W. Bush, 43rd Vice President (1981–1989)," U.S. Senate website, http://senate.gov/artandhistory/history/generic/vp_george_bush.htm.

209 *GDP growth rate of 3.86 percent:* Sutch and Carter, Table Ca9-19.

209 *below 1 percent:* Measuringworth.com.

209 *high of 5.88 percent of GDP:* "US Federal Deficit as Percent of GDP in United States 1900–2010—Federal State Local," http://www.usgovernmentspending.com/federal_deficit_chart.html.

210 *nearly 5 percent of GDP:* Ibid.

210 *Reagan's deficit:* Ibid.

210 *4.58 percent of GDP:* Ibid.

210 *unemployment rose to 7.4 percent:* Sutch and Carter, 3–84.

210 *up from 5.3 percent in 1989:* Ibid.

210 *"The totalitarian era is passing":* "George Bush, Inaugural Address, Friday, January 20, 1989," http://www.bartleby.com/124/pres63.html.

211 *approval rating to above 90 percent:* DeCell, "Lucky George."

CHAPTER 11: THE POST–COLD WAR PRESIDENTS

PAGE

212 *"No historian":* Sean Wilentz, "The Worst President in History?," *Rolling Stone,* April 21, 2006.

213 *unemployment stood at 7.4 percent:* Sutch and Carter, 3–84. Subsequent percentages come from the same source.

215 *43 percent mandate:* Moore, Preimesberger, and Tarr, Vol. I, 686.

215 *43 percent victory in 1968:* Ibid., 680.

215 *"Just sixteen days":* Ronald D. Elving, *Conflict and Compromise: How Congress Makes the Law* (New York: Simon & Schuster, 1995), 11.

216 *journalists noted at the time:* Merry, "A Rule for Presidents: Go Centrist or Perish," *Congressional Quarterly Weekly Report,* October 26, 1996.

216 *"misery index" lowest:* Merry, "Referendum Politics: Dole's Campaign," *Congressional Quarterly Weekly Report,* August 10, 1996.

216 *4.2 percent increase in GDP:* Ibid.

216 *deficit of just 1.37 percent of GDP:* "US Federal Deficit as Percent of GDP in United States."

216 *49.2 percent of the popular vote:* Moore, Preimesberger, and Tarr, Vol. I, 687. Dole and Perot percentages come from the same source.

217 *GDP growth through Clinton's second term:* Measuringworth.com.

217 *"the purblind rich":* Merry, "A Rule for Presidents."

219 *"Still, even in the absence":* Schlesinger Jr., "Editor's Note: The American Presidency," preface to John Seigenthaler, *James K. Polk* (New York: Times Books, Henry Holt, 2003), xv.

220 *"I may not have been the greatest":* "Bill Clinton Quotes," thinkexist.com, http://thinkexist.com/quotation/i_may_not_have_been_the_greatest_presi dent-but_i.336958.html.

220 *"History," he replied. "We don't know":* Quoted in Wilentz, "The Worst President in History?"

220 *"Fellow citizens":* Quoted in ibid.

220 *"headed for colossal historical disgrace":* Ibid.

223 *"Given a choice":* Stefan Halper, *The Beijing Consensus: How China's Authoritarian Model Will Dominate the Twenty-First Century* (New York: Basic Books, 2010), x.

224 *51 percent of the popular vote:* "CNN.com Election Results: U.S. President," http://www.cnn.com/election/2004/pages/results/president/.

224 *a mere thirty-five ballots:* Ibid.

224 *GDP growth averaged only about 2.1 percent:* Measuringworth.com.

224 *just over 1 percent:* Ibid.

224 *3.47 percent in the reelection year:* Ibid.

225 *negative growth rate in the 2008:* Ibid.

226 *"high-flown pronouncements":* Quoted in Wilentz, "The Worst President in History?"

226 *"No other president":* Wilentz, "The Worst President in History?"

226 *rating in the Gallup Poll:* "United States Presidential Approval Rating," Wikipedia, http://en.wikipedia.org/wiki/United_States_presidential_approval _rating.

226 *independent vote, which Bush split:* "CNN.com Election Results: U.S. President," http://www.cnn.com/election/2004/pages/results/president.

227 *"shellacking"*: "After Shellacking, Obama Laments Disconnect with Voters," MSNBC.com, http://www.msnbc.msn.com.

228 *$787 billion stimulus:* "What Was the Stimulus Package," about.com, US Economy, http://useconomy.about.com/od/candidatesandtheeconomy/a/Obama_Stimulus.htm.

229 *"You never want a serious crisis"*: Quoted in Gerald F. Seib, "In Crisis, Opportunity for Obama," *Wall Street Journal,* November 21, 2008.

229 *$16.2 trillion by 2012:* "United States Public Debt," Wikipedia, http://en.wikipedia.org/wiki/United_States_public_debt.

231 *"Part of the reason"*: Quoted in Peter Baker, "The Charge That Obama Can't Shake," *New York Times,* "Week in Review," October 31, 2010.

231 *"flagrant hypocrisies"*: Shelby Steele, "The Referendum on the Redeemer," *Wall Street Journal,* October 28, 2010. Further quotes are from the same article.

232 *a feeble 37 percent:* Cited in ibid.

232 *Democrats' loss of sixty-three House seats:* "Obamanomics Takes a Holiday," editorial, *Wall Street Journal,* December 8, 2010.

232 *six in the Senate:* "Election Results, Senate Map," *New York Times,* http://elections.nytimes.com/2010/results/senate.

232 *on the wrong track:* Andy Barr, "Poll: 62% of Americans Say U.S. on Wrong Track," *Politico,* June 24, 2010, http://www.politico.com/news/stories/0610/38961.html.

232 *77 percent:* "Right Direction or Wrong Track," Rasmussen Reports, October 26, 2011, http://www.rasmussenreports.com/public_content/politics/mood_of_America/right_direction_or_wrong_track.

232 *independent vote split 56 percent for Republican:* "CNN.com Election Results," 2010, CNN.com.

232 *Two years earlier, Obama garnered:* Ibid., 2008.

CONCLUSION: CLEAR AND PRESENT DANGER
PAGE

235 *"They talk about the power"*: Quoted in *Time,* "Man of the Year: Lyndon B. Johnson, the Paradox of Power," January 5, 1968.

237 *"one of the few truly successful"*: Rossiter, 13.

237 *"both more and less than a king"*: Laski, 11.

239 *"a second-class intellect"*: Quoted in Robert H. Bork, "Franklin Delano Roosevelt," chapter in Taranto and Leo, 156.

Bibliography

BOOKS

Adams, Henry. *The Education of Henry Adams.* Boston: Houghton Mifflin, 1974. (Originally published in 1918 by the Massachusetts Historical Society.)

Ambrose, Stephen E. *Eisenhower: Soldier and President.* New York: Simon & Schuster, 1990.

Bailey, Thomas A. *Presidential Greatness: The Image and the Man from George Washington to the Present.* New York: Irvington, 1878.

Baker, Jean H. *James Buchanan.* New York: Times Books, Henry Holt, 2004.

Barone, Michael, Grant Ujifusa, and Douglas Matthews. *The Almanac of American Politics 1980.* New York: Dutton, 1979.

Bauer, Jack K. *Zachary Taylor: Soldier, Planter, Statesman of the Old Southwest.* Baton Rouge: Louisiana State University Press, 1985.

Bell, Jeffrey. *Populism and Elitism: Politics in the Age of Equality.* Washington, D.C.: Regnery, 1992.

Bemis, Samuel Flagg. *John Quincy Adams and the Foundations of American Foreign Policy.* New York: Knopf, 1949.

Benedict, Michael Les. *A Compromise of Principle: Congressional Republicans and Reconstruction, 1863–1869*. New York: W. W. Norton, 1974.

Bessette, Joseph M., and Jeffrey K. Tulis. *The Constitutional Presidency*. Baltimore: Johns Hopkins University Press, 2009.

Bose, Meena, and Mark Landis, eds. *The Uses and Abuses of Presidential Ratings*. New York: Nova Publishers, 2003.

Bowen, Catherine Drinker. *Miracle at Philadelphia: The Story of the Constitutional Convention, May to September 1787*. Boston: Little, Brown, 1966.

Bowers, Claude G. *Jefferson in Power*. Boston: Houghton Mifflin, 1967.

Brands, H. W. *Andrew Jackson: His Life and Times*. New York: Doubleday, 2005.

Brinkley, Alan, and Davis Dyer, eds. *The American Presidency: The Authoritative Reference*. Boston: Houghton Mifflin, 2004.

Buchanan, Patrick J. *A Republic, Not an Empire: Reclaiming America's Destiny*. Washington, D.C.: Regnery, 1999.

Cronin, Thomas E., ed. *Inventing the American Presidency*. Lawrence: University Press of Kansas, 1989.

Dallek, Robert. *Flawed Giant: Lyndon Johnson and His Times, 1961–1973*. New York: Oxford University Press, 1998.

Dalton, Kathleen. *Theodore Roosevelt: A Strenuous Life*. New York: Knopf, 2002.

Diller, Daniel C., and Stephen L. Robertson. *The Presidents, First Ladies, and Vice Presidents: White House Biographies, 1789–1997*. Washington, D.C.: Congressional Quarterly, 1997.

Donovan, Robert J. *Conflict and Crisis: The Presidency of Harry S Truman, 1945–1948*. New York: W. W. Norton, 1977.

———. *Tumultuous Years: The Presidency of Harry S Truman, 1949–1953*. New York: W. W. Norton, 1982.

Eland, Ivan. *Recarving Rushmore: Ranking the Presidents on Peace, Prosperity, and Liberty*. Oakland, Calif.: Independent Institute, 2009.

Ellis, Joseph J. *His Excellency: George Washington*. New York: Knopf, 2004.

Ellis, Richard E. *Andrew Jackson*. Washington, D.C.: CQ Press, 2003.

Elving, Ronald D. *Conflict and Compromise: How Congress Makes the Law*. New York: Simon & Schuster, 1995.

———, ed. *Congress and the Great Issues, 1945–1995*. Washington, D.C.: Congressional Quarterly, 1996.

Felzenberg, Alvin Stephen. *The Leaders We Deserved (And a Few We Didn't): Rethinking the Presidential Rating Game*. New York: Basic Books, 2008.

Gartner, Michael, ed. *Outrage, Passion, and Uncommon Sense*. Washington, D.C.: National Geographic, n.d.

Gay, Sydney Howard. *James Madison*. New Rochelle, N.Y.: Arlington House, n.d.

Germond, Jack W., and Jules Witcover. *Wake Us When It's Over: Presidential Politics in 1984.* New York: Macmillan, 1985.

———. *Whose Broad Stripes and Bright Stars? The Trivial Pursuit of the Presidency.* New York: Warner Books, 1989.

Halper, Stefan. *The Beijing Consensus: How China's Authoritarian Model Will Dominate the Twenty-First Century.* New York: Basic Books, 2010.

Heckscher, August. *Woodrow Wilson: A Biography.* New York: Scribner, 1991.

Horn, Charles F. *The Story of Our American People.* Vol. II. New York: National Alumni, n.d.

Israel, Fred L. *Student's Atlas of American Presidential Elections, 1789 to 1996.* Washington, D.C.: Congressional Quarterly, 1997.

James, Marquis. *The Life of Andrew Jackson.* Garden City, N.Y.: Garden City Publishing Co., 1938.

Johnson, Paul. *A History of the American People.* New York: HarperCollins, 1998.

Kennedy, David M. *Freedom from Fear: The American People in Depression and War, 1929–1945.* New York: Oxford University Press, 1999.

Klein, Philip S. *President James Buchanan: A Biography.* Newtown, Conn.: American Political Biography Press, 1995. (Originally published by Pennsylvania State University Press, 1962.)

Langguth, A. J. *Driven West: Andrew Jackson and the Trail of Tears to the Civil War.* New York: Simon & Schuster, 2010.

Larrabee, Eric. *Commander in Chief: Franklin Delano Roosevelt, His Lieutenants, and Their War.* New York: Harper & Row, 1987.

Laski, Harold J. *The American Presidency: An Interpretation.* New York: Harper & Brothers, 1940.

Lichtman, Allan J., and Ken DeCell. *The 13 Keys to the Presidency: Prediction Without Polls.* Lanham, Md.: Madison Books, 1990.

MacMillan, Margaret. *Paris 1919: Six Months That Changed the World.* New York: Random House, 2001.

Madison, James, Alexander Hamilton, and John Jay. *The Federalist Papers: The Classic Original Edition.* New York: SoHo Books, n.d.

McCullough, David. *Truman.* New York: Simon & Schuster, 1992.

———. *John Adams.* New York: Simon & Schuster, 2001.

McDonald, Forrest. *The American Presidency: An Intellectual History.* Lawrence: University Press of Kansas, 1994.

McPherson, James M. *To the Best of My Ability: The American Presidents.* New York: Dorling Kindersley, 2000.

Meacham, Jon. *American Lion: Andrew Jackson in the White House.* New York: Random House, 2008.

Merry, Robert W. *Taking On the World: Joseph and Stewart Alsop—Guardians of the American Century.* New York: Viking, 1996.

———. *Sands of Empire: Missionary Zeal, American Foreign Policy, and the Hazards of Global Ambition.* New York: Simon & Schuster, 2005.

———. *A Country of Vast Designs: James K. Polk, the Mexican War, and the Conquest of the American Continent.* New York: Simon & Schuster, 2009.

Milkis, Sidney M., and Michael Nelson. *The American Presidency: Origins and Development, 1776–2007.* 5th ed. Washington, D.C.: CQ Press, 2008.

Moore, John L., Jon P. Preimesberger, and David R. Tarr. *Congressional Quarterly's Guide to U.S. Elections.* 2 vols. 4th ed. Washington, D.C.: CQ Press, 2001.

Morgan, Ted. *FDR: A Biography.* New York: Simon & Schuster. 1985.

Murray, Robert K., and Tim H. Blessing. *Greatness in the White House: Rating the Presidents from George Washington Through Ronald Reagan.* University Park: Pennsylvania State University Press, 1994.

Neal, Steve. *The Eisenhowers: Reluctant Dynasty.* Garden City, N.Y.: Doubleday, 1978.

Nevins, Allan. *Ordeal of the Union: A House Dividing, 1852–1857.* Vol. II. New York: Scribner, 1947.

Parrington, Vernon L. *Main Currents in American Thought.* Vol. II, *The Romantic Revolution in America, 1800–1860.* New York: Harcourt, Brace & World, 1927.

Parrish, Thomas. *Roosevelt and Marshall: Partners in Politics and War.* New York: Morrow, 1989.

Potter, David M. *The Impending Crisis, 1848–1861.* Completed and edited by Don E. Fehrenbacher. New York: Harper & Row, 1976.

Priestly, Herbert Ingram. *The Mexican Nation: A History.* New York: Macmillan, 1923.

Reeves, Richard. *President Nixon: Alone in the White House.* New York: Simon & Schuster, 2001.

———. *President Reagan: The Triumph of Imagination.* New York: Simon & Schuster, 2005.

———. *Daring Young Men: The Heroism and Triumph of the Berlin Airlift, June 1848–May 1949.* New York: Simon & Schuster, 2010.

Remini, Robert V. *Andrew Jackson and the Course of American Empire, 1767–1821.* Vol. I. New York: Harper & Row, 1977.

———. *Andrew Jackson and the Course of American Freedom, 1822–1832.* Vol. II. New York: Harper & Row, 1981.

———. *Andrew Jackson and the Course of American Democracy, 1833–1845.* Vol. III. New York: Harper & Row, 1984.

———. *Henry Clay: Statesman for the Union.* New York: W. W. Norton, 1991.

Rossiter, Clinton. *The American Presidency.* Rev. ed. New York: New American Library, 1960.

Russell, Francis. *The Shadow of Blooming Grove: Warren G. Harding in His Times.* New York: McGraw-Hill, 1968.

Sabato, Larry J. *A More Perfect Constitution: 23 Proposals to Revitalize Our Constitution and Make America a Fairer Country.* New York: Walker & Co., 2007.

Schlesinger, Arthur M., Jr. *The Age of Jackson.* Boston: Little, Brown, 1945.

———. *The Cycles of American History.* Boston: Houghton Mifflin, 1986.

Seigenthaler, John. *James K. Polk.* New York: Times Books, Henry Holt, 2003.

Shogan, Robert. *Hard Bargain: How FDR Twisted Churchill's Arm, Evaded the Law, and Changed the Role of the American Presidency.* New York: Scribner, 1995.

Silbey, Joel H. *Martin Van Buren and the Emergence of American Popular Politics.* Lanham, Md.: Rowman & Littlefield, 2002.

Smith, Jean Edward. *Grant.* New York: Simon & Schuster, 2001.

Solberg, Carl. *Riding High: America in the Cold War.* New York: Mason & Lipscomb, 1973.

Stevenson, Elizabeth. *Henry Adams: A Biography.* New York: Macmillan, 1956.

Strober, Deborah Hart, and Gerald S. Strober. *Reagan: The Man and His Presidency: The Oral History of an Era.* Boston: Houghton Mifflin, 1998.

Strozier, Charles B. *Lincoln's Quest for Union: Public and Private Meanings.* New York: Basic Books, 1982.

Taranto, James, and Leonard Leo, eds. *Presidential Leadership: Rating the Best and the Worst in the White House.* New York: Free Press, 2005.

Thach, Charles C., Jr. *The Creation of the Presidency, 1775–1789: A Study in Constitutional History.* Indianapolis: Liberty Fund, 2007. (Originally published by Johns Hopkins Press, 1922.)

Thomas, Benjamin P. *Abraham Lincoln.* New York: Knopf, 1952.

Tugwell, Rexford G. *The Democratic Roosevelt: A Biography of Franklin D. Roosevelt.* Garden City, N.Y.: Doubleday, 1957.

Twain, Mark. *Pudd'nhead Wilson.* Printed in *The Family Mark Twain.* New York: Harper & Row, 1972.

Van Deusen, Glyndon G. *The Rise and Decline of Jacksonian Democracy.* New York: Van Nostrand Reinhold, 1970.

Wanniski, Jude. *The Way the World Works: How Economies Fail—and Succeed.* New York: Basic Books, 1978.

Watt, Richard M. *The Kings Depart: The Tragedy of Germany: Versailles and the German Revolution.* New York: Simon & Schuster, 1968.

Wellman, Paul I. *The House Divides: The Age of Jackson and Lincoln, from the War of 1812 to the Civil War.* Garden City, N.Y.: Doubleday, 1966.

White, Theodore H. *In Search of History: A Personal Adventure.* New York: Harper & Row, 1978.

———. *America in Search of Itself: The Making of the President, 1956–1980.* New York: Harper & Row, 1982.

Whitney, David C. *The American Presidents: Biographies of the Chief Executives from Washington Through Ford.* Garden City, N.Y.: Doubleday, 1975.

Wilentz, Sean. *The Rise of American Democracy: Jefferson to Lincoln.* New York: W.W. Norton, 2005.

Wills, Garry. *Lincoln at Gettysburg: The Words That Remade America.* New York: Simon & Schuster, 1992.

Wood, Gordon S. *Empire of Liberty: A History of the Early Republic, 1789–1815.* New York: Oxford University Press, 2009.

MAGAZINE AND JOURNAL ARTICLES

Anderson, Harry, with Rich Thomas and Pamela Lynn Abraham. "The U.S. Economy in Crisis." *Newsweek,* January 19, 1981.

Church, George, reported by William Blaylock and Michael Moritz. "The Biggest Challenge." *Time,* January 19, 1981.

DeCell, Ken. "Lucky George." *Washingtonian,* September 1992.

Howe, Daniel Walker. "The Ages of Jackson." *Claremont Review of Books,* Spring 2009.

Kendall, Willmoore. "Equality: Commitment or Ideal?" *Intercollegiate Review,* Spring 1989.

Lichtman, Allan J. "How to Bet in '84: The Only Presidential Election Guide You'll Ever Need." *Washingtonian,* April 1982.

———. "President Bill?" *Washingtonian,* October 1992.

Lichtman, Allan J., and Ken DeCell. "How to Bet in November." *Washingtonian,* May 1988.

"Man of the Year: Lyndon B. Johnson: The Paradox of Power." *Time,* January 5, 1968.

"The Man Who Beat Communism: Ronald Reagan Was Fond of a Nap and No Intellectual. Oddly Enough, He Had What It Took." *The Economist,* June 12, 2004.

Merry, Robert W. "The Pedernales Gatsby." *National Review,* August 20, 1976.

———. "The Political Outlook of Teddy White." *Congressional Quarterly Weekly Report,* September 9, 1989.

———. "Presidential Politics and the Big Picture." *Congressional Quarterly Weekly Report,* May 5, 1990.

———. "Populism and Elitism: The Clinton Model." *Congressional Quarterly Weekly Report,* May 1, 1993.

———. "Politics of the Future Beckons Democrats." *Congressional Quarterly Weekly Report,* November 26, 1994.

———. "Referendum Politics: Dole's Campaign." *Congressional Quarterly Weekly Report,* August 10, 1996.

———. "A Rule for Presidents: Go Centrist or Perish." *Congressional Quarterly Weekly Report,* October 26, 1996.

———. "The Reagan Legacy." *CQ Weekly,* June 12, 2004.

Nixon, Richard M. "Asia After Viet Nam." *Foreign Affairs,* October 1967.

Piereson, James. "The Forgotten Man by Amity Shlaes." *Commentary,* September 2007.

Schlesinger, Arthur M., Jr. "The Ages of Jackson." *New York Review of Books,* December 7, 1989.

———. "The Ultimate Approval Rating." *New York Times Magazine,* December 15, 1996.

———. "History and National Stupidity." *New York Review of Books,* April 27, 2006.

Wilentz, Sean. "The Worst President in History?" *Rolling Stone,* April 21, 2006.

NEWSPAPER ARTICLES

"Arthur M. Schlesinger Sr., Historian, Dies at 77." *New York Times,* October 31, 1965.

Baker, Peter. "The Charge That Obama Can't Shake." *New York Times,* "Week in Review," October 31, 2010.

Friedman, Thomas L. "Bring Back Poppy." *New York Times,* July 30, 2011.

Martin, Douglas. "Arthur Schlesinger, Historian of Power, Dies at 89." *New York Times,* March 1, 2007.

Meacham, Jon. "Rocking the Vote, in the 1820s and Now." *New York Times,* October 24, 2010.

Merry, Robert W. "History and Gerald Ford." *National Observer,* January 22, 1977.

———. "The Post-Industrial Campaign." *Wall Street Journal,* October 3, 1984.

———. "Growth Agent: Reagan Transformed." *Wall Street Journal,* September 13, 1985.

———. "Finance Panel Can Look Back: Jefferson, Jackson, and Lincoln." *Wall Street Journal,* May 6, 1986.

————. "Don't Count Bush In Yet." *Memphis Commercial Appeal* (distributed by Scripps Howard News Service), October 4, 1991.

————. "Today's Political Map Leads to Suburbs." *Quincy (Illinois) Herald-Whig* (distributed by Scripps Howard News Service), June 24, 1992.

————. "Reagan Legacy Is Dead." *Memphis Commercial Appeal* (distributed by Scripps Howard News Service), August 19, 1992.

————. "Our Greatest Retreat." *Wall Street Journal*, April 27, 1994.

————. "Urban Cowboy: A Biography of Theodore Roosevelt Stresses His Adventurous Spirit." *New York Times Book Review*, October 27, 2002.

————. "The Myth of the One-Time Wonder." *New York Times*, February 14, 2010.

Nevins, Allan. "At the Roots of Democracy." *New York Times*, September 16, 1945.

"Obamanomics Takes a Holiday." Editorial, *Wall Street Journal*, December 8, 2010.

Seib, Gerald F. "In Crisis, Opportunity for Obama." *Wall Street Journal*, November 21, 2008.

Steele, Shelby. "The Referendum on the Redeemer." *Wall Street Journal*, October 28, 2010.

Wilentz, Sean. "Into the West: James K. Polk Engineered the Triumph of Manifest Destiny." *New York Times Book Review*, November 22, 2009.

————. "Who's Buried in the History Books?" *New York Times*, March 14, 2010.

WEB SITES

http://www.americanwarlibrary.com

http://www.andrewjohnson.com

http://www.answers.com/topic/myers-v-united-states

http://www.archives.gov

http://www.claremont.org

http://www.clinton4.nara.gov

http://www.cnn.com

http://www.dlc.org

http://eh.net

http://www.highbeam.com

http://www.huppi.com

http://www.measuringworth.com

http://www.msnbc.msn.com

http://www.online.wsj.com

http://www.pbs.org

http://www.politico.com
http://www.presidency.ucsb.edu
http://www.rand.org
http://www.senate.gov
http://www.spartacus.schoolnet.co.uk
http://www.stratfor.com
http://supreme.justia.com/us/272/52/
http://www.taxpolicycenter.org
http://www.thefastertimes.com
http://www.thinkexist.com
http://www.truth-out.org
http://www.usgovernmentspending.com
http://www.wikipedia.org

Index

Page numbers in *italics* refer to illustrations.

ABC News, xv, 12
abolitionist movement, 101, 178
abortion issue, 200
Acheson, Dean, 134
Adams, Abigail, 169
Adams, Henry, 24, 73, 164–65, 170, 176
Adams, John, xvi, xx, 44, 169
  Alien and Sedition acts and, 75, 78, 170
  electoral judgment of, 79
  French undeclared naval war and, 77–78
  historical judgment of, 4, 5, 7, 8, 9, 10, 38, 77–79, 125
  Madison and, 24, 73
  Murray-Blessing ranking and, 9
  Neal ranking and, 8
  Schlesinger Jr. survey and, 10
  Schlesinger Sr. surveys and, 4, 5
  U.S. Historical Society ranking of, 7
  Wall Street Journal ranking and, 12
Adams, John Quincy, xx, 93, 113, 120, 147, 171, 173, 225
  Murray-Blessing survey and, 9
Adams, Sherman, 109
Afghanistan, 195
African Americans, 79, 80, 81, 83, 105, 128, 157
Age of Jackson, The (Schlesinger), 20–23, 30, 31–33
Agnew, Spiro T., 93
Agricultural Adjustment Act (1933), 184
AIDS (Acquired Immune Deficiency Syndrome), 199, 200
Alabama, University of, 11
Albemarle, C.S.S., 85–86

Alien and Sedition acts (1798), 75, 78, 170
al Qaeda, 218
Alsop, Joseph, 136, 137, 154
Alsop, Stewart, 136
Alvernia College, 8
Ambrose, Stephen E., 153
America in Search of Itself (White), 57
American Lion: Andrew Jackson in the White House (Meacham), 35
American Political Science Association, 204
American Revolution, 45, 74, 168, 179
Americans with Disabilities Act (1990), 206
American System, 27, 33
American University, 53
Andrew Jackson: His Life and Times (Brands), 35
Angola, 195
anti-Federalists, 168, 169
    see also Democratic-Republican Party
Appleby, Joyce, 171
Arthur, Chester A., xx, 5, 11, 197
Articles of Confederation (1781), 167
"Asia After Viet Nam" (Nixon), 159–60
Atlanta, Ga., 85
atomic bomb, 63, 134
Austria, 130
automobiles, 153

Babcock, Orville E., 82
Bailey, Thomas A., 5–7, 13, 70, 174
Baker, Jean H., 103
Baltimore, Md., 176
Bank of the United States, Second, 22, 28, 31, 32, 33, 37, 76, 201
banks, banking:
    Clinton and, 219
    financial crisis and, 228
    Grant and, 82
    Great Depression and, 111, 183, 184
    Hamilton proposal for, 168–69, 170
    Jackson and, 22, 28, 31, 32, 33, 37, 201
    Madison and, 76, 172
    Monroe and, 173
    War of 1812 and, 74
    Wilson and, 148

Barnes, Fred, 123
baseball, 61
Bell, John, 178
Benson, Allan L., 127
Benton, Thomas Hart, 37
Berlin Airlift (1948–49), 64, 136
Berlin Wall, 203
Blaine, James G., 67
Bleeding Kansas, 101, 102–3, 176
Blessing, Tim H., xix*n*, 8–10, 11, 197–98
Bloody Bloody Andrew Jackson (Friedman and Timbers), 22
Bowers, Claude G., 25, 106
Brady Bill (1993), 219
Brands, H. W., 35
Breckinridge, John C., 178
Bretton Woods Conference (1944), 63
Brezhnev, Leonid, 193–94
"Bring Back Poppy" (Friedman), 206
Bristow, Benjamin H., 82
Britton, Nan, 91
Brown, Dee, 34
Bryan, William Jennings, 70, 127
Buchanan, James, xx, 90, 94, 99–103, *100,* 112, 219, 226
    Bailey's ranking of, 7
    historical ranking of, 7, 10, 103
    Murray-Blessing survey and, 10
    Polk and, 100–101
    slavery issue and, 101–3
    Southern secession and, 103
Buchanan, Patrick J., 207, 210
Buckley, William F., Jr., 226
Bundy, McGeorge, 138
Burns, James MacGregor, 185–86
Burr, Aaron, 172
Bury My Heart at Wounded Knee (Brown), 34
Bush, George H. W., xx, 56, 119, 195, 196, 205–11, 213, 227
    election of 1992 and, 206, 207, 213
    electoral judgment of, 196, 206
    historical judgment of, 211
    Persian Gulf War and, 141–43, 206, 210–11
    Soviet collapse and, 206, 210
    "vision thing" remark of, 208

Bush, George W., 40, 212, 213, 220–27, *221*
  election of 2000 and, 221
  election of 2004 and, 224, 226, 233
  Iraq invasion and, 119, 221, 222–24, 225
  split-decision presidency and, 146, 147
  tax cuts of, 225
  veto and, 225
  Wall Street Journal survey and, 13

Calhoun, John C., 37, 121–22
California, 37, 38, 95–96, 118, 199
Cambodia, 140–41
Canada, 215
"cap and trade," 229
capital gains taxes, 209
Caro, Robert A., 158
Carranza, Venustiano, 149
Carter, Jimmy, 62, 65, 147, 188–89, 199–200, 226, 227, 238
  electoral judgment of, 93
  Murray-Blessing ranking and, 9
  Porter ranking and, 8
  Schlesinger Jr. survey and, 11
Cass, Lewis, 37, 98
Census, U.S., 108
Central America, 99, 137, 195, 199, 203
Central Intelligence Agency (CIA), 64, 153
Chase, Salmon P., 85
checks and balances, 46, 48–49
Cherokees, 23, 29
Chicago Tribune poll, xix*n,* 8, 104, 112, 123, 150, 158
China, People's Republic of, 14, 64, 135, 137, 154, 160–61, 223
Churchill, Winston S., 127, 152, 237
Civil Rights Act (1964), 156
civil rights movement, 14, 105, 156, 188
Civil War, U.S., 17, 81, 85–86, 105, 118, 119, 122–23, 174–79
Clarus Research Group, 12
class warfare, 217–18
Clay, Henry, 95, 172, 181, 201
  Jackson and, 26–27, 33, 173, 184–85
  Polk and, 37

  Roosevelt and, 32, 33
  War of 1812 and, 120
Clayton Antitrust Act (1914), 148
Clemenceau, Georges, 129
Cleveland, Grover, xvi, *68,* 220
  background of, 67
  Bailey ranking of, 7, 70
  Eland on, 16
  electoral judgment and, 67–71, *68,* 72
  historical judgment of, 4, 5, 7, 10, 23–24, 67–71, 72, 77, 125
  Porter survey and, 7
  presidential veto and, 17
  Schlesinger Jr. survey and, 10, 70
  Schlesinger Sr. surveys and, 4, 5, 23, 70
  Wall Street Journal ranking of, 70
Clinton, Bill, xx, xxi, 94–95, 213–20, *214,* 227
  bank deregulation and, 219
  election of 1992 and, 215
  election of 1994 and, 204–5, 214–15, 216, 219, 228, 233
  election of 1996 and, 216, 218, 233
  government shutdown and, 216
  healthcare reform and, 215, 216, 218
  historical judgment of, 219–20
  impeachment of, 109, 218
  personal scandals of, 214, 218
  Schlesinger Jr. survey and, 219
  split-decision presidency and, 146, 213
  Wall Street Journal survey and, 219
  welfare reform and, 216
coal industry, 128
Cold War, 133, 136–38, 152–53, 154–55, 159–63, 188, 193–94, 195, 202–3, 210
  see also Soviet Union; *specific presidents*
Colombia, 88
Compromise of 1850, 95–96
Congress, U.S., 7, 44, 45, 46, 58, 60, 220
  Andrew Johnson and, 104–7, *104*
  constitutional powers of, 49
  election of 1866 and, 106
  election of 1994 and, 204–5, 214–15, 216, 219
  energy policy and, 229, 230
  government shutdown and, 216

Congress, U.S. (*cont.*)
  Harding and, 91
  healthcare reform and, 54, 216, 230
  immigration and, 108
  Jackson and, 27
  Jefferson and, 75, 171
  J. Q. Adams and, 93
  Lyndon Johnson and, 156
  Obama and, 230
  Persian Gulf War and, 141–42
  Polk and, 38, 117, 118
  presidential term and, 62
  Radical Republicans and, 25, 79–80,
    104–7
  Reagan and, 202
  Roosevelt Court packing scheme and,
    186
  slavery issue and, 95–96
  tariffs and, 69
  Theodore Roosevelt and, 87, 88
  War of 1812 and, 120, 121
  Washington and, 167, 168, 169
  World War I and, 128, 129
  see also House of Representatives, U.S.;
    Senate, U.S.
Congressional Quarterly Weekly Report, 52
Constitution, U.S., 17, 27, 96, 170, 197,
    201
  Lincoln and, 174–75, 178–79, 189
  ratification of, 58, 59–60
  slavery and, 178–79
  Thirteenth Amendment to, 178
  Fourteenth Amendment to, 105
  Fifteenth Amendment to, 80
  Sixteenth Amendment to, 182
  Twenty-Second Amendment to, 48, 72
Constitutional Convention (1787), xviii,
    xxi, 43–50, 59, 74, 166
Constitutional Union Party, 178
Continental Congress, 77
Contras, 204
Coolidge, Calvin, xx, 109–10, 238
  electoral judgment of, 72, 86, 110
  historical judgment of, 72, 87, 92, 94
  Reagan and, 86–87, 110
Copperheads, 176
corporations, 180, 182, 202, 208, 228

Country of Vast Designs, A (Merry), 39
Cox, James M., 131
C-SPAN, 12
Cuba, 98, 99, 124–25, 137, 180–81
Cuomo, Mario, 11
Czechoslovakia, 130

Daily Union, 98
Dalton, Kathleen, 181, 189
Daniels, Mitch, 225
Daugherty, Harry, 107
Davis, Jefferson, 98
Dayton Peace Accords (1995), 219
debt, national, 229, 232
DeCell, Ken, 51–55, 57–58, 60, 64, 68,
    81, 85–86, 93, 156, 186, 206, 207
Declaration of Independence (1776), 179
Defense Department, U.S., 63–64
de Gaulle, Charles, 164, 189
Delaware, 178
Democratic Party, 37, 55, 65, 67, 81, 97,
    101, 174, 177
  election of 1854 and, 98–99
  election of 1920 and, 130–31
  election of 1930 and, 111
  election of 1952 and, 136
  election of 1994 and, 204–5, 214–15,
    216, 233
  election of 2008 and, 232
  election of 2010 and, 227, 232, 233
  slavery issue and, 98–99, 103
Democratic-Republican Party, 77, 170,
    172, 173
deregulation, 219
Detroit, Mich., riot (1967), 157
Dewey, George, 125
District of Columbia, 96, 196
Dole, Robert, 216
Douglas, Stephen A., 35, 97–98, 176, 177
draft, military, 128
Dred Scott v. Sanford (1857), 102
Dukakis, Michael, 56
Dulles, John Foster, 137
Dunning, W. A., 25

Earned Income Tax Credit, 219
Economist, 130, 203

Egypt, 137, 154
Eisenhower, Dwight D., 18, 89, 109, *151,*
    237
  electoral judgment of, 155
  historical ranking of, 155–56
  interstate highway system and, 153
  Korean War and, 119, 136–37, 152
  Murray-Blessing ranking and, 9–10
  Neal ranking and, 8
  New Deal legacy and, 165–66, 188
  Porter survey and, 7
  Rossiter critique of, xiii–xiv, 6, 212
  Schlesinger Jr. survey and, 10, 156
  Schlesinger Sr. surveys and, 5, 6, 15
  Soviet Union and, 137, 152, 153, 154, 155
  split-decision presidency and, 146,
    150–56
  Wall Street Journal ranking and, 12
  World War II and, 151
Eland, Ivan, 16–18
elections, midterm, xvii, 61
  of 1854, 98–99
  of 1858, 177
  of 1866, 106
  of 1914, 148
  of 1918, 150
  of 1930, 111
  of 1938, 186
  of 1966, 157
  of 1994, 204–5, 214–15, 216, 219, 228,
    233
  of 2010, 227, 231, 232, 233
elections, presidential:
  of 1800, 24, 79
  of 1816, 76–77
  of 1820, 77
  of 1824, 173
  of 1844, 36–37
  of 1852, 97
  of 1860, 53, 123, 177–78
  of 1864, 85–86, 104, 123
  of 1872, 81
  of 1876, 82–83, 221
  of 1884, 67, 69
  of 1888, 68, 69
  of 1892, 69
  of 1896, 70

  of 1904, 88
  of 1912, 147, 182
  of 1916, 126, 127, 149
  of 1920, 130–31, 150
  of 1924, 86
  of 1928, 86
  of 1932, 86, 111
  of 1936, 186
  of 1940, 186
  of 1944, 133
  of 1948, 62, 64, 228
  of 1952, 65, 136
  of 1956, 154
  of 1960, 55, 154, 155
  of 1964, 145
  of 1968, 55, 158, 215
  of 1972, 159, 161, 162
  of 1976, 56, 65, 93, 193, 199
  of 1980, 65, 199–200
  of 1984, 55–56, 196, 201–2
  of 1988, 56, 196, 208
  of 1992, 206, 207, 213, 215
  of 1996, 216, 218, 233
  of 2000, 213, 218, 221
  of 2004, 224, 226, 233
  of 2008, 232, 233
  mass media and, 55, 56
  money's influence in, 52
  negative advertising and, 52
  polling and, 55
  referendum character of, xviii, 51–66,
    71, 76
Electoral College, 48, 68, 69, 77, 83, 97,
    196, 213, 218, 224
Elving, Ronald D., 215
Emancipation Proclamation (1863), 178
Emanuel, Rahm, 229
Equal Opportunity Act (1964), 156
era of good feelings, 76

Fall, Albert, 107
Family and Medical Leave Act (1993),
    215
Fass, Paula S., 90
*Fathers and Children: Andrew Jackson and
    the Subjugation of the American Indian*
    (Rogin), 34

Faucheux, Ron, 12
Federal Deposit Insurance Corporation
    (FDIC), 184
Federalist Papers, 59–60
Federalist Party, 75, 77, 78, 79, 120, 168,
    170, 171
Federalist Society, 11
Federal Reserve, 148, 202
Felzenberg, Alvin Stephen, 13–16, 18
Fifteenth Amendment (1870), 80
Fillmore, Millard, xx, 94, 95–96, 112
financial crisis, 228–30
financial industry, 219, 228
    see also banks, banking
fireside chats, 184
Florida
    election of 1876 and, 83
    election of 2000 and, 213
Foner, Eric, 25
Ford, Gerald R., 65, 93–94, 141, 199
    Schlesinger Jr. survey and, 11
Fordney-McCumber Tariff (1922), 108
Foreign Affairs, 159–60
Forgotten Man, The: A New History of the
    Great Depression (Shlaes), 185
Forrestal, James, 64
Fourteen Points, 129
Fourteenth Amendment (1868), 105
France, 74, 75, 77, 168
    Mexico and, 121
    Reign of Terror in, 78
    Suez crisis and, 154
    U.S. undeclared naval war with, 77–78
    World War I and, 127, 129
free silver movement, 70
Friedman, Thomas L., 206
Fugitive Slave Act (1850), 96

Gadsden Purchase (1854), 99
Gallup poll, 5, 15, 226
Garfield, James A., xx, 3
gay rights issue, 200, 215
George III, King of England, 45, 169
Georgia, Native American removal from,
    22, 23, 29, 32, 34, 35
German Empire, World War I and,
    126–28, 129–30

Germany, Nazi, 132–33, 187
Germond, Jack, 55–56, 57
Gettysburg Address (1863), 179
Ghent, Treaty of (1814), 75
Gilded Age, 24
Glass-Steagall Act (1933), 184, 219
Gorbachev, Mikhail, 194, 196, 198, 203
Gore, Albert, Jr., 39, 213
Grant, Ulysses S., xv–xvi, xx, 79–84, 80,
    112, 146
    Bailey ranking of, 7
    Civil War and, 123
    electoral judgment of, 72, 81, 107
    historical judgment of, 4, 5, 7, 10, 12,
        24–25, 72, 83–84, 92, 94, 104, 107, 109
    Murray-Blessing survey and, 10
    Porter ranking and, 7
    Reconstruction and, 79–81, 105
    scandals in administration of, 82, 109
    Schlesinger Sr. surveys and, 4, 5
    Wall Street Journal ranking and, 12
Great Britain, 77, 81, 168
    Oregon and, 37
    in Suez crisis, 154
    in War of 1812, 74–75, 120–21
    in World War I, 126–27, 129
    in World War II, 133, 187
Great Depression, xx, 6, 86, 87, 155,
    182–86, 216, 217, 238
Greatness in the White House: Rating the
    Presidents from George Washington
    Through Ronald Reagan (Murray and
    Blessing), xixn
Great Society, 14, 156, 157, 188, 229
Great White Fleet, 88
Greece, 136
Greeley, Horace, 178
Greenfield, Kent Roberts, 132
Gross Domestic Product (GDP), xvi, 92,
    128, 148, 155, 156, 162, 182, 186,
    195, 196, 209–10, 216, 217, 224, 228
Grover Cleveland: A Study in Courage
    (Nevins), 23–24, 70
Guam, 84, 125, 181

habeas corpus, writ of, 80–81, 175
Halper, Stefan, 223

Hamilton, Alexander, 33, 79, 171
  bank proposal of, 168–69, 170
  Constitutional Convention and, 43–44,
    48, 59
  death of, 172
  Federalist Papers and, 59–60
Hard Bargain (Shogan), 187
Harding, Warren G., xvi, xx, 86, *91,*
    107–9, 110, 112, 131, 226
  Congress and, 91
  historical and electoral judgments of,
    90–92, 94, 107, 109
  Murray-Blessing survey and, 10
  Schlesinger Sr. surveys and, 4, 5
  Teapot Dome scandal and, 90, 91, 109
Harrison, Benjamin, 11, 68, 69, 92, 113,
    197
Harrison, William Henry, 3, 62
Harris poll, 232
Hawaii, 84, 125, 181
Hay, John, 125
Hayakawa, S. I., 88
Hayes, Rutherford B., xx, 62, 220
  Eland's ranking of, 16
  election of 1876 and, 83
Haymarket riot (1886), 69
Hays, Will, 107
healthcare reform, 54, 215, 216, 218, 229
Hearst, William Randolph, 124
Heller, Walter, 195
Hepburn Act (1903), 87
highways, 153
*History of the United States of America
    During the Administrations of Thomas
    Jefferson and James Madison* (Adams),
    24, 73
Hitler, Adolf, 130, 132
Hofstadter, Richard, 31, 33
Holmes, Oliver Wendell, Jr., 239
Homestead Act (1862), 123
Hong Kong, 160
Hoover, Herbert C., 86, 219, 238
  electoral judgment of, 110, 111, 112
  Harding and, 108
  historical judgment of, 9, 23, 92–93, 94,
    111, 112
  Murray-Blessing survey and, 9, 23

Hopkins, Harry, 132
House of Representatives, U.S., 48, 53, 81,
    97, 147, 206
  Andrew Johnson impeachment and,
    104, 106
  Clinton impeachment in, 109, 218
  election of 1854 and, 98–99
  election of 1876 and, 83
  election of 1920 and, 131
  election of 1930 and, 111
  election of 1932 and, 111
  election of 1938 and, 186
  election of 1964 and, 145
  election of 1994 and, 204–5, 214–15,
    216, 219
  election of 2008 and, 232
  election of 2010 and, 227, 232
  Obama and, 230
  Reagan and, 202
  see also Congress, U.S.; Senate, U.S.
housing bubble, 228, 229
Huerta, Victoriano, 148–49
Hughes, Charles Evans, 108, 127
Humphrey, Hubert H., 55, 158
Hussein, Saddam, 141–43

Idaho, 174
immigration, 87, 108
impeachment, 44, 47, 49, 61, *104,* 106,
    109, 218
impressment, 74, 75, 120, 121
income inequality, 236
income taxes, 111, 123, 128, 148, 158,
    182, 219
independent voters, 226, 232
Industrial Revolution, 31, 33
inflation, 65, 74, 128, 153, 159, 162, 195,
    196, 202
In Search of History: A Personal Adventure
    (White), 57
Interstate Commerce Act (1887), 68
Interstate Commerce Commission (ICC),
    87, 181
Iran, 137, 142, 195, 199, 204
Iran-Contra scandal, 54, 196, 204, 205
Iraq, 119, 141–43, 211, 221, 222–24, 225
Islamic fundamentalism, 236

isolationist movement, 187
Israel, 142, 154
Italy, 134

Jackson, Andrew, *21*, 96, 201, 219
  background of, 26
  Bailey ranking of, 7
  Clay and, 26–27, 33, 173, 184–85
  Eland on, 16
  electoral judgment of, 72, 89
  historical judgment of, xix, 4, 5, 7, 9,
    10, 12, 20–23, 25–36, 89
  as Leader of Destiny, 165, 173–74
  Murray-Blessing ranking of, 9, 23
  National Road and, 27, 33
  Native Americans and, 22, 23, 26, 29,
    32, 34, 35
  nullification and, 28–29, 31
  Polk and, 25
  populism of, 20, 26–28, 30, 32, 33, 173
  Roosevelt compared with, 21–22, 23, 32
  Schlesinger biography of, 20–23, 30,
    31–33, 34, 35
  Schlesinger Jr. survey and, xix, 10
  Schlesinger Sr. surveys and, 4, 5, 22
  Second Bank of the United States and,
    22, 28, 31, 32, 33, 37, 201
  slavery and, 22, 23, 32, 35
  spoils system and, 29–30
  tariffs and, 27, 29
  Texas and, 16–17
  U.S. Historical Society ranking of, 7
  Van Buren and, 25
  veto and, 27–28, 33
  Wall Street Journal ranking and, 12
  War of 1812 and, 26, 74
  women's rights and, 22, 23
James, Marquis, 30–31, 35
Japan, 63, 99, 132, 133, 134, 160, 186–87
Japanese Americans, 133
Jay, John, 59
Jay Cooke & Company, 82
Jay Treaty (1794), 168
Jefferson, Thomas, 201, 219, 229
  Bailey ranking of, 7
  Congress and, 75, 171
  Eland on, 16

electoral judgment of, 72, 79, 89
historical judgment of, xix, 4, 5, 7, 10,
  12, 38, 72, 89
as Leader of Destiny, 165, 169–73, 189
neutrality policy of, 75, 172
partisan strife and, 78
Schlesinger Jr. survey and, xix, 10
Schlesinger Sr. surveys and, 4, 5
Sherman and, 44
U.S. Historical Society ranking of, 7
Wall Street Journal ranking and, 12
Johnson, Andrew, xx, 62, 94, 104–7, *104*,
  112
  historical ranking of, 5, 10, 104, 106, 107
  impeachment of, *104*, 106
  Murray-Blessing survey and, 10
  Reconstruction and, 79, 104–7
  Schlesinger Sr. surveys and, 5, 104
  veto and, 105
Johnson, Louis, 134
Johnson, Lyndon B., 62, 109, 125, 147,
  155, 217, 220, 222, 229
  electoral judgment and, 145
  Murray-Blessing ranking and, 9, 23,
    158
  Porter ranking of, 8, 158
  Schlesinger Jr. survey and, 10, 158
  split-decision presidency and, 144–45,
    146, 156–58
  Vietnam War and, 14, 39, 119, 138–40,
    157, 158, 188, 223, 237
  Wall Street Journal survey and, 13, 158
Jomini, Henri, 123
Jones, Charles O., 204
Jordan, 142
Justice Department, U.S., 80

Kansas, 97, 99, 101, 102–3, 176
Kansas-Nebraska Act (1854), 96, 97–99,
  102, 176, 177, 230
Kemp, Jack, 199
Kendall, Willmoore, 179
Kennedy, David M., 133
Kennedy, John F., 55, 77, 125, 154–55,
  156, 188
  Murray-Blessing survey and, 9
  Schlesinger Jr. survey and, 10

Vietnam and, 138–39
Wall Street Journal survey and, 13
Kentucky, 178
Kerry, John F., 226
Khrushchev, Nikita S., 155
King, Martin Luther, Jr., 159
King, Rufus, 77
Kings Depart, The (Watt), 129
Knights of Labor, 69
Komatsu, Sylvia, 39
Korea, North, 134, 136, 152
Korea, South, 134, 152, 160
Korean War, 64, 118–19, 134–37, 152, 223
Kosovo, 219
Ku Klux Klan, 80, 81, 108–9
Ku Klux Klan Act (1871), 80
Kuwait, 141, 142

labor movement, 69, 70, 128, 184, 185
LaFeber, Walter, 125
land grants, 81, 123
Laos, 137
Larrabee, Eric, 132
Laski, Harold J., xiv, 237
Leaders of Destiny, xviii, 164–90
*Leaders We Deserved (And a Few We
    Didn't), The: Rethinking the
    Presidential Rating Game*
    (Felzenberg), 13–16, 18
League of Nations, 130, 181
Lebanon, 204
Lee, Fitzhugh, 124
Leff, Mark, 183
Leo, Leonard, xixn
Lewinsky, Monica, 214, 218
Lichtman, Allan J., 51–55, 57–58, 60, 64,
    68, 81, 85–86, 93, 156, 186, 206
Life, xixn, 3, 4, 22
Life of Andrew Jackson (James), 30–31, 35
Life of Andrew Jackson (Parton), 29–30
Lincoln, Abraham, xx, 53, 84, *175*, 184,
    219, 238–39
    Bailey ranking of, 7
    Civil War and, 17, 85–86, 118, 119,
        122–23, 174–79, 189
    Constitution and, 174–75, 178–79, 189
    Eland on, 16, 17

election of 1858 and, 177
election of 1860 and, 53, 123, 177–78
electoral judgment of, 72, 85–86, 89
historical judgment of, xix, 4, 5, 7, 9,
    10, 12, 38, 72, 85, 89
history comment by, 220
as Leader of Destiny, 165, 174–80, 182,
    189
Murray-Blessing survey and, 9
Reconstruction and, 79
Schlesinger Jr. survey and, xix, 10
Schlesinger Sr. surveys and, 4, 5
secession and, 174
slavery issue and, 176–79
U.S. Historical Society ranking of, 7
Wall Street Journal ranking and, 12
Whig Party and, 27, 103
Lincoln at Gettysburg (Wills), 179
Lindgren, James, 12
Lloyd George, David, 129
Lodge, Henry Cabot, 130
Longworth, Alice Roosevelt, 92
Lotto, Mark, xiv–xv
Louisiana, election of 1876 and, 83
Louisiana Purchase (1803), 171
Lovett, Robert, 64
Lowell, Mass., 32

MacArthur, Douglas, 64, 135–36
McCain, John, 232
McCarthy, Eugene, 144, 145
McCoy, Drew R., 24
McCullough, David, 15, 78
McDonald, Forrest, 11, 170
McDonald, John A., 82
McGinniss, Joe, 55
McGovern, George, 162
McKinley, William, 87, *124*, 156
    electoral judgment of, 72, 125
    historical judgment of, 8, 10, 11, 72,
        84–85, 123, 125
    Murray-Blessing survey and, 10, 123
    Neal ranking and, 8
    Schlesinger Jr. survey and, 11, 84–85,
        123, 125
    Spanish-American War and, 84, 119,
        123–25, 180–81

MacMillan, Margaret, 130
McNamara, Robert S., 138, 139
Madison, James, xxi, *73*, 170, 172
    Adams and, 24, 73
    Constitutional Convention and, 46, 47,
        74
    electoral vs. historical judgment of, 24,
        72, 73–77, 79
    Federalist Papers and, 59
    neutrality issue and, 120, 121
    War of 1812 and, *73*, 74–75, 119,
        120–21
Mahan, Dennis Hart, 123
Main Currents in American Thought
    (Parrington), 30
Maine, 97
Maine, U.S.S., 125, 181
Making of the President, The (White), 55
Malaysia, 160
Manifest Destiny, 40
Marcy, William, 98
Marshall, George C., 64, 131, 132
Marshall Plan, 63, 136
Maryland, 176, 178
mass media, 55, 56
Maysville Road (National Road), 27, 33
Meacham, Jon, 22, 35
Meat Inspection Act (1906), 87
Medicaid, 156
Medicare, 156
Mellon, Andrew W., 108
Melville, Herman, 35
Mexican War, 38, 39, 40, 95, 97, 117–18,
    119, 121–22, 174
Mexico, 17, 37–40, 99, 117, 121, 148–49,
    174, 215
Meyers, Marvin, 26
Middle East, 223, 236
minimum wage, 153
Minnesota, 196
misery index, 65, 216
missile gap, 154
Mississippi River, 26
Missouri, 97, 102
Missouri Compromise (1820), 97–98, 102,
    176
Mondale, Walter, 55, 201–2

money, currency, 22, 27, 28, 70, 74, 76, 92,
    162, 170, 208
Monroe, James, 172–73, 220
    electoral judgment of, 72, 76–77, 79
    historical judgment of, 72, 77, 125
    Neal ranking and, 8
    Schlesinger Jr. ranking of, 10–11
Montana, 174
Morris, Gouverneur, 46–47, 48, 59
mortgage crisis, 228, 229
muckrakers, 87
Murray, Robert K., xix*n*, 8–10, 11, 94,
    197–98
Muslims, 224
Myers v. United States (1926), 106*n*
"Myth of the One-Term Wonder, The"
    (Merry), xv

Napoleon I, Emperor of France, 75
National Bank Act (1863), 123
National Industrial Recovery Act (1933),
    184
National Labor Relations Act (Wagner
    Act) (1935), 184, 185
national park system, 88
National Road (Maysville Road), 27, 33
National Security Act (1947), 63–64
National Security Council (NSC), 64
Native Americans:
    Jackson and, 22, 23, 26, 29, 32, 34, 35
    War of 1812 and, 120
Navy, U.S., 78, 86, 88, 99, 125
Neal, Steve, xix*n*, 8, 123, 150, 158
Nebraska, 97, 176
negative advertising, 52
neutrality, U.S., 75, 120, 121, 126–27, 168,
    172, 187
Neutrality Act (1939), 187
Nevins, Allan, 23–24, 46, 70, 98
Newark, N.J., riot (1967), 157
New Deal, 21–22, 23, 32, 33, 152, 153,
    165, 186, 188
New England, 74, 75
New Hampshire, 1992 Republican
    primary in, 207
New Mexico, 96, 118
New Orleans, Battle of (1815), 26, 74

Newsweek, 195
New York Review of Books, 23, 33
New York Times, xiv-xv, 22, 84, 206
New York Times Magazine, xix*n*, 4–5,
  10–11, 14
New York Tribune, 178
Ngo Dinh Diem, 138, 139
Nicaragua, 204
Nixon, Richard M., 55, 92, 94, 155, 156,
  161, 204, 215
  Asia policy and, 159–61
  Felzenberg and, 13–14
  Ford and, 93
  historical judgment of, 162
  Murray-Blessing ranking and, 9, 10, 23,
    162
  Porter ranking and, 8
  Soviet Union and, 160, 161–62
  split-decision presidency and, 146,
    158–63
  Vietnam War and, 119, 140–41, 159,
    160, 163
  Watergate and, 14, 65, 92, 109, 112,
    141, 159, 161, 162, 188
Nobel Peace Prize, 88
Noriega, Manuel, 206, 210
North American Free Trade Agreement
  (NAFTA) (1994), 215
North Atlantic Treaty Organization
  (NATO), 64, 219
Northwestern University, 12
nullification, 28–29, 31

Obama, Barack H., xv, xviii, 119, 204,
  213, 227–33, 238
  Clarus poll and, 12
  economic stimulus plan and, 228,
    229–30
  election of 2010 and, 227, 231, 232,
    233
  energy policy and, 229, 230
  financial crisis and, 228–29
  healthcare reform and, 54, 229
  mortgage crisis and, 228, 229
  Truman model and, 227, 228
O'Brien, Lawrence, 144–45, 157
Occupy Wall Street movement, 217

oil embargo, Arab (1973–74), 93, 162
oil industry, 93, 142, 162
OPEC (Organization of Petroleum
  Exporting Countries), 162
Oregon, 174
  election of 1876 and, 83
Oregon Territory, 37, 174

Pacific Railway Act (1862), 123
Palmer, A. Mitchell, 128
Panama, 206, 210
Panama Canal, 88
Panic of 1837, 22
*Paris 1919: Six Months That Changed the
  World* (MacMillan), 130
Parker, Alton B., 88
Parrington, Vernon L., 30
Parton, James, 29–30
Pearl Harbor attack (Dec. 7, 1941), 132,
  187
Pendergast, Thomas J., 109
Pennsylvania State University, 8
Perot, H. Ross, 207, 210, 215, 216
Perry, Matthew C., 99
Persian Gulf War, 141–43, 206, 210–11
Philippines, 84, 88, 125, 181
Phillips, Carrie, 91
Pierce, Franklin, xx, 96–99, 112, 177
Poland, 130
Polk, James K., xv, xviii–xix, *36*, 71, 96,
  100–101, 147, 219, 222, 226
  Bailey ranking of, 7
  Buchanan and, 100–101
  Eland on, 16, 17
  historical judgment of, 36–40, 89, 94,
    125
  Jackson and, 25
  Mexican War and, 38, 39, 40, 117–18,
    119, 121–22, 174
  Murray-Blessing survey and, 9, 10
  Neal ranking and, 8
  Schlesinger Jr. survey and, xix, 10
  Schlesinger Sr. surveys and, 4, 5, 38
  single term chosen by, xix
  slavery issue and, 39, 40, 174
  tariff reduction and, 37
  Texas and, 17

Polk, James K. (*cont.*)
  U.S. expansionism and, 37–40
  U.S. Historical Society ranking of, 7
  Wall Street Journal ranking and, 12
popular sovereignty, 176
populism:
  Jackson and, 20, 26–28, 30, 32, 33, 173
  Morris and, 46–47
  Reagan and, 208, 209, 210
Porter, David L., xix*n*, 7–8, 123, 150, 158
Potsdam Conference (1945), 134
Presidential Greatness (Bailey), 5, 70
President Reagan: The Triumph of Imagination (Reeves), 199
presidents, presidency:
  Bailey ranking of, 5–7
  Constitutional Convention and, xviii, xxi, 43–50, 59, 74, 166
  constitutional powers of, 49
  electoral compared with historical judgment of, 67–89
  failures in, 90–113
  foreign vs. domestic policy and rankings of, 13–14
  judgment of history and, 3–19, 67–89
  as Leaders of Destiny, xviii, 164–90
  Murray-Blessing ranking of, 8–10, 11, 12, 23, 111, 123, 150, 158, 162, 197–98
  political bias and rankings of, 5–6, 13
  Porter survey of, xix*n*, 7–8, 123, 150, 158
  post-Cold War period and, 212–34
  power vs. encumbrances of, 235–39
  Schlesinger Jr. survey of, xix, xix*n*, 10–11, 14, 15, 70, 83, 84–85, 107, 111, 123, 125, 150, 156, 158, 162, 196, 211, 219
  Schlesinger Sr. rankings of, xix*n*, 3–7, 13, 14, 15, 22, 23, 38, 70, 104, 111, 123, 150
  Siena Research Institute ranking of, 16
  "split-decision" phenomenon of, xviii, 144–63
  term duration and, 58–62
  vagaries of history and, 20–40

veto and, 17, 27–28, 33, 44, 105, 167, 172, 225
Wall Street Journal ranking of, xix*n*, xx–xxi, 11–13, 16, 18, 70, 84, 85, 107, 111, 112, 123, 150, 155, 158, 162, 211, 219
war and, 117–43
see also specific presidents
progressive movement, 87, 88, 91, 147, 150, 184
Progressive Party, 147, 182
Prohibition, 108
Proposition 13, 199
Public Works Administration (PWA), 184
Puerto Rico, 84, 125, 181
Pulitzer Prize, 20, 30, 70
Pure Food and Drug Act (1906), 87–88

Radical Republicans, 25, 79–80, 104–7
railroads, xx, 33, 68–69, 81, 87, 97, 123, 128, 189
Rasmussen Reports, 12
Reagan, Ronald W., xviii, 18, 84, 94, 189, 193–205, *194*, 213, 214–15, 219, 229, 238, 239
  ABC News poll and, 12
  Congress and, 202
  Coolidge and, 86–87, 110
  C-SPAN viewer poll and, 12
  Eland on, 16
  election of 1976 and, 193
  election of 1980 and, 65
  election of 1984 and, 55–56
  electoral judgment of, 72, 195, 198, 199
  historical judgment of, 89, 195, 196–98
  Iran-Contra scandal and, 54, 196, 204, 205
  Jackson as progenitor of, 33
  Murray-Blessing survey and, 12, 197–98
  Rasmussen Reports poll and, 12
  Schlesinger Jr. survey and, 10, 11, 15, 196
  Soviet Union and, 193–94, 195, 196, 198, 202–3
  Wall Street Journal ranking and, 12, 13
Reagan Democrats, 208

Reagan Revolution, 205
*Recarving Rushmore: Ranking the
    Presidents on Peace, Prosperity, and
    Liberty* (Eland), 16–18
Reconstruction, 25, 79–81, *80,* 83, 104–7,
    104, 180
Reeves, Richard, 198–99, 201, 202, 203,
    204, 205
Reign of Terror, 78
Remini, Robert, 33
Reno Gazette, 204
Republican Party, 67, 81, 83, 121, 177,
    179–80
    election of 1994 and, 204–5, 214–15,
        216, 219
    election of 2008 and, 232
    election of 2010 and, 227
    federal government shutdown and, 216
Rhee, Syngman, 134, 152
riots, 128, 157, 159
Ritchie, Donald A., 10
Rogers, Will, 94
Rogin, Michael Paul, 34
Rolling Stone, 220–21, 225
Roosevelt, Franklin D., xvii-xviii, *63,* 64,
    86, 111, 153, *183,* 195, 201, 204,
    217, 219
    activist style of, 87, 88
    Bailey ranking of, 7
    banks and, 32, 183, 184
    Clay as progenitor of, 32, 33
    Eland on, 16
    electoral judgment of, 72, 89, 133, 186
    fireside chats and, 184
    historical judgment of, xix, 4–6, 7, 9,
        10, 12, 38, 72, 89
    Holmes on, 239
    Jackson as progenitor of, 21–22, 23, 32
    as Leader of Destiny, 165, 182–88, 189
    Murray-Blessing survey and, 9
    Schlesinger Jr. survey and, xix, 10
    Schlesinger Sr. surveys and, 4, 5, 6
    Supreme Court and, 186
    U.S. Historical Society ranking of, 7
    Wall Street Journal ranking and, 12
    World War II and, 119, 131–33, 152,
        186–88

Roosevelt, Theodore, xv, 87–89, 147, 150,
    184, 219, 239
    election of 1912 and, 147, 182
    electoral judgment of, 72, 86, 88–89
    historical judgment of, xix, 4, 5, 9, 10,
        38, 72, 86, 88–89
    as Leader of Destiny, 165, 180–82, 189
    Murray-Blessing ranking and, 9
    Schlesinger Jr. survey and, xix, 10
    Schlesinger Sr. surveys and, 4, 5
    U.S. Historical Society ranking of, 7
    Wall Street Journal ranking and, 12
Rossiter, Clinton, 237
    Eisenhower critiqued by, xii–xiv, 6, 212
Royall, Kenneth, 64
Rural Electrification Administration
    (REA), 184
Rusk, Dean, 138
Russell, Francis, 109
Russell, Richard, 139
Russia, 101, 120
Russo-Japanese War, 88

Sabato, Larry J., 62
Saturday Evening Post, 148
Saudi Arabia, 141
Sawyer, Diane, xv, 227
Schlesinger, Arthur M., Jr., 3, 25, 221
    Harding and, 91–92
    Jackson and, 20–23, 26, 30, 33, 34, 35
    presidential survey of, xix, xixn, 10–11,
        14, 15, 70, 83, 84–85, 107, 111, 123,
        125, 150, 156, 158, 162, 196, 211,
        219
Schlesinger, Arthur M., Sr., presidential
    surveys of, xixn, 3–7, 13, 14, 15, 22,
        23, 38, 70, 104, 111, 123, 150
Schroeder, John H., 39
Scott, Winfield, 97, 122
secession, 74, 103, 174
Seigenthaler, John, 219
Selling of the President, The (McGinniss),
    55
Senate, U.S., 44, 48, 49, 97
    Clinton trial in, 218
    election of 1876 and, 83
    election of 1920 and, 131

Senate, U.S. (*cont.*)
  election of 1932 and, 111
  election of 1938 and, 186
  election of 1964 and, 145
  election of 2010 and, 232
  Jay Treaty and, 168
  Johnson trial in, *104,* 106
  League of Nations and, 130
  Mexican War and, 117, 118
  Obama and, 230
  Radical Republicans and, 79
  Wilson and, 147–48
  see also Congress, U.S.; House of
    Representatives, U.S.
Serbia, 219
Seward, William, 103, 238–39
Sheridan, Philip, 85
Sherman, Roger, 44, 45, 47, 48
Sherman, William T., 85, 123
Shiite Muslims, 224
Shlaes, Amity, 185
Shogan, Robert, 187
Siena Research Institute, 16
Simões, Jayme, 99
Simon, Paul, 11
Singapore, 160
Sixteenth Amendment (1913), 182
slaves, slavery, 22, 23, 32, 35, 39, 40,
    95–96, 97–99, 101–3, 105, 174,
    176–79
Smith, Richard Norton, 93
Smoot-Hawley Tariff (1930), 110
Social Security, 153, 184, 185
South Carolina:
  election of 1876 and, 83
  nullification and, 28–29, 31
Soviet Union, 130, 133
  Eisenhower and, 137, 152, 153, 154,
    155
  George H. W. Bush and, 206, 210
  Nixon and, 160, 161–62
  Reagan and, 193–94, 195, 196, 198,
    202–3
  Truman and, 63, 136
Spain, 99, 124–25, *124,* 180–81
Spanish-American War, 84, 119, 123–25,
    124, 180–81

split-decision presidents, xviii, 144–63,
    213
spoils system, 29–30
Sputnik, 154
Stalin, Joseph, 133, 134, 152
Stanford University, 5
Stanton, Edwin M., 106
states' rights issue, 105, 170
Steele, Shelby, 231–32
Stevenson, Adlai E., 136, 154
Stevenson, Elizabeth, 24
Stilwell, Joseph W., 132
stock market, 87, 180, 182, 232
Story, Joseph, 173
strikes, 70, 87, 128
submarines, 127
Suez crisis (1956), 154
Sunni Muslims, 224
"supply side" economics, 199
Supreme Court, U.S.:
  election of 1876 and, 83
  election of 2000 and, 221
  Roosevelt and, 186
  slavery issue and, 102
  Tenure of Office Act and, 106, 106*n*

Taft, William Howard, xv, xx, 62, 106*n,*
    108, 147, 181–82, 220
Taiwan, 160
Taney, Roger B., 175
Taranto, James, xix*n*
tariffs, 27, 29, 37, 69, 76, 87, 92, 108,
    110–11, 147, 172, 173, 201
taxes, taxation, 37, 82, 87, 170, 199–200,
    209, 219
  Eisenhower and, 153
  Franklin Roosevelt and, 185
  George W. Bush and, 225
  Harding and, 108
  Hoover and, 111
  Jackson and, 27
  Jefferson and, 171
  Johnson and, 156, 158
  Lincoln and, 123
  Reagan and, 195, 196, 197, 208
  Theodore Roosevelt and, 182
  Wilson and, 128, 148

Taylor, Zachary, xx, 94, 95, 112, 121, 197
Teapot Dome scandal, 90, 91, 109
telegraph, 128, 182
telephones, 128, 182
Tennessee, 26, 35, 178
Tennessee Valley Authority (TVA), 184
Tenure of Office Act (1867), 106
terrorism, 218, 222, 225, 236
Tet Offensive (1968), 139, 140
Texas, 16–17, 38, 96, 121, 174
Texas State Historical Association, 39
13 Keys to the Presidency, The (Lichtman
    and DeCell), 51–55, 57–58, 60, 64,
    68, 81, 85–86, 93, 154, 155, 156, 158,
    186, 206–7
Thirteenth Amendment (1865), 178
Tilden, Samuel J., 82–83
Time, 34, 196
Trail of Tears, 22, 23, 29
Treasury Department, U.S., 37, 81, 82
treaties, 49
Trist, Nicholas, 117
Truman, Harry S., 63, 109, 133–36, 150,
    152, 155, 222, 227, 228
  Bailey ranking of, 7
  Eland on, 16
  Felzenberg and, 15
  historical vs. electoral judgments of,
    62–65, 89, 134, 150
  Korean war and, 118–19, 134–36, 223
  Murray-Blessing survey and, 9
  popular rating of, 5, 15
  presidential power evaluated by, 235
  Schlesinger Jr. survey and, xix, 10
  Schlesinger Sr. surveys and, 5
  Soviet Union and, 63, 136
  split-decision presidency and, 146,
    158–63
  U.S. Historical Society ranking of, 7
  Wall Street Journal ranking and, 12
  World War II and, 134
trusts, 68–69, 87, 147
Turkey, 136
Turner, Frederick Jackson, 30
Twain, Mark, xiii, 77, 88
Twenty-Second Amendment (1951), 48,
    72

Tyler, John, 16, 17, 96, 197
Tyler, Ron, 39

U-2 spy planes, 155
"Ultimate Approval Rating, The"
    (Schlesinger), 10–11
unemployment, 65, 82, 148, 153, 155, 162,
    182, 186, 195, 196, 210, 230, 232
Union Party, 104
United Nations (UN), 63
  Korean War and, 134–35
  Persian Gulf War and, 141–42
United States Historical Society, 7
USA Today/Gallup poll, 15
Utah, 96

Vallandigham, Clement L., 176
Van Buren, Martin, xx, 37, 92, 113, 220
  Eland's ranking of, 16
  Jackson and, 25
Vandenberg, Arthur, 187
Veracruz, Mexico, U.S. occupation of, 149
Versailles, Treaty of (1919), 129–30
veto, 17, 27–28, 33, 44, 105, 167, 172, 225
vice presidents, 49, 65, 93
Vietnam, North, 137, 139, 141, 157
Vietnam, South, 137, 138, 157, 188
Vietnam War, 14, 38, 39, 93, 119, 137,
    138–41, 154, 157, 158, 159, 160, 163,
    188, 223, 237
Villa, Francisco "Pancho," 149
Volcker, Paul, 202
voting rights, 22, 23, 156
Voting Rights Act (1965), 156

Wagner Act (National Labor Relations
    Act) (1935), 184, 185
Wake Us When It's Over (Germond and
    Witcover), 55–56
Walker, Robert, 102
Wallace, George C., 158
Wallace, Henry C., 108
Wall Street Journal, 229, 231–32
Wall Street Journal poll, xixn, xx–xxi,
    11–13, 16, 18, 70, 84, 85, 107, 111,
    112, 123, 150, 155, 158, 162, 211,
    219

Wanniski, Jude, 111
War of 1812, 26, *73*, 74–75, 119, 120–21
war on poverty, 156
war powers, 49
Washington, 174
Washington, D.C., British burning of, 74
Washington, George, xxi, 26, *167*
  Bailey ranking of, 7
  Congress and, 167, 168, 169
  electoral judgment of, 72, 77, 89
  historical judgment of, xix, 4, 5, 7, 9,
    10, 12, 72, 89
  as Leader of Destiny, 165, 166–69, 182,
    189
  Murray-Blessing ranking and, 9
  Schlesinger Jr. survey and, xix, 10
  Schlesinger Sr. surveys and, 4, 5
  U.S. Historical Society ranking of, 7
  U.S. neutrality and, 168
  veto and, 167
  Wall Street Journal ranking and, 12
Washington, Treaty of (1871), 81
Washingtonian, 53, 206
Washington Post, 181
Watergate scandal, 14, 65, 92, 109, 112,
    141, 159, 161, 162, 188
Watt, Richard M., 129
Watts riot (1964), 157
weapons of mass destruction (WMDs),
    222
Webster, William, 142
welfare reform, 216
Westmoreland, William, 139
westward expansion, 27, 30, 37–40, 121,
    174
Whig Party, 27, 33, 37, 95, 97, 99, 103,
    118, 177
Whiskey Rebellion (1794), 167–68
Whiskey Ring, 82
White, Theodore H., 55, 56–57
White House tapes, 159

Whitney, David C., 79
*Whose Broad Stripes and Bright Stars?: The
    Trivial Pursuit of the Presidency*
    (Germond and Witcover), 56
Wilentz, Sean, 84, 212, 220–21, 225,
    226
William Penn College, 7
Wills, Garry, 179
Wilson, Woodrow, xvi, 39, 50, 87, 89, 108,
    113, *126,* 151, 155, 182, 184, 223,
    226
  Eland on, 16
  electoral judgment of, 149–50
  Federal Reserve and, 148
  Fourteen Points of, 129
  Harding as nullifier of, 91, 92
  Mexico and, 148–49
  Murray-Blessing survey and, 9, 150
  neutrality issue and, 126–27
  Schlesinger Jr. survey and, xix, 10, 150
  Schlesinger Sr. surveys and, 4, 5, 150
  split-decision presidency and, 146–50
  strokes of, 129, 130, 150
  tariffs and, 147
  U.S. Historical Society ranking of, 7
  Wall Street Journal ranking and, 12, 13,
    150
  World War I and, 39, 119, 125–30, 149
Witcover, Jules, 55–56, 57
women's rights, 22, 23
Woodward, Bob, 220
Works Progress Administration (WPA),
    185
World War I, 39, 108, 119, 125–30, 149
World War II, 6, 39, 63, 119, 131–33,
    134, 151, 152, 186–88, 202
Wyoming, 174

Yalta Conference (1945), 152
yellow press, 124
Yemen, 142